salt-water aquarium fishes

Chelmon rostratus. Photo by Earl Kennedy.

dr. herbert r. axelrod
and warren e. burgess

Distributed in the U.S.A. by T.F.H. Publications, Inc., 211 West Sylvania Avenue, P.O. Box 27, Neptune City, N.J. 07753; in England by T.F.H. (Gt. Britain) Ltd., 13 Nutley Lane, Reigate, Surrey; in Canada by Clarke, Irwin & Company, Clarwin House, 791 St. Clair Avenue West, Toronto 10, Ontario; in Southeast Asia by Y. W. Ong, 9 Lorong 36 Geylang, Singapore 14; in Australia and the south Pacific by Pet Imports Pty. Ltd., P.O. Box 149, Brookvale 2100, N.S.W., Australia. Published by T.F.H. Publications, Inc. Ltd., The British Crown Colony of Hong Kong.

CONTENTS

Dedicated to Dr. John Randall for the originality and dependability of his extensive writings on marine fishes, and his great contribution to the education of marine ichthyologists.

This underwater photograph of *Heniochus acuminatus* was taken by Rodney Jonklaas in the coral reefs around Ceylon. The beauty of coral fishes has intrigued hobbyists for years, and it is only recently, with the advent of synthetic resin filters and artificial marine salts, that the hobby has grown to include millions of people all over the world.

1

WHY A SALT-WATER AQUARIUM?

"That butterflyfish is seven years old."

"The damselfish in that tank was purchased five years ago."

"I raised that angelfish from one inch to six inches in a couple of years."

"My clownfish spawned."

The marine aquarists have done it! They've broken through the salt-water barrier. For many years it has been the dream of aquarists to try their hand at the gorgeously colored marine fishes that inhabit the coral reefs. Until recently, this feat has been considered fraught with difficulties and almost always doomed to failure or, at best, a short-lived success.

A clean, healthy marine aquarium can be a beautiful addition to your home. Photo by Dr. Herbert R. Axelrod.

Our hats are off to the pioneers of the hobby. They had to adapt and use equipment specifically designed and suited for fresh-water fishes. Items, metal or otherwise, that would remain inert in contact with fresh-water became sources of deadly poison when in contact with highly corrosive salt-water. The water itself was purchased and shipped to the aquarist who had to keep it clean and healthy, *or else*! Some lucky individuals living near a source of clean sea water could change the water when necessary by hauling it back, usually in 5-gallon carboys, from the sea. Fishes were bought on the basis of color appeal, no information being available as to their disposition, habits, food requirements or the special techniques needed to properly maintain them. Almost all of the marine fishes were high priced; a mistake, usually fatal, was costly. Marine diseases were all new to the pioneer salt-water aquarist, and the fresh-water cures did not work. Home remedies were usually the cure-or-kill type. But even with all of the problems they presented, the appeal of these fishes was so great that marine aquarists did not give up, and one by one the major problems were solved.

ELIMINATING PROBLEMS

The major obstacle in the beginning was supply and demand. With only a few hardy souls able (or willing) to keep a marine tank going, development of new products was economically unproductive. Aquarium books dedicated at best a single chapter to marine aquaria, mostly emphasizing the difficulty and complexity of maintaining them.

But there were pioneers in the business world as well. As interest in marine fish-keeping grew, more marine-oriented products, including entire books on the subject, hit the market. Synthetic sea water, high-powered filters, protective coatings for exposed metal were developed, and finally all-plastic and all-glass tanks were produced. New foods were packaged, new cures developed, and specialized items such as UV light for aquaria and protein skimmers were invented.

With more knowledge came more success; with more success came more knowledge. The marine aquarium hobby blossomed. A book *"Sea-water Systems for Experimental Aquariums"* edited by John and Roberta Clark disclosed all the "secrets" of the professionals and the hobby was on its way!

MARINE FISHES AND DECORATIONS

Despite the advances in marine fish-keeping equipment, the problems of the fishes themselves and the decorations for the tank remained. As each fish had to be captured and shipped (none of the marine fishes had been raised in captivity), they were very high in price. As new

Ostracion meleagris can exude a toxic mucus or slime when disturbed and kill its tankmates or fishes in the same shipping container. Photo by Klaus Paysan.

and faster shipping methods were developed and greater quantities of fishes were shipped safely, the prices dropped. Prices are still high when compared to prices of freshwater fishes, but at least they are now within the range of many more enthusiasts.

Losses were cut as knowledge spread. Toxic fishes* were discovered, as well as those with nasty dispositions and big appetites. Fishes which could never become acclimated to captivity were abandoned in favor of the more hardy and adaptable species. Some fishes became easier to keep and lived longer as their food requirements became known.

Decorations were difficult to obtain, high in price, and often outright dangerous. Corals, the favorite decoration of most marine aquarists, were delicate and heavy, both disadvantageous characteristics when it comes to shipping. In addition, not all corals were properly cured; some caused a great deal of damage to marine aquaria by fouling the tank or releasing poisonous substances that killed the fish. Rocks and

---

*See Russell's *Poisonous Marine Animals*.

A beautiful marine aquarium. Decorations not suitable for use inside the tank can be placed below (as shown) or behind the tank in a shadow box. Photo by Robert P. L. Straughan.

other hard objects may also contain substances that dissolve in sea water and are toxic to fishes. The increased knowledge as to which rocks are safe and which may upset the chemical balance of the aquarium aided the marine aquarist considerably when choosing these decorations. In 1969 the author (HRA) developed and patented plastic coral suitable for the salt-water aquarium.

The larger the marine aquarium is the better chances the aquarist has of keeping his fishes healthy. This Hawaiian family is enjoying their "personal coral reef." Photo by Dr. Herbert R. Axelrod.

The use of plants in a marine aquarium is dangerous, even though some marine plants are available. The plants in this aquarium did well under the expert care of Earl Kennedy. Photo by Kennedy.

A coral reef is like a living picture with the ever-changing colors of the brilliantly hued fish life darting everywhere. Photo by Rodney Jonklaas.

OBTAINING MARINE FISHES

Since very few marine fishes have been spawned and raised in captivity specifically for the aquarium trade, practically all must be collected from their natural environment. Because their natural environment is usually the coral reef, the collector often has a tough job. Just look closely at a photo of a coral reef. Can you imagine chasing a small, agile fish through that? When you see a high price on a reef fish, just remember the collector catching it with only small hand nets at his disposal! It takes a lot of practice and patience to coax a fish out of its hiding place. Most of us would probably face financial chaos if we had to depend on collecting fish for a living.

The professional collector has many additional problems. The trip to the holding tanks and the wait before shipping usually take a high toll. Those fishes that have injured themselves or cannot adjust to captivity either die or have to be discarded. Then there is the actual shipping. Although transport is faster and more efficient now, the long distances involved are still dangerous, not only because of oxygen depletion in the bags but also because of the possibility of rapid temperature changes.

One has to admire the great collectors like Earl Kennedy of the Philippines and Rodney Jonklaas of Ceylon, who have been able to get good, healthy marine fishes to us from these far-off places.

Imagine trying to capture an elusive fish in this growth of coral.
The coral is very sharp and soon makes shreds of your net as well
as your hands. Photo taken in the Maldive Islands by Scheer.

This is how a natural coral reef looks. When alarmed the small
school of fishes in the foreground disappears, as if by magic, into
the coral. Photo by Dr. Wolfgang Klausewitz.

Rodney Jonklaas attempts the difficult feat of herding a group of Clownfish, *Amphiprion polymnus*, into his net.

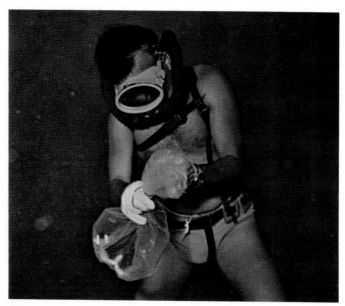

Once Jonklaas captures a fish, he keeps it in a plastic bag, adding new specimens as quickly as he catches them. It may take hours to collect even one specimen.

The day is not counted successful until these fishes are brought back safely and placed in holding tanks. Many difficult-to-obtain fishes are lost between the collecting grounds and home. Photo by Rodney Jonklaas.

A school of young parrotfishes passing over the dense growths of coral on a reef. Photo by John Pederson.

2

SETTING UP YOUR MARINE AQUARIUM

INITIAL CONSIDERATIONS

A little thought beforehand will save much grief afterwards when setting up a salt-water aquarium. You should remember that the aquarium you set up can be a thing of great beauty and that giving it the proper location takes a bit of planning. Besides consideration of ease of performing the routine maintenance (feeding, cleaning, etc.), the amount of sunlight and balance of room decor are important. It is definitely inadvisable to place an aquarium on a bookcase or over electronic equipment like a television or a hi-fi set. No matter how careful you are, there is bound to be some spillage, and glass panels of aquaria do break occasionally, so be prepared for the worst and pick your location accordingly.

Some of the requirements for a marine aquarium are similar to those for a fresh-water aquarium. A solid base must be provided, preferably a stand especially built for aquarium use. The tank should be kept away from drafts or heat-producing units such as radiators. It should also be kept away from direct sunlight, since the bright light favors algal growth in marine aquaria just as it does in fresh-water tanks. Since you can use aquarium equipment to supply all the heat and light needed for the aquarium, a dark corner is an ideal spot. Make sure that a power outlet is within easy reach. See to it that metals which may possibly come into contact with the salt-water or salt spray are protected, possibly through use of one of the available epoxy spray coatings.

The receding tide uncovers many interesting spots in the tropics, where collecting small fishes is a lot easier than diving for them. Photos by Dr. Herbert R. Axelrod, taken in the Fiji Islands.

A look at a coral bottom in shallow water.

Earl Kennedy's immense concrete aquarium in the Philippines.
Photo by Earl Kennedy.

SIZE OF THE TANK

Choosing the size of the tank is easy. *Get the biggest one you can afford.* A tank of less than 20 gallons capacity is not practical if you want to keep most of the coral fishes so enticingly displayed at your favorite pet shop. You can get smaller tanks, of course, but they severely limit the amount and type of animals you can keep. Smaller aquaria are best used for special animals that are not compatible with others in the larger aquaria or for very small ones, such as dwarf sea horses, with low space requirements. These small tanks foul very easily and quickly and need more intense care. Salt-water aquarium fishes entail a fair-sized investment, so why not get off on the right foot with the proper tank?

TYPE OF AQUARIUM

The ideal aquarium is one in which no metal or other toxic substances can come into contact with the salt-water or salt spray. A few years ago practically all available aquaria were metal-framed. This meant that the metal of the frames had to be coated with some protective substance such as black asphaltum varnish before the tank could be used as a marine tank. In addition, it was found that some of the aquarium cements, although safe for fresh water, broke down and released toxic substances after long contact with salt water. The inner joints then also had to have a protective coating. Unfortunately, these coatings did not last, so the tanks had to be completely broken down and repainted periodically.

All metals are potentially dangerous, even such "safe" or relatively inert metals as lead or stainless steel. Hard rubber is relatively safe, and a number of plastics can be used (but not *all* plastics).

This gloomy picture has been brightened recently by the production of all-glass and all-plastic bonded aquaria. These are safe for both fresh and salt water and are now competitively priced; until comparatively recently, they were much more expensive than metal-framed aquaria.

It should be noted here that copper is one of the metals that reacts to salt water by releasing a toxic substance. Like other substances, however, the toxicity varies depending on its strength, killing weaker or more susceptible organisms first and stronger animals like fishes last. Copper is less toxic in sea water than in fresh water and less in hard, alkaline fresh water than in soft, acidic fresh water. The toxic properties of ionic copper are often used as a medication or cure for certain fish diseases. At low levels of concentration some disease organisms and parasites are eradicated without affecting the fishes. Invertebrate animals are more sensitive to copper than fish and succumb very quickly. Several large public aquaria use copper in low concentrations as an algicide to keep the large tanks clear of unwanted algae, as well as a control on the parasite *Oodinium*.

THE BACKGROUND

Among the favorite aquarium backgrounds is the colorful aquarium crystal paint. It comes in various colors, is easily applied and the designs it creates are very pleasing. Some aquarists are content to apply it to the rear glass of the tank, others continue it around to the sides. It is easily scraped off with a razor blade when one wants a change of color to show off better some new inhabitants of the tank. Full color, yet inexpensive, decals or printed scenes, can be applied to the back of an aquarium, and removed easily when a change of scenery is desired.

Synthetic 3-dimensional printed plastic backgrounds depicting many types of underwater scenery are available commercially. They provide a nice, scenic background with a minimum of effort since they are also easy to replace or change.

For the more artistic aquarist the shadow-box is a challenge and a sight to behold. It adds depth to the aquarium and provides space for decorations that ordinarily cannot be placed in the tank itself. There are two basic methods of constructing a shadow-box: (1) using a curved background from one rear edge of the aquarium to the other and provided with flooring, and (2) using a square, box-like background extending from the edges of the tank (an equal-sized aquarium with the front glass removed can be employed for this). The shadow-box is decorated with sea fans, coral, dried starfish, shells, fish-netting, etc. It is best to continue decor of the aquarium itself to provide the greatest illusion of depth. Be sure that the sand inside and outside are of equal level so that there is no perceived break in the continuity of the substrate.

THE SAND

After the aquarium is in place the first consideration is the sand. Cleanliness is of utmost importance. New sand should be washed thoroughly until all foreign matter and impurities are removed. Beach sand, which comes in various textures and colors, can be used. There is always some contamination in beach sand such as bits of dead crustaceans or seaweeds which must be removed. Thorough washing not only does away with much of the foreign matter but it also removes the dust-fine particles which would otherwise mar the perfect clarity of the water.

A good way to wash sand entails the use of a container (plastic bucket) and an ordinary garden hose. Place the container where the overflow won't hurt anything and regulate the stream of water from the hose so that you can stir the sand up vigorously without splashing too much or

The Saunders admire an aquarium set up for them by Lee Chin Eng in Indonesia. The aquarium is made of cement and tile and is very effective for marine use. Photo by Edgar Smith, I.C.A.

washing the sand itself out of the bucket. For best results keep the bucket only one-half to one-third full of sand. Poke the nozzle of the hose into the sand and move it around until nothing but clear water flows out over the edge of the bucket. To hasten the cleaning, the top layer of dirty water can be poured off. Drain the sand thoroughly. If time and space permit the sand should be spread out on a flat, clean surface to dry in the sun. The sun's ultra-violet rays will help sterilize the sand to some extent.

This beautful red-tailed *Chaetodontoplus mesoleucus* is in an aquarium. It almost looks as if the fish were in its native habitat. This photo was taken by the *Malaya Straits Times* in the Raffles Museum.

This marine aquarium was placed in front of another, giving a greater depth of view. Photo by Dr. Wolfgang Klausewitz.

The coarseness of the sand is important. In fresh-water aquaria the substrate is used to support rooted plants and must be chosen accordingly. In marine aquaria the particle size should be selected with two things in mind. Firstly, if a sub-sand or undergravel filter is used the sand should not be so fine as to fall through or clog up the slots. If fine sand is desired a coarse layer can be placed between it and the filter. Secondly, coarse sand might trap bits of uneaten food and detritus that fall onto it and remain there to decay and cause foulness. If a sub-sand filter is not present fine grain sand that packs tightly can be used. All foreign matter should stay on top from where it can easily be removed.

The depth of sand has to be considered. A deep layer is more likely to become contaminated than a shallow one. All that is needed in an aquarium is about one-half inch or so, that is, enough to cover the bottom unless you have burrowing fishes in your tank. On the other hand a sub-sand filter requires a deeper layer of sand. The types of fishes kept have to be taken into consideration as well. Most marine fishes do not need any great depth of sand and the half inch will suffice. Even flat-fishes lie on the surface with only a light covering over the edges of their fins to provide protection through camouflage. Wrasses and eels are great burrowers and dive into the sand when danger threatens. For these fishes a greater depth of sand must be provided depending on their size.

ROCKS AND CORAL

Naturally, you don't want a bare tank with just water and sand. Correctly placed pieces of rocks and coral will not only improve the appearance of your set-up but will also provide protection and hiding places which your animals need even in their natural environment.

Again, you must be extremely careful. After going to the trouble of keeping metals or other toxic substances away from the aquarium it would be disastrous to include rocks with soluble mineral content or other kinds of contaminants. Porous rocks can provide lodging places for all sorts of things including uneaten food and detritus. Use rocks like granite, marble or glass. It is possible to use natural rocks from the sea but chances are you may introduce unwelcome materials or visitors into your tank as well.

Coral is one of the most beautiful decorations for marine aquaria. It is the "skeleton" produced by hundreds of minute living animals closely related to the sea anemones and jellyfishes. It is used only after proper

Here is another way to achieve depth. A piece of coral is placed behind the rear glass, making the tank look much deeper than it actually is. N.Y.Z.S. Photo.

A great variety of life can be kept in a healthy marine aquarium. Besides the two fishes (Blue Devil and Clownfish), there is a sponge crab on the left, two species of scallops at right center and a group of living corals at upper right. Photo by Robert P. L. Straughan.

These corals, probably in the genus *Dendrophyllium*, come in all colors from bright yellow through red to dark brown. Photo by G. Marcuse.

curing. Boiling the coral in water followed by several rinsings removes all the organic matter, including the coral polyps themselves and other organisms using the coral as a home. Coral is very delicate and breaks easily so it should be handled with the utmost of care. It also has many sharp edges that can cut or scrape your hand.

There are many different types of coral, practically all candidates for the aquarium. They range from the flat, oval or rounded Button Coral (*Fungia*) to the tree-like, many-branched Stags Horn Coral (*Acropora*). Brain Coral is attractive but some part of the substrate is usually attached to the coral itself thereby making cleaning much more difficult than the high, branching coral which can be broken off above the point of attachment. Although 90% of cured coral is white, or a variation of white, some species have highly colored skeletons as the Organ Pipe

The bizarre Shrimp Fish are easily kept, and their strange head-down method of swimming makes them an excellent "contrast fish."
Photo by Edgar Smith, I.C.A.

Branching corals are very decorative but also difficult to clean. Debris or dead fishes may remain hidden in this coral and form a source of pollution. Photos by Dr. Herbert R. Axelrod.

The unbranched corals are less trouble, although uneaten food will still find its way into the spaces between the septa. Photos by Dr. Herbert R. Axelrod.

The photo above was taken by Edgar Smith in Indonesia. It shows one of Lee Chin Eng's "natural method" aquaria. There is no filtration and only a bit of aeration to keep the water moving. Note the variety of colors and the extreme intensity of coloration in the fishes. On the facing page is a photo by Franz Lazi which shows the "old method" of keeping marine fishes. This photo was taken in Germany and the tank is heavily filtered. Everything is meticulously clean and the fish have a "sterile" coloration. Both types of marine aquaria are successful, but if you have success with Lee Chin Eng's method, your fishes are much more colorful and your marine aquarium is more interesting and educational.

Such a profusion of fishes can only be presented in large tanks, like those of the New York Aquarium, where this picture was taken. N.Y.Z.S. Photo.

Coral (red) and Blue Coral (blue). These make a pleasant contrast to the white corals. Due to the many tube-like openings of the Organ Pipe Coral where pollutants can accumulate it is perhaps wiser to place this species in the shadow-box instead.

OTHER ORNAMENTS

If you've ever seen fishes around a coral reef you will realize at once the importance of a good hiding place for the general well-being and survival of the fishes. Fish psychologists (usually referred to as ethologists or animal behaviorists) all agree that a sense of security is important to the fish's health as it is to the human being's. Along with coral and rocks, sea shells have been used for this purpose.

It must be repeated that cleanliness is very important. The outside of the shell may be a source of fouling as well as any internal or animal matter. The coiled shells of snails are quite attractive but unwanted materials are easily trapped within the spiral and are hard to clean out. Clam shells make good decorations. They are easy to obtain, come in many different sizes and colors, are easy to clean, and can also provide a smooth surface for gobies or damselfishes on which to lay their eggs.

Plastic coral, sea fans, etc., are now available commercially. They look very realistic and are usually lower-priced than the genuine article. With less chance of foreign matter being carried into the tank on these plastic items they are generally safer to use.

China or porcelain articles in the form of shells, figurines, etc., are brightly colored and have been fired in a kiln and should, therefore, be inert in salt water. Fancy and decorative pieces are available in most flower and gift shops but be sure that they are free of harmful coatings or substances that may possibly leach out in salt-water.

For additional information consult your local fish dealer for suggestions regarding the type of decoration and hiding places best suited to your fish stock.

PLANTS

Plants comprise a major part of a fresh-water aquarium but are not really necessary in a marine aquarium. The addition of some lush green marine plants is a great temptation. This is fine at first but as the plants begin to deteriorate, as they almost always do, there will be some cleaning chores ahead.

However, some types may thrive successfully for a period of time. Algal plants of the genus *Caulerpa* are now being imported and kept in marine aquaria by many aquarists. It won't be long before other varieties make their appearance. Red or green plants are less likely to cause trouble than the brown ones. If you are collecting the plant yourself be careful not to damage the roots. If the plant is anchored to a rock, chip off the piece of rock with the roots attached. It is more apt to survive than if it is pulled off and replanted. Use plants sparingly and watch them closely for signs of new growth, an assurance that they are thriving. The proper amount of light is just as important as in fresh-water plants. Too much light may cause unwanted algal growth, too little inhibits growth and the plants soon die. The actual light requirements are mostly unknown and must be determined by trial and error. At present marine plants are not recommended, at least until some experience is gained in caring for them in a tank separate from that in which the valuable fishes are kept.

Lee Chin Eng of Djakarta, Indonesia, the discoverer of the "natural method" for keeping marine fishes with living corals and living plants and invertebrates. The success of his method led to the first successful spawnings of marine fishes, though none have ever been raised to maturity in captivity. Photo by Edgar Smith, I.C.A.

For those who insist on having more greenery in their aquaria artificial plastic marine plants are available. They are relatively inexpensive, replaceable, and can be removed periodically for cleaning. See to it that they are specifically designed for marine aquaria and constructed out of "safe" material. Some are plastic on wire and should not be used. For those decorations that are potentially dangerous but very attractive there is always the shadow-box for their placement.

THE "NATURAL METHOD" OF LEE CHIN ENG

While in Djakarta, Indonesia, Lee Chin Eng   discovered and promoted a "natural system" for keeping marine aquaria. He places living pieces of coral, complete with all its associated plant and animal life, into his large tanks. He spurns the use of filters and just adds a small air stone with a few bubbles coming from it to give some slight movement to the water. The water remained crystal clear, the corals grew, and the fishes thrived. Small crustaceans and other animals could be seen darting in and out amongst the corals. Eventually some of his fishes even spawned. Lee Chin Eng's methods have been imitated with some aquarists achieving success, others having disastrous results. Obviously, those who were successful lauded the achievements of Lee Chin Eng, those who failed said the system could never work. For people who are adventurous (and have easy access to the marine animals and water) it provides a new challenge, for those who rely on the local shops for their fish and equipment the more "sterile" method should be used.

3

WATER — THE MAIN INGREDIENT

The most important item which contributes to a fish's well-being is, of course, the medium in which it lives. As long as the water is kept clean and without chemical changes and the proper temperature is maintained, the fishes have a very good chance to live a reasonable length of time. It is therefore vital that you provide the best and cleanest water possible, *and keep it that way!*

OCEAN WATER

The most inexpensive source of salt-water for the marine aquarist is the ocean. After all, if the fishes in the aquarium came from the ocean what better medium is there than the water from which they were taken? But it is not that simple!

When sea water is taken from the ocean changes occur even after it has been filtered. There is a tremendous "bloom" of bacteria with accompanying chemical changes. Foremost among the deleterious effects are reduction of oxygen and increase in carbon dioxide resulting in decreased pH (discussed elsewhere in more detail). The bloom lasts about two weeks after which the bacterial population becomes reduced to tolerable limits. It is suggested that after filtration and aeration the sea water be stored in clean glass containers in the dark for at least two weeks (but preferably up to six weeks). Besides filtration and dark storage, accepted methods of bacterial control include ultra-violet and ozone treatments, and addition of antibiotics. The ultra-violet and ozone treatments will be discussed later in this chapter. Antibiotics such as Chloromycetin and Streptomycin reduce the bacterial counts drastically but they are selective as to which bacterial strain they kill and it is also not known what the full effects of these substances are on some invertebrates. When using antibiotics follow the instructions carefully and proceed with caution.

A word of warning when collecting your own sea water. NEVER use a metal container. There is always danger of chemical contamination even when the container has an enameled surface. A small chip in the enamel is enough to cause trouble. Plastic or glass carboys, such as those used for transporting acid, are ideal containers. Glass is of course breakable, and when wet, heavy carboys are slippery so they should be handled with care.

Plastic shipping bags which fit into insulating boxes of Styrofoam or corrugated cardboard boxes are also good collecting containers. Most commercial dealers handle these products. The plastic bags are easily punctured so double them up for safety, especially when transporting spiny animals.

SYNTHETIC SEA WATER

Sea water for inland aquarists was naturally difficult to obtain. That which was shipped to the dealers was usually quite expensive. For many years aquarists and laboratory technicians made numerous attempts to produce synthetic sea water by recombining the various chemicals found in ocean water. The results were not always gratifying, as the mixtures were not satisfactory all the time.

At present there are several preparations on the market which give uniformly good results. It is merely necessary to take these salts, mix them with soft tap water and you have water which in many cases is superior to the natural kind. Large inland aquaria around the world are now using artificial sea water for their marine tanks.

Synthetic sea water, having no micro-organisms to contaminate it, does not have to go through the seasoning process required for natural sea water. As soon as all the salts have thoroughly combined with the tap water it is ready for use.

When salts are mixed according to directions the specific gravity should be about 1.025. This can be adjusted according to requirements, more tap water to reduce the specific gravity and more salts to raise it. The best artificial salts are buffered to the correct pH.

The former major problem in creating synthetic sea water involved the loss of the minute trace elements, present in natural sea water but neglected in the preparation of the older synthetic mixtures. The newer formulae take these into account and today, anyone, anywhere, who has all the other necessities can set up and maintain a marine aquarium.

The development of artificial sea water is another step closer to the day when economically successful propagation of these much-coveted marine beauties is a reality. Already there is encouragement with more reports of spawnings occurring in artificial sea water. The raising of these fishes is still a problem but as our knowledge and experience increase and more and more of the "skilled" freshwater breeders turn their talents towards the challenge of rearing these fishes, it won't be long before "tank-bred" marine fishes are here. They will be hardier (having been able to adapt to tank life since hatching) and in turn much easier to breed than the original parents from the wild.

SPECIFIC GRAVITY

Specific gravity is the ratio of the mass of a liquid to the mass of an equal volume of distilled water at 4° Centigrade. The mass of distilled water at that temperature is considered as 1.000. Since sea water is heavier than distilled water, the greater weight being that of the dissolved salts, the specific gravity will be above 1.000. When we use a figure like 1.020 as that of the ideal specific gravity, it means simply that the water in question is 1.020 times as heavy as an equal volume of distilled water. The arithmetic need not concern us since special hydrometers are sold in pet shops or laboratory equipment supply companies with which you can easily measure the specific gravity of your sea water.

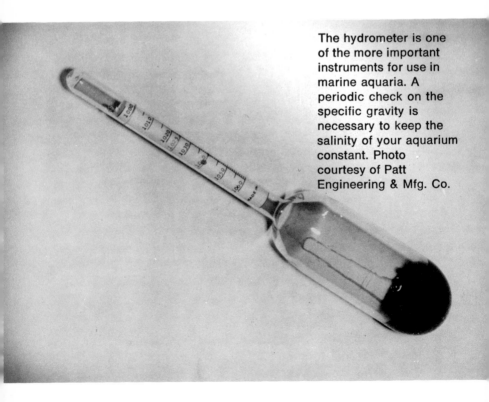

The hydrometer is one of the more important instruments for use in marine aquaria. A periodic check on the specific gravity is necessary to keep the salinity of your aquarium constant. Photo courtesy of Patt Engineering & Mfg. Co.

A specific gravity of 1.020 is considered optimum for the successful maintenance of small marine fishes. Some variation is allowable but care should be exercised that the specific gravity stays within a range from 1.016 to 1.025 for reef-type fishes. This may not seem very large but remember that the difference between distilled water and pure sea water is only 0.02, very small in range. Some fishes have a wide salinity tolerance and can live in anything from pure fresh to pure sea water, as long as the change is not too rapid. If you are collecting your own fishes, ascertain the specific gravity of the water from which they come. If purchased, the proper specific gravity can be obtained from the dealer.

The specific gravity does not change very rapidly but it does change. Evaporation is taking place in all aquaria all the time. The water is the only part that leaves, the salts remain. Ideally, the amount of water that evaporates should be replaced by an equal amount of distilled water to keep the specific gravity constant. If you cannot get distilled water and your tap water is not very hard, it may be used to replace the evaporated water. Keep a constant watch on the specific gravity of your aquarium with your hydrometer. Some people rely on a line drawn at the initial level of the water, adding tap water when the water level falls below the line. In an emergency this method can be used but do not rely too much on it.

pH

The acidity or alkalinity of an aquarium (usually called pH) is very important to the well-being of your fishes. Normally, after a period of time marine aquarium water will tend to drop in pH (toward the acid side). This is caused by the metabolic processes of the fish and invertebrates. Aside from their respiration, which uses up oxygen and releases carbon dioxide, all excretions of the animals are oxidized, an acid-producing process. The pH is chemically tied in with a series of reactions involving carbon dioxide, carbonic acid, sodium bicarbonate, and sodium carbonate. In nature these processes are kept in equilibrium and the pH of sea water is maintained around 8.0, seldom dropping to 7.5 or exceeding 8.4. Since carbon dioxide and fish excretions contribute towards lowering the pH, a drop would indicate that too many animals are being kept in an aquarium.

Kits measuring the pH are now available at your pet supply or chemical supply companies. They range from simple, inexpensive, not too accurate kits, to very accurate (and very expensive) electronic analyzers. One of the moderately priced colorometric (color comparison) sets will do nicely. The pH of your water should be checked periodically, perhaps weekly, to see if it is at the proper level of 8.1-8.2. Try not to

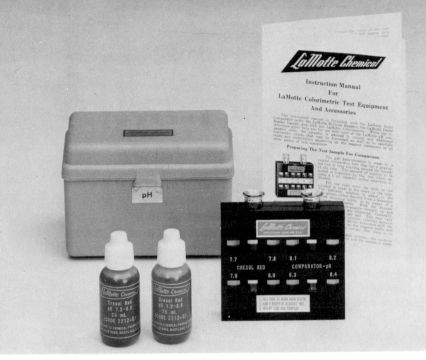

Your pH kit can be as simple or as complicated as your pocketbook can stand. A colorimetric kit such as the one shown is very popular because of the simplicity of use and general accuracy.

let the pH drop below 7.9 since this will cause problems in readjusting it, although some fishes can easily withstand a drop to 6.8.

There are several ways of compensating for a drop in pH. Calcium carbonate in the form of coral, shells, coral sand, or marble chips will help keep the proper balance. The decorations you choose therefore take on an added importance. Freshly slaked lime and sodium bicarbonate are added periodically to some public aquaria for the purpose of maintaining the right pH. For the home aquarium you can add about an ounce of sodium or calcium bicarbonate to a 20-gallon aquarium filter every month. The amount should be adjusted for different sized tanks and for different conditions in the aquarium. This can be determined by monitoring the pH closely and increasing or decreasing the amount of bicarbonate accordingly.

FILTERING DEVICES

One of the principal waste products of marine fishes and invertebrates and the main nitrogenous substance resulting from the decay of plants and animals is ammonia. Ammonia is a colorless gas. Some of it escapes into the atmosphere but most of it remains behind to be oxidized by bacteria to nitrates and nitrites. Some of these bacteria are found inside the aquarium while large numbers turn up in the filters where the wastes accumulate. If the bacteria are plentiful enough the ammonia will be eliminated. Unfortunately nitrates are thought to be the cause of respiratory problems in marine animals, particularly the invertebrates. They also act as fertilizer for unwanted algae which invade the marine aquarium.

It is possible to remove much of the droppings with the aid of a diptube or bottom siphon. They can be decreased by feeding sparingly and making sure no uneaten food remains in the tank. This is often impossible to do or too time-consuming for the average aquarist. Besides, poking around with a dip-tube or siphon frightens the fish unnecessarily. This does not mean you can over-feed, but sometimes, to make sure the slow feeder gets its share, extra portions are given and some of the extra food accumulates on the bottom.

The filter is one answer to cleanliness in a marine tank and it should be selected with this job in mind. Use a filter which would be slightly oversized for a comparable fresh water tank. For example, a filter which would be used in a 20-gallon aquarium with fresh water would be about right for a 10-gallon marine aquarium. A good sized filter is important because it can handle a large volume of undesirable wastes and at the same time create a small current in the aquarium.

Diatomaceous earth filters are powerful filters used for filtering out the finer material from the aquarium. Photo courtesy of Vortex Products.

Undergravel filters help keep the sand or gravel clean by drawing oxygen containing water through it.

Some people do not choose between an outside or sub-sand filter — they use them both. Others have two outside filters, one at each end of the aquarium to assure better cleaning action. Inside filters (not the sub-sand type) are not as good as the outside variety, are difficult to clean, and take up valuable space in the tank.

A very efficient filter is the so-called "high-lift type." This consists of a unit resembling an ordinary outside filter except that it has an outlet at the bottom. The water, after passing through the filtering medium, drains into this outlet to a plastic tube which hangs below the level of the aquarium. It then comes up to return to the aquarium on the other end. At the low point of this return there is an air intake into the filtering system which gives a tremendous lift because of the stream of bubbles traveling through this long tube before being released. This type of filter is capable of handling many times the capacity of an ordinary filter and has been found exceptionally good for a large marine aquarium.

Power filters are excellent for marine aquaria. A pump is attached to the filter where it pumps back the filtered water into the tank. The siphon tubes (usually two) are of different lengths to pick up the water to be filtered at different levels of the aquarium. This type of filter is efficient and handles large volumes of water as well.

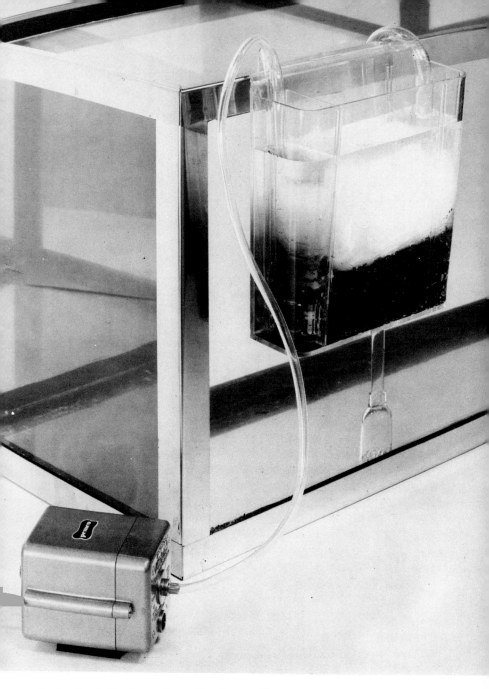

A standard filtering set-up showing a vibrator-type pump operating an outside filter. This arrangement is an excellent one for a small home marine aquarium. Photo courtesy of Patt Engineering Co.

Other styles of filters are shown in the accompanying photos. Your dealer should be able to help you select the best one for the particular job you wish it to do.

The filter intake tubes should be those with small slots in them. Those with larger openings are apt to "filter" some of your more inquisitive fishes out of the aquarium. Even larger fishes that do not fit through the tube may become victims of the siphon current. Coral fishes love to hide in small cracks and crevices and you might lose many valuable fishes by having them get stuck in the intake stem.

Positioning of the filter will depend upon the aquarium set-up. The small currents that it generates should direct the greatest amount of detritus to the siphon rather than into the coral or other decorations. Vary its position until the most efficient site is found.

The usual filtering medium in a marine aquarium is a layer of charcoal topped by glass wool. Sand, gravel, or any inert material are suitable substitutes as long as they do the job of mechanically cleaning the water passing through them. A good filter will remove many of the wastes from an aquarium but remember, the wastes are in the filter and as they break down, they can return to the aquarium by way of the filtered

This is the proper method of hooking up a pump, filter and airstone. Photo by Mervin F. Roberts.

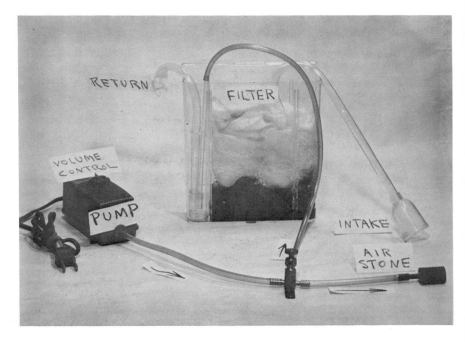

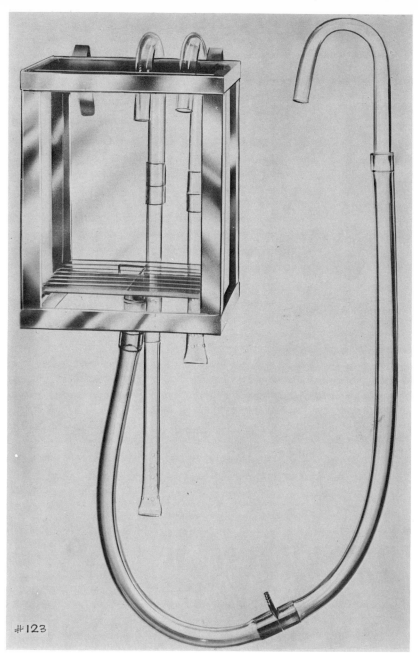

#123

A better method of filtering as well as circulating the water is this "high-lift" filter. The long air-lift tube for returning clean water can be placed so that it will enter on one side of the tank while the dirty water is being picked up on the other. All metal parts exposed to the water must be coated with a rust preventive.

water. To completely get rid of the unwanted material the filter medium must be cleaned as often as possible. In addition, changing some of the water in the tank periodically will help prevent the build-up of the various metabolites.

It goes without saying that only plastic (no metal) filters or filter parts should come in contact with the sea water.

AERATION

An airstone or two in a marine tank goes hand in hand with the filter. It can help by causing currents which bring the wastes within reach of the filter siphons.

The many tiny bubbles from an air stone create additional surface area where gaseous exchange can occur. Most aquarists believe they use an airstone to "pump" oxygen into the aquarium. Actually it is air (which of course contains oxygen) that is being pumped through the aquarium. Remember also that the air used is that immediately around the air pump. Dangerous fumes such as smoke, paint fumes or some of the aerosol bug sprays can be sucked in by the pump and pumped into the aquarium even if it is tightly covered.

Perhaps more important than adding oxygen is the removal of carbon dioxide. Fishes gasping at or near the surface are sometimes victims of the build-up of carbon dioxide rather than the lack of oxygen as tests of the water have shown.

Most aquaria with efficient filters do not require much additional aeration. A good filter not only cleans the water but keeps it circulating, insuring proper gaseous exchange. But an airstone, in the right place, is beneficial.

SYNTHETIC RESINS

Various filtering media were used in the filter in an attempt to "purify" the water before returning it to the aquarium. It is impossible to say exactly who was the person primarily responsible for the application of the combination of synthetic resins and special bone charcoal to marine aquariums. Mr. Richard "Dick" Boyd marketed a product for a while and in Germany another product appeared under the name "Ionic Marin" which made the same claims that the Boyd product did. The German product seemed to work a bit better, but was quite a bit more expensive. Essentially the synthetic resin/charcoal mixture was able to keep artificial sea water in perfect condition for two or three years without changing it. It was also designed to remove the "fright substances" from the water thereby making the fishes less subject to panic.

It would be best to try the synthetic resins on your less expensive fishes until you determine if the claims are justified. A little caution when dealing with any new, highly touted product is advisable.

ULTRA-VIOLET LIGHT, OZONIZERS, AND PROTEIN SKIMMERS

Ultra-violet light rays kill certain strains of bacteria. This attribute has been used in marine aquaria to greatly reduce the bacterial count, therefore reducing the chances of infection and spread of disease. A typical set-up includes a couple of six to fifteen watt low pressure ultra-violet tubes backed by a reflector set over a trough with the aquarium water flowing past. The water need not be more than one inch deep. Another popular method is to enclose the ultra-violet tube within a

This is a so-called "power filter," which pumps back the filtered water, while two siphon tubes pick up the dirty water at separate levels. The power filter is by far the most powerful of all aquarium filters and is perfect for marine aquaria. Photo courtesy of Eugene Danner Mfg., Inc.

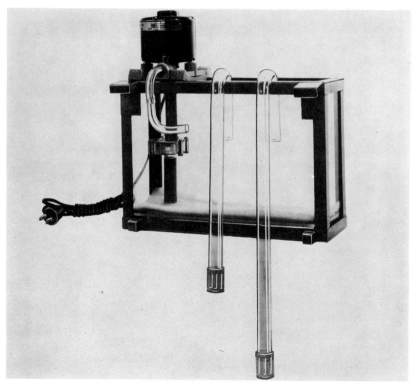

larger tube where the aquarium water can completely surround the UV tube itself. In all methods the ultra-violet treatment is applied to the water that has already been filtered and is on its way back to the tank.

Not only does UV light help to control diseases that have inadvertently entered the aquarium, it helps to check its spread from fish to fish. Any bacteria or protozoa that are free in the tank are bound to be taken into the filtering system where the ultra-violet light can do its work.

Be sure to check the active life of the UV bulb. Its efficiency decreases with time and the beneficial effects could be lost if it is kept going beyond its recommended life expectancy.

Ultra-violet light treatment is still in the experimental stage and should not be attempted by anyone who is not familiar with its characteristics and possible hazards not only to the fish but to man.

Since the sun emits ultra-violet light some aquarists have an arrangement where the water is somehow exposed to the sun's rays before being returned to the main aquarium. An auxiliary holding tank exposed to sunlight is one method.

Ozonizers are available commercially for the marine aquarist. They are devices which produce ozone, a molecule which contains three atoms of oxygen (O_3) instead of the usual two (O_2). Ozone is a powerful oxidizing agent which acts in a way similar to hydrogen peroxide (bleach) and is lethal to bacteria and protozoa. Too much ozone is deleterious to fishes and invertebrates so care should be taken to keep the amounts of ozone introduced into the water at safe levels. To do this limit the time the ozonizer is running, perhaps to a few hours per day or to a couple of days per week. Some plastic tubings decompose when exposed to O_3 for extended periods.

As with ultra-violet light the ozone should be released into the water after it leaves the filtering system.

Have you ever noticed that as aquarium water ages the bubbles from the air stone take longer and longer to burst at the surface? Protein skimmers were designed to remove the substance that causes this and which threatens to eventually foul the aquarium. It is a remarkably simple device that uses air bubbles to collect this material and bring it to the surface. There, the bubbles burst but in a container above the water's surface which traps the unwanted material. It is still a rather new device and all the benefits are not yet known. What is known is that it helps keep the marine aquarium cleaner and that the fishes seem to do much better after its installation.

LIGHTING YOUR MARINE AQUARIUM

The lack of marine plants in your aquarium makes the lighting problems fade considerably. The light is basically used to show off your fishes to better advantage. The choice of type and color of bulbs can be determined more by artistic values than as an attempt to keep or grow certain plants. Of course, with too much light, algae can become a problem so some caution is advised.

Incandescent light gives a good, natural light which can be controlled as to brightness by changing wattages of bulbs. If a change in light quality is desired, several other colors of bulbs are available, in various wattages. With incandescent lighting however there are the disadvantages of producing too much heat for the aquarium water and for the cover glass. Fluorescent lighting is more economical to use since it gives more light per watt of power consumed and has the added advantage of giving off much less heat. The initial equipment is a little more expensive but in the long run there is a saving.

The usual choice of a fluorescent tube is one whose wavelength is towards the red end of the spectrum such as the type known as "warm white." This is close to the color of incandescent lighting and gives us a natural-looking illumination which enhances the reds and yellows. The "Daylight" tube, on the other hand, gives off a more bluish light. Recently fluorescent lights have been selected to "show off" to best advantage the particular fishes of the aquarium. Some glow-lights, as they are sometimes called (pinkish in shade), are used in both fresh-and salt-water aquaria to bring out neon-like qualities in the colors of some of the fishes.

The metal parts inside the plastic shield of the reflector must be protected from salt water. The spray from the filter or airstone may come in contact with the metal and drip back into the aquarium with disastrous results. In addition the metal parts of the reflector will become rusted or corroded and eventually cease to function, perhaps causing a short circuit or fire. This is prevented by placing a cover glass over the aquarium and setting the reflector on this. WARNING: - Incandescent lamps become hot and may crack the glass. If an air space is left between glass and lamp air may circulate and keep the temperature down to a safe level. The space can be created by placing small wedges of wood near the back of the reflector, the size of the wedges being determined by common sense, but at least one inch thick.

With proper lighting your fishes will look better than they do in the depths of the reefs. As a diver descends in the water the quality of light changes drastically. With depth light is filtered out selectively due to the differences in wave-length, the red end of the spectrum being lost early. At about 30 feet deep all that appears to be left are shades of blue or green. You must have noticed that most underwater photographs taken without the aid of flash equipment predominantly contain colors at the blue end of the spectrum. Divers who cut themselves on coral or other sharp objects are used to seeing gray-colored blood, the natural red color being filtered out by the water. Perhaps a bright red color in an animal is a protection in these regions, and it is Nature's intention that these "roses" are born to blush unseen.

TEMPERATURE CONTROL

The correct temperature for an aquarium should be that in which the fishes normally live. Tropical fishes do best in high temperatures; temperate fishes in cooler temperatures. There is a great deal of tolerance to temperature in most fishes and an average temperature of 65° to 75°F for all tropical fishes usually should be sufficient, whereas a temperature of 50° to 65° is better for the temperate fishes. Temperatures higher than normal will usually cause some distress in the tanks.

Your aquaria should be located where outside influences, except that of the normal room heating, are at a minimum. The aquarium heater should be regarded as a device which, rather than raising the temperature, is merely to prevent the water from chilling when the room temperature drops. Water conserves heat very well and a large aquarium will cool off very slowly if the room heating is turned off at night. The heater will serve as a sort of "cushion" when the dangerous rapid drops take place. For example, if the temperature of your aquarium is 73°F and at night the temperature drops to 65°F or lower, the thermostat can be set at 70°F to prevent harmful chilling.

Cool water fishes have the reverse problems. In the summer months they are apt to suffer from too high a temperature. If a refrigerating unit is not available (they usually are expensive and bulky) the best that can be done is to keep them in the coolest place available out of the path of direct sunlight. High aeration is desirable and the aquarium lights should be used as little as possible.

FISH CAPACITY OF THE TANK

Salt-water fishes cannot be crowded. Even with aeration only about half the normal number of fishes can be kept in a marine aquarium than in a comparable fresh-water aquarium. Basically this means about two gallons of water are needed for each inch of fish or about $3\frac{1}{2}$ gallons for the average sized fish. For example, a 20-gallon aquarium should not contain more than five 2-inch fishes. There are always exceptions to this rule. Species like sea horses and pipefishes, which are not very active, can be more crowded, perhaps ten 2-inch individuals in a 20-gallon tank. When deciding on the inhabitants of any aquarium their

In a small, uncrowded tank it is possible to make use of a small inside filter, as is shown here. These can be concealed by cutting away a recess in a lump of soft, porous coral. Photo by Douglas Faulkner.

A behind-the-scenes view, showing the pipe-organ coral which has been hollowed out, with the filter concealed in it. All that can be seen from the front are the bubbles! Photo by Douglas Faulkner.

size, type, disposition, and oxygen utilizing characteristics must be correlated with the aeration, filtration, circulation, and general cleanliness of the aquarium.

Keep one question in mind when tempted to add that "extra" fish or two: will your fish survive if the electricity suddenly goes off and the filter, airstones, and heater stop functioning?

4

SOME PRINCIPLES AND PRACTICES OF WATER MANAGEMENT FOR MARINE AQUARIUMS

BY DR. JAMES W. ATZ *

Despite a tradition that goes back to the ancient Romans and a lively, uninterrupted history of more than a century, the keeping of marine animals in captivity remains more of an art than a science. The most valuable attribute an experimentally minded marine biologist can have is a wet thumb. Of course, the more he is able to apply precise, reproducible techniques to the maintenance of his subjects, the greater are his chances of success, but there will inevitably remain some intangibles, indescribable and unpredictable, that he, as scientist, can only attribute to the complexity of the subject he is dealing with.

Central to the problem of keeping marine animals alive in aquariums is the maintenance of sea water in such confined bodies. In his classic elucidation of the coordinate roles played by the fitness of the environment and the fitness of the individual in the evolution of life, Henderson (1913) points out that in no other habitable place on the earth are so many conditions so stable and so enduring as in the ocean. This eon-embracing stability of the sea as an environment of life is the fundamental cause of the difficulties that marine laboratories, public aquariums, and home aquarists alike have in keeping marine fishes and invertebrates. Because these animals evolved in a world that has remained practically constant in temperature, osmotic pressure, alkalinity, and chemical composition, they have developed few mechanisms to isolate themselves from these environmental factors and little toler-

---

*From *"Sea-water Systems for Experimental Aquariums,"* by John and Roberta Clark, TFH, 1971.

50

ance for change. In captivity, they perforce must be provided with an environment that at least approaches in stability their natural one. But once sea water has been removed from the ocean, it begins to change and to lose some of its capacity to support delicate marine life. This is directly and indirectly the result of its no longer being part of a body of water that is to all intents and purposes infinitely large. The best that any marine aquarium practices seem to be able to do is merely to slow down the rate of this deterioration.

MATERIALS SUITABLE FOR SEA-WATER SYSTEMS

Any discussion of water as an environment, artificial as well as natural, ought at least to mention the attributes that intimately connect this unique substance with life, namely its great specific heat, latent heats of fusion and evaporation, and thermal conductivity, its high surface tension and dielectric constant, its transparency, and its tremen-

A small all-plastic aquarium will hold only a few small fish, but is leak-proof, non-toxic and ideal for a small marine aquarium. Photo by Robert P. L. Straughan.

dous solvent power combined with chemical stability. These characteristics were first penetratingly analyzed by Henderson (1913), and they
have been reviewed by Sverdrup, Johnson, and Fleming (1942). Of
them, only water's close approach to being the universal solvent presents
any special problems in aquarium management.

Because of water's ability to dissolve a wide variety of toxic substances
and because of the extreme sensitivity of most aquatic animals to them,
the only certain way to keep water suitable for most marine life is to
use chemically inert materials throughout the water system. Copper is a
good example of a problem material. This heavy metal is acutely toxic
to fresh-water fish in concentrations of a few parts per hundred million,
but in hard alkaline waters its toxicity is considerably reduced (Doudoroff and Katz, 1953). In sea water, as might therefore be expected,
copper is somewhat less toxic, and at the New York Aquarium and the
John G. Shedd Aquarium, prophylactic doses of 0.20 to 0.25 p.p.m.
(parts per million) are considered safe for the great majority of marine
fishes (Carleton Ray, personal communication; Braker, 1961). At the
Steinhart Aquarium, however, a number of marine fishes have been
found to be sensitive to concentrations of less than 0.20 p.p.m. (Herald
et al., 1962).

Invertebrates are much more sensitive; for example, sea-urchin larvae
were strongly affected by 0.03 p.p.m. of copper (Wilson and Armstrong,
1961). Surprisingly little metallic copper need be exposed to sea water
to produce a dangerous concentration of dissolved copper. Braker (1961)
placed two U.S. pennies in a system containing 6 gallons of sea water
with 1 gallon per hour flowing over the copper coins. He found a concentration of 0.1 p.p.m. of copper in the ambient sea water at the end
of 12 hours, and 0.58 p.p.m. at the end of 48. (At this rate, it would
take more than 5 years for the coins to dissolve.) We have received
several reports that fresh sea water flowing through a single copper, brass,
or bronze fixture can pick up enough copper to kill larvae. One reason
for the acute sensitivity of fishes and aquatic invertebrates to a heavy
metal under these conditions is that they act as biological accumulators,
removing the metal from solution and retaining it.

Few determinations of the toxicity of substances in sea water have
been made, but materials toxic in fresh water are usually also toxic in
sea water, although somewhat less so. Exceptions are known. Boëtius
(1960) found that although mercuric chloride is less toxic to small fish
in sea water than it is in fresh, phenylmercuric acetate is more toxic in
sea water. Certain aquarium cements, whose performance in fresh water
is satisfactory, break down in salt water and release substances that kill
fish. In general, all metals should be avoided, even those like lead and

stainless steel that are sometimes considered safe. Wood and other questionable materials may be covered with several coats of a good grade of black asphaltum varnish, but this protective coating will not last indefinitely and requires periodic checking. Cement is inert, but only after it has been "cured," a process that may take months. Chemically ideal for sea-water systems is hard rubber, also called vulcanite and ebonite, the use of which was first recommended by Michael Faraday in 1857 (Lloyd, 1871). In recent years, a number of plastics have also proved satisfactory. Not all plastics are safe to use, however. In fact, if there is any doubt about the suitability of a material, it ought to be rigorously tested, by the animals themselves, as recommended and described by MacGinitie (1947).

NATURAL CONSTITUENTS OF SEA WATER

Overlying the differences between sea water in nature and in confinement is the basic similarity of its composition the world over. The ratios between the nine ions which constitute more than 99 percent of its dissolved salts are virtually constant (Sverdrup, Johnson, and Fleming, 1942; Harvey, 1955). This is a fortunate circumstance that permits a great deal of uniformity in approach and procedure by aquarists and experimentalists as well as oceanographers. On the other hand, at least 52 elements have been found in natural sea water, and this complexity has led to some irrational ideas about its chemical composition, particularly in connection with its duplication in the laboratory as artificial sea water. A fundamental difficulty is that conventional chemical notation cannot represent a mixture of many anions, cations, and molecules, all in dynamic equilibrium. There is perhaps no more striking illustration of this and its relation to life in the sea than the observation that a volume of sea water allowed to evaporate to dryness and then reconstituted with the proper amount of distilled water will not support the variety of marine life it originally would.

Moreover, as found in nature, sea water is not only an inorganic complex. An ever-increasing number and variety of organic substances are being found in it. Although there is very little organic matter in sea water quantitatively speaking, evidence is accumulating that the little there is exerts an important influence on marine life (Collier, 1953; Lucas, 1955; Nigrelli, 1958). Among the various types of organic substances that have been found in sea water are enzymes, vitamins, pigments, amino acids, antibiotics, and toxins, most of them presumably produced as external metabolites or ectocrines by plants and animals in the sea. The role that such minute constituents of sea water can play in maintaining marine life in captivity has been determined for only a few microorganisms, and their fate, when subjected to the changes that "captive" sea water undergoes, is unknown. Nevertheless, their existence is noted here because of the good possibility that some of them may be important in the culturing of larval forms and macroscopic invertebrates.

Whatever may be their bases, the differences between various natural sea waters can be extraordinarily subtle, as the decade of painstaking work by Wilson and Armstrong has shown. Faced with similar mysteries, aquarists have attributed a sort of *élan vital* to sea water and called it "living"—for instance, when they have observed that artificial sea water had to be inoculated with some of the natural stuff before most invertebrates and some fishes would live in it. Vitalism is not the answer, of course, but there are vital constituents of sea water that are still unrecognized.

CHANGES OCCURRING IN SEA WATER REMOVED FROM THE SEA

Within 30 minutes after a volume of sea water has been taken from the sea, detectable chemical changes have occurred in it (Collier and Marvin, 1953). Biotic activity is responsible for this, the forerunner of a series of profound changes that are brought about in stored sea water by bacteria. Although the sea contains a widely distributed microscopic fauna and flora consisting of protozoans, algae, fungi, yeasts, and bacteria, only bacteria have as yet been found to be important in sea water maintained in vessels or water systems (ZoBell, 1946, 1959; Harvey, 1955). When fresh, filtered sea water is stored, there is a tremendous increase in the number of bacteria, a maximum population of from 2 million to 100 million per cc. being attained in 3 to 6 days at room temperature (ZoBell and Anderson, 1936). In about 2 weeks the initial growth phase is over, and the population then fluctuates from a few thousand to more than 100,000 per cc. At the same time, the number of species of bacteria is drastically reduced to less than half a dozen. Sea water stored for 4 years at 2° to 6° C. still contained more than 200,000 bacteria per cc. (ZoBell and Anderson, 1936), while that stored at room temperature became practically sterile in 6 months (MacGinitie, personal communication).

During the period of the precipitous growth and decline in number of bacteria and for some time thereafter, stored sea water is lethal to the more delicate creatures reared in marine laboratories (MacGinitie, 1947). Because of similar difficulties, aquarists using natural sea water in small aquariums (up to about 100 gallons) subscribe to the procedure of storing the water in glass in the dark for 6 weeks before use. The lethal effect appears to result from the presence of bacterial metabolites, since aeration is not supposed to relieve the condition. In contrast, public aquariums have never reported any difficulties with fresh sea water, perhaps because of the much greater volumes of water, more effective filtration, and lack of delicate forms in their establishments.

The control of bacteria must be one of the principal objectives in the management of salt-water systems and aquariums, but so little is known about the forms that occur in these artificial habitats that any approach is largely empirical. Although sea water has well-recognized bactericidal effects, it also provides an excellent medium for some bacteria, and when enriched with organic matter, may contain billions per cc. These microorganisms can reduce the amount of dissolved oxygen. They can also produce asphyxiating amounts of carbon dioxide and in this way, as well as others, may dangerously lower the pH. Under anaerobic conditions, they produce methane and hydrogen sulphide, the latter of which is known to be strongly toxic to fish (Doudoroff and Katz, 1950). Quite possibly they produce metabolites that are inimical to higher forms. Although this has never been demonstrated, Harvey (1925) found that sea water in which a worm had putrified or to which enough peptone had been added to make it become cloudy was toxic to a species of copepod for some days, even after it had been filtered through a Berkfeldt candle several times and also well aerated.

A *sine qua non* of bacterial control in confined bodies of sea water is cleanliness, achieved by avoiding overfeeding and overcrowding and by practicing systematic but not stereotyped cleaning procedures. In addition, four methods of reducing the number of bacteria have been used, viz., filtration, storage in the dark, ultra-violet treatment, and addition of antibiotics. The efficacy of filtration and storage had been well known long before Stowell and Clancey (1927) found, at the London Aquarium, that storage in the dark for 28 days eliminated "66 per cent. of the ordinary bacteria and 97 per cent. of the so-called 'blood-heat' organisms and bacteria of the human intestinal type," and Lackey (1956) determined that passage through the filters at Marine Studios (Marineland) generally removed more than half of the circulating bacteria. Herald et al. (1962) found that exposure to ultra-violet reduced demonstrable bacterial populations of 1,200 to 2,000 per cc. to practically zero. Marshall and Orr (1958) successfully used chloromycetin and streptomycin to prevent the bacterial multiplication that occurs when fresh sea water is put into aquariums, but there were indications that antibiotics may sometimes harm invertebrates exposed to them.

The importance of microorganisms, especially bacteria, to the state of the water in marine aquariums can scarcely be over-emphasized, and not until we have a better understanding of bacterial activities can we hope to develop a truly rational technique of taking care of it. The fundamental difference between the behavior of small standing fresh-water aquariums and those containing sea water lies with their micro-biology. The real "balance" of the former consists in the relatively stable condition of its microbial population, even in the presence of quite large amounts of organic material. The basis for this phenomenon is not definitely known. Breder (1931) has suggested that it may be partly the development of buffering capacity by the water and the appearance of bacteriophage, while studies of Dr. Seymour Hutner have indicated that the development of a dominant population of predatory protozoans is largely responsible. The situation in fresh water may well be excep-tional, but the reasons for its absence in sea water would nevertheless be of interest. For example, bacteriophages have been found in the ocean (Spencer, 1960), but they do not seem to have been looked for in marine aquariums or other artificial environments.

CHANGES OCCURRING IN SEA WATER AFTER LONG USE

The outstanding changes occurring in sea water that has been kept in circulatory systems for months or years are two: a permanent lowering of the pH and an accumulation of nitrates. After 20 years of use, an analysis of the sea water in the New York Aquarium revealed that the nitrate content had increased more than 250-fold and that the pH had dropped below neutrality (Townsend, 1928). Similar data, involving similar or shorter periods of time, have been reported for the London Aquarium (Stowell, 1926a; Brown, 1929; Oliver, 1957), the Amsterdam Aquarium (Honig, 1934; Sunier, 1951), and the Ueno Aquarium (Saeki, 1958).

In nature, the pH of sea water seldom exceeds 8.4 or drops below 7.5 (Sverdrup, Johnson, and Fleming, 1942). It is regulated by a series of chemical equilibria involving carbon dioxide, carbonic acid, sodium bicarbonate, and sodium carbonate which forms a buffer mechanism and makes possible the addition of relatively large amounts of acid or alkali before the pH is appreciably altered (Harvey, 1928, 1955). If enough acid is added, all the excess base (alkali reserve) will be destroyed, but this occurs at a pH of 5.5, a far stronger acidity than the vast majority of marine fishes and invertebrates can endure. There has been disagree-ment as to the exact source of the acidity brought about by the meta-bolism of fish, in addition to that caused by the carbon dioxide they produce, but it is agreed that oxidation is the ultimate fate of practically all the excretions of fish — which is, of course, an acid-producing process.

Three methods of maintaining the pH in marine circulations have been used. At the Plymouth Aquarium, freshly slaked lime ($Ca(OH)_2$) is periodically added to the reservoir (Brown, 1929; Atkins, 1931; Wilson, 1952, 1960). At the New York Aquarium, sodium bicarbonate ($NaHCO_3$) was added continuously to the circulating water (Breder and Howley, 1931), and modifications of this procedure have been used by other aquariums including the John G. Shedd Aquarium and the London Aquarium. At the Amsterdam, London, Ueno, and New York Aquariums, quantities of some form of calcium carbonate ($CaCO_3$) such as bi-valve shells, marble chips, coral sand, or calcite, are kept in contact with the circulating water (Sunier, 1951; Oliver, 1957; Saeki, 1958). The relative merits of treatment with slaked lime or sodium bicarbonate were briefly argued by Breder and Howley (1931), Atkins (1931), Breder and Smith (1932), and Cooper (1932). One noteworthy aspect of this is the great importance that Breder (1934) attributed to the calcium ion in keeping captive marine fishes.

Although there are differences of opinion whether ammonia is the characteristic excretory product of aquatic organisms (Smith, 1953), it is agreed that this substance is at least one of the principal waste products of fish and aquatic invertebrates. It is also the main nitrogenous substance resulting from the bacterial decomposition of plant and animal tissues under both aerobic and anaerobic conditions in sea water (ZoBell, 1959). Since ammonia is highly toxic to fish in fresh waters, particularly alkaline ones (Doudoroff and Katz, 1950), and there is every reason to believe that it is comparably toxic in sea water, the fate of this metabolite is of considerable concern to the marine aquarist. Some ammonia passes into the atmosphere; the remainder, which is undoubtedly the bulk of it, is oxidized by bacteria to nitrites and nitrates. Large numbers of these bacteria are found in aquarium filters, but some also live on the walls of the tanks (Saeki, 1958). In a quantitative experiment concerning the nitrogenous substances in closed sea-water circulations, Saeki (1958) found that about 25 percent of the decrease in ammonia resulted from oxidation in the filter by its *Schmutzdecke*. Storage of aquarium water in the dark also reduces its ammonia content (Stowell, 1926b). The latter may be the result of direct chemical oxidation as well as biotic activity (Harvey, 1955; Vaccaro, 1962). There are bacteria that reduce nitrates and nitrites to nitrogen and others that reduce nitrates to nitrites, but what significant part, if any, they play in the nitrogen cycle of aquariums is unknown.

In fresh water, nitrates are hardly more toxic to fish than chlorides (Trama, 1954), and no adverse effects on marine species have ever been reported. According to Oliver (1957), however, nitrate can interfere

57

with the respiratory processes of some animals, in particular marine invertebrates. Effects of nitrite do not ever seem to have been described. Oliver (1957) has pointed out that there is no chemical way of removing nitrate, and to accomplish this some adaptation of the denitrifying activities of bacteria appears to offer the most promise. Indeed, Honig (1934) was able practically to eliminate nitrite and nitrate in an experimental marine system by encouraging the multiplication of denitrifying bacteria, but Sunier (1951) reported that the practical application of her method presented difficulties. In a 6,600-gallon sea-water system at the Wuppertal zoological gardens, the combination of filtration by a pressure filter charged with activated carbon and a specially encouraged growth of marine algae kept nitrite and nitrate concentrations within the range of natural sea water (Seiffge, 1941).

The reduction of nitrate and nitrite to ammonia and the formation of ammonia from bacterial decomposition of proteinaceous substances causes an increase in the pH of sea water, while bacterial oxidation of ammonia to nitrite or nitrate causes a decrease (ZoBell, 1959). These relationships require consideration, for Saeki (1958) has reported that a low pH inhibits the oxidation of ammonia in aquariums.

DISSOLVED RESPIRATORY GASES

Sea water can dissolve about 20 percent less oxygen than fresh water; at 20°C, for example, oxygen-saturated sea water (salinity 36 parts per thousand) contains 7.12 p.p.m. of that gas, as compared with 8.84 for distilled water (Truesdale, Downing, and Lowden, 1955). A survey of the literature has shown that the minimum oxygen requirements of marine fishes range from 3.3 to 0.1 p.p.m. At the London and Plymouth aquariums, Brown (1929) found that the sea-water systems were 60 to 90 percent saturated with oxygen. No temperatures are given, but at 20°C, this would correspond to at least 4 p.p.m., and at 30°C, to 3.6 p.p.m., which may be considered adequate for the majority of fishes.

The carbon dioxide content of sea water influences the respiration of fish by reducing the amount of oxygen carried by their red blood corpuscles (Fry, 1957). This is also a pH effect, and it would therefore be expected that sea water whose pH was low — whether from an accumulation of carbon dioxide or a loss of alkali reserve — would inflict respiratory stress on various fishes. Although general aquarium experience bears this out, no experiments to demonstrate the phenomenon have ever been reported. A pH of 7.8 or more appears to be safe for all fishes, while one of 7.0, or even 6.8, is adequate for some of them (Oliver, 1957). One important characteristic of carbon dioxide and its passage between the sea and the atmosphere is that the process takes place relatively slowly, and even with artificial aeration may require several hours (Harvey, 1928, 1955).

Marine fishes that are exposed to sea water supersaturated with air frequently develop gas-bubble disease in which bubbles, mostly of nitrogen, appear under the skin, especially on the fins, and within various vital organs, causing exophthalmia, loss of equilibrium, and death. The supersaturation generally results from a leaky pump or pipeline which permits air to enter and mix with water that is put under pressure, or from a sudden, relatively great increase in water temperature. Marsh and Gorham (1905) first described the disease and its cause in detail, and their account was based on its occurrence in fishes living in a sea-water circulatory system. Since then, all investigations appear to have been carried out on fresh-water species (Harvey and Smith, 1961). Dr. Ross F. Nigrelli, Pathologist of the New York Aquarium, has suggested that denitrifying bacteria may be a source of nitrogen that causes gas-bubble disease.

For the aquarist or experimentalist with a physicochemical background, the papers by Downing and Truesdale (1955, 1956) and Haney (1954) provide basic and theoretical data on the aeration of aquariums.

MARINE CIRCULATORY SYSTEMS

From the preceding account, there can be little doubt of the complexity of inter-relations between captive marine macro- and microorganisms and the sea water in which they live (see fig. 1). Early aquarists considered their aquariums and water systems to be microcosms whose elements behave in the same way as they do in the whole earth's grand economy (e.g., Lankester, 1856; Mather, 1880), and this attractive but erroneous idea has persisted for many years (see Stowell, 1926a). As a consequence, the early aquarists who discovered such vital techniques as circulating the sea water, storing it in the dark, and aerating it, attributed their usefulness to quite incorrect reasons (Lloyd, 1871; Newman, 1873). Standing on the shoulders of these pioneers, we now recognize many significant differences between the bionomics of aquarium systems and the sea.

The need for constant treatment of sea water in order to keep it satisfactory for marine life is apparent. At the very least, sea water must be areated continuously, but unless it is to be replaced often and unless the ratio of volume of water to volume of animals living in it is extremely large, circulation, filtration, and storage in some sort of reservoir are also necessary In a typical circulatory system, the water flows from tank (exhibition, holding, or experimental) to filter, to reservoir, and back to tank (see fig. 2). Aerators are frequently located

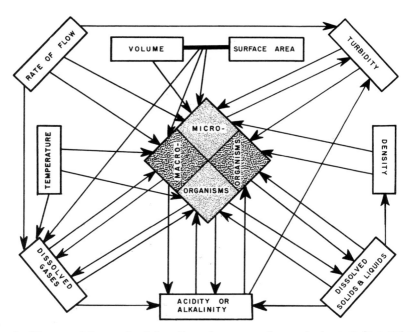

FIGURE 1.—Diagram of the complex interactions of macroorganisms and microorganisms and environment in a marine aquarium or sea-water system. Arrows point from the agent or influencing factor to the item changed or influenced.

between each of these units and the next. The pump is placed after the reservoir because it is least likely to become clogged with animals, sand, or solid wastes at this spot. A gravity tank greatly facilitates the regulation of water flow into the animals' tanks and lessens the chance of introducing water supersaturated with air.

Systems in which the water is recirculated, being used over and over, are called "closed." A typical "open" sea-water system has been described by Hinton (1958). In this, the water is used once and then discarded. The tanks of such a system should be connected in parallel to the water source, not in series, so that each tank receives the same kind of water, and disease cannot be spread through the water from tank to tank. Both Hinton (1958) and MacGinitie (1947) point out that the storage tank, which provides an emergency supply of water if the pumps fail and also acts as a settling tank, should not contain more than a 36-hour supply and that a 24-hour supply is usually sufficient.

In order to prevent the spread of disease and facilitate water treatment, each tank should have its own circulatory system with an individual pump, filter, and reservoir, but the expense of initial installation

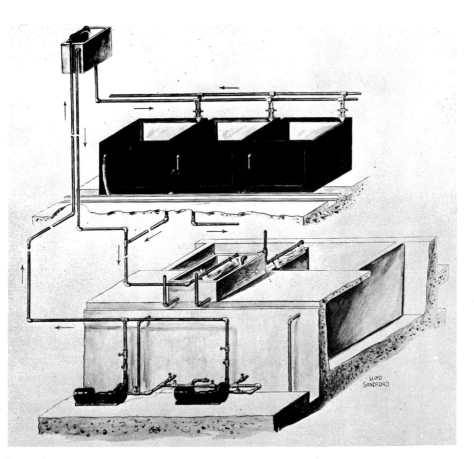

FIGURE 2.—Typical closed sea-water circulatory system. The water flows as follows: Holding tank (black) to return trough and pipeline, to manifold aerator, to filter, to manifold aerator, to reservoir, to pump, to supply riser, to gravity tank, to supply pipeline, to holding tank. Note that all service units, except the gravity tank, are in duplicate and that valves are arranged to provide complete flexibility—that is, all possible combinations of units. The holding tanks are connected to two supply pipelines, and a length of flexible hose from each overflow makes it possible to use either return trough.

and of maintenance may preclude this ideal arrangement, especially if large tanks are involved. When the units have been small enough (less than 1,000 gallons) that they could be provided adequate circulations by means of air lifts, individual sea-water circulatory systems have been set up in public aquariums, for example, at Wuppertal (Wiedemann, 1943) and Bern (Hediger, 1944). Ingenious modifications of filters and aquariums making them more suitable for individual circulations have been described by Wiedemann, by Chin (1959), and by Kelley and Moreno (1961).

In some sea-water systems, there is no filter; instead the water is allowed to pass slowly through a large settling tank or reservoir. Herald et al. (1962) have compared this type with the one using filtration, and they indicate that the latter carries a greater proportion of animals, viz., about 50 gallons of sea water per pound of living animals as compared with about 450 gallons for a system depending on sedimentation alone. Wilson (1952, 1960) has described a typical filterless system. In his later paper, he stresses the importance of having a reservoir that is correctly designed, and he provides the details of a successful one now in use at the Plymouth Aquarium. One advantage of sedimentation over filtration is that filter-feeding invertebrates do better in unfiltered water (Wilson, 1952).

Filtering tests that were made on beds consisting of uniform-sized silica sand by William E. Kelley of the Cleveland Aquarium (unpublished report) and of a graded series of quartz or quartzlike filtrants by Herald et al. (1962) showed that practically all of the filtering was accomplished in the top few inches of the bed. Conventional deep filters would therefore appear not to be necessary in sea-water systems. Saeki (1958), however, has determined the amount of sand that will provide space for the bacteria necessary to oxidize the waste products of a fish, and he states that as a minimum the filtrant should weigh 30 times as much as the fish. Evidently volume as well as surface should be considered in calculating filter requirements. An example of a shallow-bed filter that uses a uniformly sized filtrant is shown in figure 3.

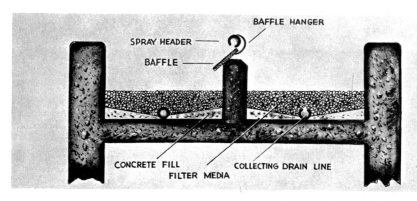

FIGURE 3.—Cross section of shallow-bed filter seen in figure 2. The spray header acts as a manifold aerator, and the baffle can be reversed to direct the water into the opposite filter chamber. Backwashing water is introduced into the collecting drain line through its elevated open end (seen in figure 2).

Hinton (1958) has discussed the problem of an optimum rate of flow in a sea-water circulation and concludes that it is difficult to have too much sea water. The water in the tanks of the aquarium at the Scripps Institution of Oceanography is changed once every 3 to 5 hours, and this has proved satisfactory. At the Plymouth Aquarium, however, a turnover of slightly more than four times a day was barely adequate (Wilson, 1960). At the Amsterdam Aquarium, an entirely different situation prevails, with the water in each tank being replaced on an average of only $1\frac{1}{2}$ times a day (Sunier, 1951). We believe that for most laboratories and aquariums, an ideal rate would be 20 to 24 changes of water a day (see Addendum).

A cardinal, though unproven, principle of sea-water management is that the greater the volume, the slower its rate of deterioration. General aquarium experience, without any doubt, abundantly supports the corollary principle that the ratio of volume of sea water to volume of animals kept in it should be as large as possible. Wilson (1952) has reported an informal experiment that was dictated by World War II at the Plymouth Aquarium: "During the war when most of our big tanks were broken and empty, the inhabitants of those which remained did noticeably better, and delicate organisms survived longer than they did before the war, or do now, and sometimes even bred." The greatest ratio ever maintained in a large sea-water circulation seems to be that in the Amsterdam Aquarium, where the tanks containing the marine animals comprise but one sixth of the total volume of the system. One way of lengthening the useful life of a volume of sea water is to divide it into two equal parts and alternatively "rest" half of the water in a dark reservoir, usually for a month or 6 weeks (Stowell and Clancey, 1927; Wilson, 1952, 1960).

Addendum

On the basis of the work of Saeki (1958) and experiments recently performed at the Cleveland Aquarium, Kelley (1963) has described the parameters of an ideal sea-water circulatory system. The relation of volume of water to weight of animals maintained in it is 100 gallons to 1 pound. The water circulates completely once every hour and passes through the filter at a rate of 1 gallon per square foot per minute. The filtrant consists of 2- to 5-mm. grains of silica gravel (75 percent) and calcareous gravel (25 percent) and there is 1 cubic foot of it for each pound of animal.

LITERATURE CITED

ATKINS, W. R. G.
1931. Note on the condition of the water in a marine aquarium. Journal of the Marine Biological Association of the United Kingdom, vol. 17, No. 2, pp. 479–481.

BOËTIUS, JAN.
1960. Lethal action of mercuric chloride and phenylmercuric acetate on fishes. Meddelelser fra Danmarks Fiskeri- og Havundersøgelser, n.s., vol. 3, No. 4, pp. 93–115.

BRAKER, WILLIAM P.
1961. Controlling salt water parasites. The Aquarium (Norristown, Pa.), vol. 30, No. 1, pp. 12–15.

BREDER, CHARLES M., JR.
1931. On the organic equilibria in aquaria. Copeia, 1931, No. 2, July 20, p. 66. Abstract of paper.

1934. Ecology of an oceanic fresh-water lake, Andros Island, Bahamas, with special reference to its fishes. Zoologica (New York), vol. 18, No. 3, pp. 57–88.

BREDER, CHARLES M. JR., and THOMAS H. HOWLEY.
1931. The chemical control of closed circulating systems of sea water in aquaria for tropical marine fishes. Zoologica (New York), vol. 9, No. 11, pp. 403–442.

BREDER, CHARLES M., JR., and HOMER W. SMITH.
1932. On the use of sodium bicarbonate and calcium in the rectification of sea-water in aquaria. Journal of the Marine Biological Association of the United Kingdom, vol. 18, No. 1, pp. 199–200.

BROWN, ELEANOR M.
1929. Notes on the hydrogen ion concentration, excess base, and carbon-dioxide pressure of marine aquarium waters. Proceedings of the Zoological Society of London, 1929, No. 44, pp. 601–613.

CHIN, EDWARD.
1959. An inexpensive re-circulating sea-water system. Progressive Fish-Culturist, vol. 21, No. 2, pp. 91–93.

COLLIER, ALBERT W.
1953. The significance of organic compounds in sea water. Transactions of the Eighteenth North American Wildlife Conference pp. 463–472.

COLLIER, ALBERT W., and KENNETH T. MARVIN.
1953. Stabilization of the phosphate ratio of sea water by freezing. U.S. Fish and Wildlife Service, Fishery Bulletin, No. 79, vol. 54, pp. 69–76.

COOPER, L. H. N.
1932. On the effect of long continued additions of lime to aquarium sea-water. Journal of the Marine Biological Association of the United Kingdom, vol. 18, No. 1, pp. 201–202.

DOUDOROFF, PETER, and MAX KATZ.
1950. Critical review of literature on the toxicity of industrial wastes and their components to fish. I. Alkalies, acids, and inorganic gases. Sewage and Industrial Wastes, vol. 22, No. 11, pp. 1432–1458.

1953. Critical review of literature on the toxicity of industrial wastes and their components to fish. II. The metals, as salts. Sewage and Industrial Wastes, vol. 25, No. 7, pp. 802–839.

DOWNING, A. L., and G. A. TRUESDALE.
1955. Some factors affecting the rate of solution of oxygen in water. Journal of Applied Chemistry, vol. 5, pp. 570–581.

1956. Aeration in aquaria. Zoologica (New York), vol. 41, No. 16, pp. 129–143.

FRY, F. E. J.
1957. The aquatic respiration of fish. The physiology of fishes, edited by Margaret E. Brown, vol. I, pp. 1–63 Academic Press, New York.

HANEY, PAUL D.
1954. Theoretical principles of aeration. Journal of the American Water Works Association, vol. 46, No. 4, pp. 353–376.

HARVEY, H. H., and S. B. SMITH.
1961. Supersaturation of the water supply and occurrence of gas bubble disease at Cultus Lake trout hatchery. Canadian Fish Culturist, No. 30, pp. 39–47.

HARVEY, HILDEBRANDE WOLFE.
1925. Oxidation in sea water. Journal of the Marine Biological Association of the United Kingdom, vol. 13, No. 4, pp. 953–969.

1928. Biological chemistry and physics of sea water. Cambridge University Press. x+194 pp.

1955. The chemistry and fertility of sea waters. Cambridge University Press. viii+224 pp.

HEDIGER, HEINI.
1944. Erfahrungen aus dem aquarium des Tierparkes Dählhölzli in Bern. Schweizerische Fischerei-Zeitung, 1944, Nos. 8/10 22 pp.

HENDERSON, LAWRENCE J.
1913. The fitness of the environment. Macmillan, New York. (Republished in 1958 by Beacon Press, Boston. xxiv+317 pp.)

ĪERALD, EARL S., ROBERT P. DEMPSTER, CLYDE
WOLTERS, and MARJORIE L. HUNT.
1962. Filtration and ultraviolet sterilization
of seawater in large closed, and semi-closed
aquarium systems. Communications Ier
Congrès International d'Aquariologie, vol. B,
pp. 49–61.

ĪINTON, SAM.
1958. The T. Wayland Vaughan Aquarium-
Museum. University of California, Scripps
Institution of Oceanography, La Jolla, Calif.
42 pp.

ĪONIG, C.
1934. Nitrates in aquarium water. Journal
of the Marine Biological Association of the
United Kingdom, vol. 19, No. 2, pp. 723–725.

ĪELLEY, WILLIAM E.
1963. Ideal configurations for a semi-closed
circulating aquarium system. Program, 50th
anniversary meeting, American Society of
Ichthyologists and Herpetologists, p. 43.
Abstract of paper.

ELLEY, WILLIAM E., and DANIEL H. MORENO.
1961. A filtering system for individual tanks.
Bulletin of Aquatic Biology, vol. 2, No. 21,
pp. 117–118.

ACKEY, ELSIE WATTIE.
1956. Some visibility problems in large
aquaria, II. A bacteriological study of the
sea water used in Marineland. Quarterly
Journal of the Florida Academy of Sciences,
vol. 19, No. 4, pp. 267–273.

ĀNKESTER, EDWIN.
1856. The Aquavivarium, fresh and marine.
Robert Hardwicke, London. 71 pp.

ĪLOYD, WILLIAM ALFORD.
1871. The Crystal Palace Aquarium. Nature, vol. 4, pp. 469–473.

ĪUCAS, C. E.
1955. External metabolites in the sea. Deep-
Sea Research, vol. 3, Supplement, pp. 139–
148.

ĀCGINITIE, G. E.
1947. Sea water systems at marine laboratories. Science, vol. 106, No. 2747, pp. 171–
173.

ĀRSH, M. C., and F. P. GORHAM.
1905. The gas disease in fishes. U.S. Bureau
of Fisheries, Report of the U.S. Commissioner of Fisheries for 1904, Appendix, pp.
343–376.

ĀRSHALL, S. M., and A. P. ORR.
1958. Some uses of antibiotics in physiological experiments in sea water. Journal of
Marine Research, vol. 17, pp. 341–346.

ĀTHER, FREDERICK.
1880. Management of public aquaria. Trans-

actions of the American Fisheries Society
(Transactions of the American Fish Cul-
tural Association), 1879, pp. 46–50.

NEWMAN, EDWARD.
1873. Official handbook to the marine aquarium of the Crystal Palace Aquarium Company (Limited). By W. A. Lloyd, Super-
intendent of the Aquarium. Fifth edition,
revised and enlarged. 1873. Review. The
Zoologist ; a Popular Miscellany of Natural
History, 2 ser., vol. 8, pp. 3661–3676, 3701–
3711, 3741–3759.

NIGRELLI, ROSS F.
1958. Dutchman's baccy juice or growth-pro-
moting and growth-inhibiting substances of
marine origin. Transactions of the New
York Academy of Sciences, 2 ser., vol. 20,
No. 3, pp. 248–262.

OLIVER, JAMES H.
1957. The chemical composition of the sea
water in the aquarium. Proceedings of the
Zoological Society of London, vol. 129, No. 1,
pp. 137–145.

SAEKI, ARITSUNE.
1958. Studies on fish culture in the aquarium
of closed-circulating system : Its fundamental theory and standard plan. Bulletin
of the Japanese Society of Scientific Fisheries, vol. 23, No. 11, pp. 684–695. (In Japanese with English abstract.)

SEIFFGE, W.
1941. Ein Beitrag zur Pflege des Seewassers.
Der Zoologische Garten, n.s., vol. 13, Nos. 3/4,
pp. 297–300.

SMITH, HOMER W.
1953. From fish to philospher. Little, Brown
and Co., Boston. xv + 264 pp.

SPENCER, R.
1960. Indigenous marine bacteriophages.
Journal of Bacteriology, vol. 79, No. 4, p. 614.

STOWELL, FLAXNEY P.
1926a. Physical and chemical conditions in
the sea-water of the Zoological Society's
aquarium—a comparison with the water of
the open sea. Proceedings of the Zoological
Society of London, 1925, No. 45, pp. 1241–
1258.

1926b. The purification of sea-water by storage. Proceedings of the Zoological Society
of London, 1926, No. 11, pp. 245–255.

STOWELL, FLAXNEY P., and VERNON J. CLANCEY.
1927. Microscopical and bacteriological in-
vestigation of the water in the Society's
aquarium. Proceedings of the Zoological
Society of London, 1927, No. 18, pp. 295–306.

Sunier, A. L. J.
1951. The circulation and chemistry of the sea water in the Amsterdam Aquarium. Minutes of the meeting of the International Union of Directors of Zoological Gardens, held in Amsterdam, 1951.

Sverdrup, H. U., Martin W. Johnson, and Richard H. Fleming.
1942. The Oceans; their physics, chemistry, and general biology. Prentice-Hall, New York. 1087 pp.

Townsend, Charles Haskins.
1928. The public aquarium; its construction, equipment, and management. U.S. Bureau of Fisheries, Document 1045; Report of the U.S. Commissioner of Fisheries for 1928 (Appendix VII), pp. 249–337.

Trama, Francesco B.
1954. The acute toxicity of some common salts of sodium, potassium and calcium to the common bluegill (*Lepomis macrochirus* Rafinesque). Proceedings of the Academy of Natural Sciences of Philadelphia, vol. 106, pp. 185–205.

Truesdale, G. A., A. L. Downing, and G. F. Lowden.
1955. The solubility of oxygen in pure water and sea-water. Journal of Applied Chemistry, vol. 5, pp. 53–62.

Vaccaro, R. F.
1962. The oxidation of ammonia in sea water. Journal du Conseil Permanent International pour l'Exploration de la Mer, vol. 27, No. 1, pp. 3–14.

Wiedemann, Eduard.
1943. Zum technischen Ausbau von Meeres aquarien. Der Zoologische Garten, n.s., vol. 15, No. 3, pp. 126–131.

Wilson, Douglas P.
1952. The aquarium and sea-water circula tion system at the Plymouth laboratory Journal of the Marine Biological Associatio of the United Kingdom, vol. 31, No. 1, pp. 193–212.

1960. The new aquarium and new sea-wate circulation systems at the Plymouth lab oratory. Journal of the Marine Biologica Association of the United Kingdom, vol. 3 No. 2, pp. 391–412.

Wilson, Douglas P., and F. A. J. Armstron
1961. Biological differences between se waters: experiments in 1960. Journal of th Marine Biological Asso iat.on of the Unite Kingdom, vol. 41, No. 3, pp. 663–681.

ZoBell, Claude E.
1946. Marine microbiology. Chronica Bota ica Co., Waltham, Mass. xv+240 pp.

1959. Introduction to marine microbiolog New Zealand Department of Scientific ar Industrial Research Information Series, N 22, pp. 7–23.

ZoBell, Claude E., and D. Quentin Anderso
1936. Observations on the multiplication bacteria in different volumes of stored s water and the influence of oxygen tensi and solid surfaces. Biological Bulletin, v 71, No. 2, pp. 324–342.

5

FEEDING SALT-WATER FISHES

One of the biggest problems in maintaining marine fishes is to provide them with proper food. Some fishes will eat almost anything that is offered whereas others refuse even their natural food when in captivity. Most fishes fall somewhere in between these two extremes, adapting to certain substitutes but refusing others. Until recently specific diets of many types of fishes were not known and aquarium fishes were offered foods they couldn't eat at all.

Finicky eaters will always be a problem. *Pterois* species and angler fishes will usually refuse anything but live food. They can sometimes be coaxed into accepting 'chunks' of fish flesh or shrimps but a supply of small fishes (goldfish or guppies) or small shrimps swimming in the tank is usually necessary. Butterflyfishes normally eat coral polyps and invertebrates associated with the coral. Several of them will refuse anything but live coral, an item that 99% of the marine aquarists cannot furnish to them regularly. It is heartbreaking to see many of these beauties become emaciated and die in front of your eyes seemingly in the midst of an abundance of food. Fortunately the time between the capture of a fish and its arrival at your dealer's tanks takes a heavy toll of these unadaptable fishes and chances are the fish you have carefully chosen (making sure it is not thin, damaged, or diseased) will survive if reasonable care is given to it.

In the early days of the hobby a great deal of reliance was placed on brine shrimp. Here was a food that was readily available and could live in the marine aquarium for several days. Unquestionably, brine shrimp in its many forms turned out to be the ideal food for marine fishes. Presently, it is prepared in several different ways, all generally accepted by marine fishes.

Of course brine shrimp was not the whole answer. Other foods were sought to help broaden the diets of marine fishes. In recent years two things helped to increase the chances for your marine fishes' survival:

Brine shrimp are the basic food for many of the marine fishes.
These are baby brine shrimp normally used for the smaller fishes.
Photo by Dr. C. W. Emmens.

(1) recent developments in the obtaining and packaging of marine fish
foods, and (2) greater knowledge in the particular feeding habits of
salt-water fishes.

Fishes can be divided into three main feeding categories: (1) carnivores, or those that eat only animal material; (2) herbivores, or those
that eat only plant material; and (3) omnivores, or those that eat both
plant and animal material.

The herbivores are specialists in feeding on the marine plants or
algae. Ideally the aquarists should determine what type of algae is
required and feed it to his fish. Normally this is not practical and since
the algae that grows on the glass or decorations of the aquarium is not
in sufficient quantities to satisfy the requirements of your fishes, additional food must be found. Frozen lettuce, spinach, and other green
vegetables are often accepted as substitutes. Wash these well before
adding them to the aquarium. Dried foods with chlorophyll content and
the fresh-water "Molly" foods are sometimes accepted. If you wish to
feed natural marine plants to your herbivores, disinfect them first as
they can carry unwanted "bugs" which can raise havoc with your prize
specimens. Herbivores, usually out of hunger, will eat animal material.
This does not necessarily mean that they will thrive. They are missing
something when they do not get their proper diet and may eventually
die for lack of it.

Carnivores are easier to feed. As mentioned above brine shrimp are readily available in several forms. For smaller specimens brine shrimp eggs can be hatched and the baby brine shrimp can be used as a staple in their diet. There are two popular varieties of brine shrimp available today probably representing two species of *Artemia*. The species from California, or San Francisco Brine Shrimp, is of better quality. It is smaller when hatched than the Salt Lake (Utah Brine Shrimp) species. According to most professionals you get twice as much yield from a gallon of San Francisco eggs as from Utah eggs. Both are hatched in a brine solution and full instructions come with every pack. Remember, brine shrimp need food and will eventually starve to death if not eaten quickly by the fishes. After a day or two the nutritional value of the brine shrimp drops very low so they should be replaced by newer ones. Try to keep the egg shells out of the aquarium, they can foul the tank, or, if eaten, cause digestive problems. Newly hatched brine shrimp comes in frozen packages.

For larger food brine shrimp adults raised by the aquarist, purchased from your dealer (when available), or bought as frozen or freeze-dried packages can be used. Those from San Francisco are collected almost all year round while the other must be collected during the summer season. In the winter months then you are better advised to get the San Francisco brine shrimp since they most likely will be fresher. Be sure that your frozen shrimp do not thaw or have not thawed and been re-frozen. When feeding take the amount that you wish to feed only, thaw, and then rinse before placing them in your tank.

Recently one of the authors (HRA) discovered the advantages of freeze-drying foods for fishes. First came freeze-dried tubifex worms which won immediate acceptance. Next came freeze-dried brine shrimp which have all but replaced the frozen type. Freeze-dried foods have an advantage in that they can be kept without refrigeration. They also have less of a tendency to foul the water and they are sterilized.

Naturally the diet of your fishes should be varied whenever possible. Some of the foods fed to fresh-water fishes will do very well for marine fishes. Freeze-dried tubifex worms, *Daphnia*, enchytrae, white worms, and mosquito larvae are all acceptable.

Of the strictly marine foods chopped clams, mussels, crabs, shrimp, or fish all are highly desirable. Frozen or freeze-dried prawns, shrimp, crabs, brine shrimp, or other crustaceans, as well as *Tubifex* worms supply a ready substitute. Dry foods like the new flake foods, crab meal, and shrimp meal are also excellent.

Not too long ago tiny copepods called *Calanus finmarchicus* were marketed under the name "Norwegian Brine Shrimp." Since copepods form one of the basic natural foods of marine fishes they are therefore ideal for marine aquarium fishes also. They are in fact more nutritious than the true brine shrimp, *Artemia salina*. The copepods are collected and cleaned in the fjords of Norway. They are rushed to the packing house where they are packed alive, cooked, and canned. The advantage of these copepods over frozen brine shrimp is that they can be stored without freezing. They do not foul the water as does brine shrimp. The latter, when it melts, gives off juices of the exploded shrimp.

Omnivores, as the definition implies will accept most all of the foods mentioned above. They can usually exist on a pure animal diet but do somewhat better if plant material is also fed. Freeze-dried *Tubifex* with *Chlorella* algae is ideal for omnivores.

Many fishes when hungry enough will eat whatever is offered. Sometimes, however, certain species are reluctant to start feeding in new and strange surroundings. If other fishes are present which are good feeders the newcomers will quickly imitate them and take their place at the "dinner table".

The type and frequency of feeding naturally depends entirely on the kinds and sizes of fishes in your aquarium. Larger fishes (over $1\frac{1}{2}$ inches) in general can be fed once per day. For smaller sized fishes at least twice a day feedings (more if possible) are recommended. For certain species, those that eat very little but often (butterflyfishes), a continuous supply of food, probably brine shrimp which can live in the tank with the fishes, must be provided. Brine shrimp are phototrophic, that is, they are attracted to light, and will accumulate where the light intensity is strongest. If brine shrimp are wanted in the lower levels of the aquarium place a small light at the desired level.

While we are on the subject of foods, here is a bit of advice which should be engraved on your memory, never to be forgotten: *Feed sparingly,* and you will have your fish for a long time; overfeed, and you may lose them overnight! Your fishes are seriously harmed when the water becomes foul due to the presence of decaying, uneaten food, the source of billions of harmful bacteria. When the water becomes foul in a freshwater tank it can be easily replaced. Marine water on the other hand is expensive to replace as it has either to be carried from the sea shore or a new batch of artificial sea water prepared. A little care when feeding can save a big headache later on.

Many aquarists have problems feeding certain delicate fishes, like *Heniochus*. A live mussel, on the half-shell, thoroughly rinsed in fresh-water, has enabled many people to maintain these hard-to-feed fishes for many years. Try it, you'll like it!

6

DISEASES OF SALT-WATER
AQUARIUM FISHES

Salt-water fishes are subject to a whole host of diseases. Now that proper marine aquarium maintenance procedures are more commonly known the aquarist can turn his attention towards identifying and eliminating the various diseases that invade his tank. Deaths from mismanagement of the aquarium are less common now. The aquarist has learned that the tank should not be overcrowded, that substances such as metals should be kept away from the marine tank or at least be protected from the effects of salt water, that overfeeding can foul a tank and kill fish, that certain fishes release poisonous substances when frightened, that aquarium chemistry (pH, salinity) is important, etc. He also remembers from keeping freshwater fishes that sudden shocks, such as turning the light on at night, can be fatal, and the air that is pumped into the aquarium comes from areas near the pump and that an ash tray set near the pump can be deadly to your fish. When the aquarium is properly managed the fishes have a very good chance of remaining free from ailments or, if stricken, of a quick recovery. Even with the best of care however, disease can strike.

AN OUNCE OF PREVENTION . . . .

Aside from proper aquarium management an aquarist can avoid many problems by choosing his fishes carefully. When ready to purchase one or several fishes look them over for any signs of trouble. Avoid fishes with lesions or wounds, spots of any sort, clamped fins, or ragged and torn fins. A fish that appears weak or thin most likely has some disorder or refuses to adapt to captivity and will not last. Many fishes go on a hunger strike for an assortment of unknown reasons. Although some start feeding again, most eventually die from starvation or malnutrition. It may be advantageous for you to be at your dealers at feeding time to observe how the fishes take to various foods.

Once fine, apparently healthy specimens are selected take some additional time and quarantine them. They should be watched for a day or two making sure no abnormalities were missed at the shop or no disease shows up. (Actually a day or two is minimum time, longer periods are recommended.) An additional precaution is to place the fish when first received into a sterilizing solution. Many importers of marine fishes use a solution of potassium permanganate and fresh water (25 mg. to a gallon of water) for sterilization. Place the fish in this solution for a few minutes. If they show signs of discomfort, remove them. Usually they can take two to three minutes in the solution without difficulty. Then place your fish in the quarantine tank. Some importers of marine fishes will tell you to use copper sulfate. This will do the job but is somewhat more dangerous to use than potassium permanganate and the latter will serve your purpose. For those who prefer copper sulfate 0.163 grams of copper sulfate crystals in 100 liters of water is the recommended dosage. This should be accompanied by a raise in temperature to about 86°F.

GENERAL TREATMENT

The potassium permanganate treatment can be used, not only as a sterilization procedure, but also as a general treatment for unknown bacterial and protozon diseases. This treatment has been found to be successful with the bacterial infections known to cause many fish diseases as well as certain other disease producing organisms.

TYPES OF DISEASES

Diseases can be caused by a host of different organisms. These organisms can generally be classified into the following categories: viruses, bacteria, protozoa, fungi, parasitic worms, and parasitic crustaceans. The viruses, bacteria, protozoa, and fungi, cause infectious diseases which invade the host and multiply uncontrolled in its tissues. The parasitic worms and crustaceans are larger organisms and invade the host where they grow but do not multiply. It must be remembered that a parasite properly adapted to its host will not kill it. If the host lives the parasite lives with it, but if the host dies, chances are the parasite will die also. Removal of the parasite then will generally be enough to "cure" the fish.

Probably the most common viral disease is *Lymphocystis*. It occurs in both marine and fresh-water fishes as whitish nodules on the body and fins. *Lymphocystis* is an infectious disease that occurs more abundantly in the summer months. It could attack fishes in a tank due to their lowered resistance caused by confinement, poor diet, too high a temperature, etc. Removal of the cause then is the best treatment. If proper tank management does not work, application of the general treatment recommended above will undoubtedly help your fishes to recover. With ozone or ultra-violet light treatment of the water this disease should not appear.

Common among the bacterial infections are lesions of all sorts and tail or fin rot. As the latter disease progresses there is increasing erosion of the tail or other fins and small red patches (hemorrhages) beneath the scales. There are many antibiotics that are known to reduce bacterial populations in salt water. The following drugs have been found to help control marine bacteria successfully:

250 mg. of Penicillin per gallon; treatment repeated every 24 hours.

250 mg. of Chloromycetin per gallon; treatment repeated every 24 hours.

250 mg. Thiolutin per gallon; treatment repeated every 24 hours.

250 mg. of Rimocydin per gallon; treatment repeated every 12 hours.

250 mg. of Polymyxin per gallon; treatment repeated every 12 hours.

250 mg. of Bacitracin per gallon; treatment repeated every 12 hours.

A mixture of 250 mg. of Chloromycetin and 250 mg. of Neomycin for every two gallons of water; keep fish in this treatment until cured, no repeat necessary.

A mixture of 250 mg. of Penicillin and 250 mg. of Streptomycin for every two gallons of aquarium water; keep fish in this solution until cured, no repeat necessary.

The best treatment of all is the combination of Chloromycetin, Penicillin and Streptomycin. Use 250 mg. of each for every three gallons of aquarium water. This treatment is effective for almost every bacterial infection of marine fishes. A single dose is effective for ten days or more depending upon conditions in the aquarium.

Ichthyophonus is a fungus infection that is caused by spores which attack the internal organs. Musculature is affected by this disease and some late symptoms are unsteady swimming, odd motion, and finally lying on the bottom. The early stages are extremely difficult to diagnose as the fish refuses to feed, clamps its fins and remains hidden most of the time. Upon dissection very small globular cysts are found. External evidence of this disease includes a bloated appearance like dropsy and possible eruptions on the body. There has been no reported cure for this disease. Since it is fungal in nature some of the above antibiotic combinations may be tried.

Brachiophillus is another infectious disease caused by an algal spore. It occurs as white spots on the gills and surrounding area. Since the gills are attacked the disease is recognized by very rapid breathing (faster gill movements) and the fish stays near the surface in an attempt to acquire oxygen (or rid itself of carbon dioxide). Potassium permanganate or copper sulfate will help combat this disease. In addition, a lowering of the temperature to 68°F is recommended.

Velvet disease of marine fishes is caused by the dinoflagellate *Amblyoodinium*. Basically it attacks the gills, causing hemorrhaging and adhesion of the gill filaments. Like the preceding disease, rapid breathing or other respiratory distress is the symptom. The disease progresses by spreading out over the skin and fins appearing like patches of velvet or areas covered with powder. It spreads in epidemic proportions throughout the tank quickly and kills within a matter of a few days. Potassium permanganate or copper sulfate is the prescribed treatment.

The white-spot disease in fresh-water fishes is well known and most aquarists are familiar with the scientific name *Ichthyophthirius*. A similar ciliate parasite, *Cryptocaryon*, is responsible for the marine white-spot disease. As in the fresh-water form the fish is covered with tiny white spots as if someone sprinkled them with salt. They drop off the host and encyst on the bottom of the tank where they will divide many times to produce large numbers of free-swimming infective stages. The cures, similar to those of fresh-water fishes infected with *Ichthyophthirius* include quinine, acriflavine, copper sulfate, etc. A commercial medication is available for the marine white-spot disease.

The microsporidian *Glugea* is a lesser known marine fish disease attacking such animals as sea horses, pipefishes and sticklebacks. Heavy infection of these cysts in the visceral area destroy the functions of the various internal organs. Try potassium permanganate or copper sulfate treatment.

Among the larger parasites are the helminths (trematodes, cestodes, nematodes, and acanthocephalans). They usually have a life cycle which occurs only partly in the fish; they do not reproduce there. As adults these parasitic worms are usually found in the digestive tract. The larvae are found in the visceral area or flesh and could be lethal. They cause metabolic disruption and retard growth in lighter infections. Once these worms are removed, without the next host in the life cycle, they cannot re-infect the fish. Potassium permanganate, copper sulfate, or sometimes immersion in fresh-water for a few minutes will help to dislodge a few of them located in vulnerable areas as the gills or skin. In nature those fishes which have survived a massive infestation of this type of parasite apparently tolerate them unless the parasites disrupt a vital function of the host. It is also a known fact that certain fishes such as the cleaner wrasses, genus *Labroides*, remove parasites from the skin, gills and mouth cavity, of other fishes to such an extent that these fishes actually solicit the cleaners for this unique service.

Other larger parasites of importance to the aquarist are the parasitic crustaceans like *Argulus*. They are generally visible with the naked eye and with a little practice they can be removed with a pair of tweezers. If this does not work the same treatment as mentioned above under parasitic worms can be applied.

The areas of bacterial infection or sites where parasites were attached usually leave raw lesions. These should be treated immediately with the permanganate solution, mercurochrome, or merthiolate applied directly to the sores. Antibiotics will help clear the aquarium of infectious bacteria or fungus.

Popeye or *exophthalmus* often occurs in marine aquaria. Many theories as to its cause have been reported. It is said that popeye is caused by: (1) hemorrhage produced by gas in the capillaries of the eye socket in turn due to supersaturation of the aquarium water with air; (2) bacterial infection; (3) improper diet; (4) use of a drug in capture; (5) overdose of copper treatment. Perhaps one or more of these theories will prove correct but until the actual cause is known nothing can be said further. Partial change of the water and treatment with an antibiotic usually takes care of this problem. There are many reports that popeye will eventually disappear of its own accord. Do not puncture the eye of your fish "to release the pressure" unless you want a fish blind in one or both eyes.

INJURIES

In general, injuries resulting from bites or damage due to collecting the fish will heal very quickly in clean water. As mentioned above, mercurochrome or other disinfectant can be applied directly to the fish to ward off infection. *Saprolegnia,* a white fungus, sometimes occurs on the injured spots or even on other parts of the skin. The above treatment can be used.

Check with your dealer when disease strikes. Many new products and "cures" are being discovered and marketed and perhaps a specific treatment for your fishes' illness is now available.

The list of diseases above is by no means inclusive. Books (such as Sindermann's *Disease of Marine Fishes*) are available describing many additional diseases. Also the treatments advanced are ones that have succeeded to a large extent in the past. It is hoped newer and more effective antibiotics will be available for specific diseases. Keep an eye on your fish and note any strange behavior or spots. Isolate the diseased fish in clean salt-water, then treat it. If all else fails try something new; you may be the discoverer of a new cure for a fish disease.

7

FISHES FOR THE
MARINE AQUARIUM

The seas of the world abound with a fantastic variety of beautiful, unusual, or interesting kinds of fishes. For centuries man has traveled to the sea with various types of collecting gear in order to capture them either for food or for scientific study. Many have been named and described by ichthyologists while others have escaped capture or recognition. There are fishes that are very common, others that are very rare, and still others that are numerous only at a particular time. They live in a vast assortment of habitats from the ocean's surface to its greatest depths. There are fishes that enter into associations with invertebrates or with other fishes. It is a strange and fascinating world under the sea. As man's knowledge of fishes grows, his curiosity and need for more information increases too. Keeping them in aquaria and observing them at close range is one way of learning more about them.

The fishes with which this book is primarily concerned are those which can be kept successfully in a home aquarium. This unfortunately excludes a great number of desirable species. Large fishes can be kept only when young, and very delicate species can hardly be kept for any length of time although they constitute a challenge to the advanced marine aquarist. Deep-water and open-water (pelagic) fishes are normally not suited to the home aquaria because of space and oxygen requirements, although a few can adapt to the much larger tanks of public aquaria. Some of the deep-water species, with their bizarre shapes and luminescent lights that flash on and off in the black depths of the ocean, could provide a spectacular display in an aquarium. Unfortunately, the conditions of temperature, pressure, etc., are extremely difficult to reproduce even in public aquaria with diverse facilities at their disposal.

The majority of fishes available to the home aquarist are reef and shore fishes. If only fishes of small enough size to reach maturity in a moderate-sized aquarium were kept these would be very few indeed. Fortunately, among the fishes that are of large size as adults but desirable as aquarium pets, there are those that are self-limiting, that is, they reach a certain size and stop growing. Aside from this stunting effect the fish does quite well. There will always be fishes that do so well in aquaria, they quickly ougrow the tank, forcing the keeper to provide larger quarters or dispose of them. And there will always be fishes that, no matter what care is provided for them, will never take to captivity.

Warm-water fishes are usually selected for the home aquarium since, besides being more colorful in general, it is easier to provide heat for a tank than it is to provide refrigeration.

COLLECTING SALT-WATER FISHES

The tropical seas of the world provide us with the coral reef fishes, among the most beautiful fishes in the world. The shallow reefs are in themselves composed (in part) of delicately constructed and brilliantly colored animals, an appropriate background for the fishes.

Collecting specimens on a coral reef is not an easy task. Anyone who has netted fishes in a tank set-up with decorations of coral knows that even in such a confined area the fish can avoid capture for a surprising length of time. At times the aquarium has to be torn down to just sand and water to capture the elusive fish. Now imagine this same fish on a reef where it has freedom to dart among the coral, sea fans, rocks or other shelter and a diver with hand nets with or without SCUBA tanks chasing it. A fish always seems to settle down or become cornered only when the air in the SCUBA tank or lungs is exhausted so that a trip to the surface becomes imperative.

Reef fishes are usually good swimmers since they have to outswim or out-dodge other fishes which have decided to have a fish dinner. Those that are poor swimmers usually have good camouflage or some distasteful aspect about them like a hard shell, long spines, or poisonous nature. The reef fishes are also familiar with their surroundings and know where to go to escape. Many times a prized specimen has been chased into a hole and, while the collector searches the hole for it, it pops out a short distance away seemingly mocking the strange, awkward creature after it.

Then of course these fishes are relatively safe if they choose certain animals to take shelter in. The Jewelfish of the Caribbean seems to prefer to swim around fire coral, and many fishes can be found swimming about the long, dangerous spines of the black sea urchin.

How then are the fishes caught? The number one attribute of a good collector is patience, followed in quick order by endurance and, of course, luck. He must be an experienced swimmer and a student of fish behavior. It helps if he has a thorough background in marine biology. As his experience increases, so will his catch!

Basically all that is needed to collect reef fishes are fins, mask, snorkel (although some collectors manage with a pair of home-made goggles), and a sturdy net or two. A holding container for the catch is necessary. For more serious collecting SCUBA equipment is a must. Before using the equipment it is imperative to take diving lessons from a qualified instructor. SCUBA tanks give the diver two main advantages over free diving: (1) not having to come to the surface every few seconds and being able to spend more time chasing a particular fish; (2) being able to probe the deeper reefs for specimens. The disadvantages are the diving hazards such as bends, air embolism, etc. When collecting with SCUBA tanks it is best to have a container for the catch with you. This can be a rather simple cage or plastic box with an entrance designed to let the fish in but not out. Some persons use a plastic bag tied to the waist, but this could be awkward and usually gets in the way. It is better to have a line from the box to the surface with a buoy marker attached. When the air runs low and the diver has to return to the surface he does not have to carry the fish with him. At the surface he can take his time retrieving his catch being careful that they do not get the bends from too quick an ascent.

The underwater world can be a very hostile environment for the collector. The physical features such as currents, surges and surf, diving hazards with SCUBA, can be just as dangerous, or even more so, as the much publicized biological ones (sharks, scorpionfish, sea wasps, etc.). A collector with a bad sunburn, cuts and bruises, stings from various animals and a chilled feeling at the end of a collecting trip is not unusual. No wonder some species of fishes are very expensive! On the other hand many species are rather easy to catch or trap and are therefore not as expensive. Drawing a seine across a grass flat usually produces something of value such as sea horses, pipefishes, puffers, or some other local fishes. Shaking *Sargassum* or brown seaweed over a net is a good method of collecting the Sargassum-fish (*Histrio histrio*), filefishes, triggerfishes, and other weed fishes. Certain species of fishes, such as the genera *Platax* and *Pterois*, rely mostly on their protective color or poisonous nature and make little or no effort to escape. Trapping has been used successfully by some of the larger fish shippers but the fishes easily become damaged either from the traps themselves or from bringing them up from too great a depth. *Centropyge potteri* is particularly subject to pressure changes and will not often survive a depth change of over 40 feet.

Problems in dealing with fishes include damage during capture, transport, holding, and handling as well as diseases and parasites that can wipe out tank after tank of fishes.

With the advent of a hurricane or typhoon the collector must sit and wait till the wind dies and the water clears before attempting a collecting trip.

The individual as well as the commercial collector are steadily building up their repertoire of fish collecting equipment. The "slurp gun," a hand suction pump of sorts for drawing a fish out of its hole, is one instrument gaining in popularity. Tranquillizers like Quinaldine or MS-222 have been used to put the fishes to "sleep" or make them groggy so that they can easily be netted. These are controversial drugs and a great debate is raging over the possible effects of their use. At the present time it cannot be stated whether they are harmless or detrimental, or harmful only when used in a particular concentration or way.

Where do these marine aquarium fishes come from? All over the world! The earliest sources for the United States were the Florida Keys and the Bahama Islands. These areas are fairly near for safe transport and supplied a colorful and popular group of fish species including such favorites as the French and Queen Angelfish, Beau Gregory, and Neon Goby. With more experience in shipping fishes, exotic reef fishes are now flown in from distant areas such as Hawaii, the Philippine Islands, East Indies, the Red Sea, and Ceylon. The famous Great Barrier Reef of Australia has a magnificent fish fauna but remains virtually untapped by collectors.

STOCKING THE HOME AQUARIUM

Many marine fishes accustomed to the vast open waters of the world's oceans gradually decline when placed in a home aquarium. If they do not die from lack of space and improper food, or their beautiful colors fade, they may become aggressive towards their tank-mates. Some fishes, such as the damselfishes, are naturally aggressive, while others, for example the angelfishes, are more aggressive towards their own kind. In some cases a "stand-off" is accomplished whereas in other instances the weaker individual will succumb. Therefore special care should be exercised in selecting the inhabitants of your aquarium.

Any new introduction into an established tank should be watched closely at first. Sometimes it is wise to separate the new one from the others by a glass or plastic partition until a mutual acceptance has been established. Small fishes will usually adapt better and faster to an aquarium and its inhabitants than larger ones.

The aquarium itself should reflect the type of fishes kept. Coral reef fishes require shelter in the form of rocks, coral, etc., sea horses need something to wrap their tails around, and flatfishes and wrasses do better with a combination of sand and rocks. Covers should be provided not only to control evaporation but to prevent fishes from jumping or climbing out.

MARINE FISH CATALOGUE

The catalogue that follows is of course not complete due to the vast number of species that are potential aquarium fishes. Common names are given whenever possible. Several common names are mentioned at times when the fish is known by different names in different parts of its range. Photographs, many of them in color, are presented to facilitate recognition.

THE SQUIRRELFISHES
Family Holocentridae

Almost all of the squirrelfishes are similarly shaped, with a deeply notched dorsal fin, forked tail, large eyes, and a very strong second spine of the anal fin. In some genera (*Adioryx, Flammeo, Holocentrus*) a strong, sharp spine is present on the cheek bone. The squirrelfishes are basically red in color, usually trimmed with a pattern of black, white, or yellow.

The large eyes and red coloration are adaptations to a nocturnal existence. Such fishes tend to be shy during the day, coming out of their hiding places in the evening to feed. They are carnivorous and will not hesitate to gulp down some of the smaller aquarium fishes if they are present.

They are provided with pharyngeal (in the throat) teeth with which they can produce clicking sounds.

Although most of the species are too large for the home aquarium as adults, young specimens are sometimes available.

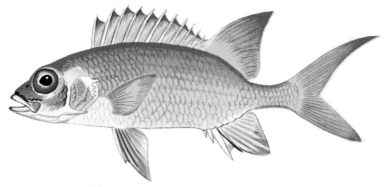

Holocentrus ascensionis from Florida.

Flammeo scythrops is a squirrelfish which is abundant around the Hawaiian Islands. Photo by Dr. Herbert R. Axelrod.

Adioryx diadema, the Barred Squirrelfish, is one of the favorites of the aquarium. Photo by Dr. Herbert R. Axelrod.

There are many common names for these fishes. A sample of these are: Squirrelfishes, Soldierfishes, Soldados, Welshmen, Matajuelos, Malais, Alaihi, etc.

SCIENTIFIC NAME: *Adioryx diadema* (Lacepede).
POPULAR NAME: Barred Squirrelfish, Alaihi Kahaloa (Hawaiian).
Illustrated on page 81.
RANGE: Red Sea to Tahiti and the Hawaiian Islands.
REMARKS: The Barred Squirrelfish is well suited to the home aquarium. It grows rather quickly, however, and soon outgrows its tank. It is also apt to eat smaller fishes placed in the aquarium with it. The Barred Squirrelfish does better with members of its own species or with other squirrelfishes. The dark colored dorsal fin is characteristic for this species.
SIZE: Attains a length of 6 inches.

SCIENTIFIC NAME: *Adioryx lacteoguttatus* (Cuvier).
POPULAR NAME: Pink Squirrelfish.
RANGE: A very wide ranging species found from the Red Sea, through the Indian Ocean, East Indies, and Pacific Ocean to the Hawaiian Islands.
REMARKS: The Pink Squirrelfish is a small species, perhaps more suited to the aquarium than some of the other species. Unfortunately it does not get the intense red coloration of most other squirrelfishes. It appears that *Adioryx lacteoguttatus* and *A. erythraeus* may be one and the same species. In Hawaii the Pink Squirrelfish may be found in water less than six feet deep.
SIZE: Reaches a length of about 5 inches.

SCIENTIFIC NAME: *Adioryx microstomus* (Günther).
POPULAR NAME: Small-mouthed Squirrelfish; Bikini Squirrelfish.
RANGE: Tropical Pacific Islands including Guam, Wake, the Hawaiian Islands, Samoa (common).
REMARKS: The greatly elongated second anal spine will help to distinguish this squirrelfish from others with a similar red and white striped pattern. The name *microstomus* when translated means small mouth.
SIZE: Attains a length of 7 inches.

SCIENTIFIC NAME: *Adioryx spinifer* (Forskål).
POPULAR NAME: Long-jawed Squirrelfish.
RANGE: New Guinea, Guam, Samoa, and possibly across the Pacific Ocean to the Hawaiian Islands; Indian Ocean to the Red Sea.
REMARKS: This is one of the largest squirrelfish. In life the colors are a pleasant blend of red with violet and yellow markings. It lacks the stripes of most other squirrelfishes.
SIZE: To about 18 inches.

SCIENTIFIC NAME: *Adioryx tiere* (Cuvier and Valenciennes).
POPULAR NAME: Palau Squirrelfish.
RANGE: Pacific Islands including the Hawaiian Islands, Tahiti, and Guam.
REMARKS: This is a beautiful species of squirrelfish. In aquarium-sized specimens (under three inches) the body is deep red spotted lightly with brown dots. The stripes show iridescent purple. The light spots on each membrane of the dorsal fin will help identify this species. This species is usually found in waters greater than 20 feet in depth.
SIZE: Reaches a length of about 10 inches.

SCIENTIFIC NAME: *Adioryx xantherythrus* (Jordan & Evermann).
POPULAR NAME: Alaihi, Alaihi Maoli (Hawaiian).
RANGE: Pacific Islands from Samoa to the Hawaiian Islands.
REMARKS: This is another striped species but the light stripes are pinkish rather than white giving it a less contrasting appearance than the white striped forms. It is found at moderate depths on the outer side of the reefs in Hawaii.
SIZE: Attains a length of about 7 inches.

SCIENTIFIC NAME: *Flammeo sammara* (Forskål).
POPULAR NAME: Squirrelfish.
RANGE: Fairly common throughout the Indo-Pacific area.
REMARKS: In the genus *Flammeo* the dorsal fins are not completely separated. In *F. sammara* the dorsal fin has a large black blotch in its anterior part. The body is silvery white with brown stripes composed of spots and with the cheek having noticeable brown spots.
SIZE: To one foot in length.

Oxymonacanthus longirostris, the Orange-spotted Filefish, is often found among the coral branches on a reef. Photo by G. Marcuse.

Monacanthus hispidus, the Common Filefish, is found along the Atlantic coast of the United States.

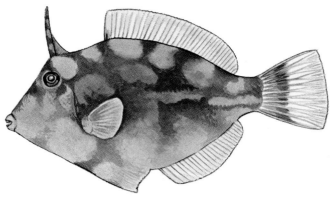

Cantherhines pardalis, a Filefish, occurs in warm waters. Photo by Dr. Herbert R. Axelrod.

Pervagor tomentosus, the Red-tailed Filefish, is native to Ceylon. Photo by Dr. Herbert R. Axelrod.

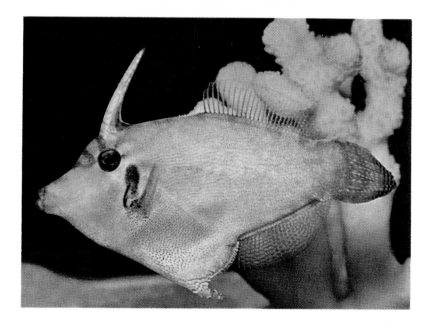

SCIENTIFIC NAME: *Flammeo scythrops* (Jordan & Evermann).

POPULAR NAME: Hawaiian Squirrelfish.

Illustrated on page 81.

RANGE: Common in the vicinity of the Hawaiian Islands.

REMARKS: This species has an elongate second anal spine, reaching almost to the base of the tail fin. It is found only in the Hawaiian Islands in relatively deep water.

SIZE: Attains a length of 10 inches.

SCIENTIFIC NAME: *Holocentrus ascensionis* (Osbeck).

POPULAR NAME: Longjaw Squirrelfish.

Illustrated on page 81.

RANGE: Caribbean Sea, common around Florida (and very likely to be included in shipments from the East Coast collectors).

REMARKS: Squirrelfishes are nocturnal and their eyes are enlarged for this purpose. Bright lights irritate this fish so shelter should be provided in the aquarium. It has an elongated air bladder which reaches all the way up to the cranium.

SIZE: Attains a length of 14 inches.

SCIENTIFIC NAME: *Myripristis chryseres* Jordan & Evermann.

POPULAR NAME: Yellowfin Soldierfish; Pauu (Hawaiian).

RANGE: Hawaiian Islands.

REMARKS: This species is easily recognized by its yellow fins in comparison to the red color in other species. The genus *Myripristis* lacks the cheek spine of the above genera. Although not very common the Yellowfin Soldierfish is still a very popular Hawaiian soldierfish.

SIZE: Reaches a length of at least 10 inches.

SCIENTIFIC NAME: *Myripristis murdjan* Forskål.

POPULAR NAME: Bigeye Squirrelfish; Mempache (Hawaiian).

Illustrated on pages 322, 325.

RANGE: Red Sea through the Indian Ocean, East Indies, and Polynesia to the Hawaiian Islands.

REMARKS: In Hawaii the natives had an interesting method of capturing this fish. A net was lowered with a live Mempache attached above it. Other Mempaches were attracted by the unusual actions of the hooked fish and gathered around it. The net was then raised with the swarm of fish inside.

SIZE: Up to one foot in length in nature.

SCIENTIFIC NAME: *Myripristis pralinus* (Cuvier & Valenciennes).
POPULAR NAME: Red Soldierfish.
RANGE: Widely distributed through the South Pacific area.
REMARKS: This is one of the more popular fishes of the squirrelfish family. It lacks the cheek spine. It still retains the nocturnal habit and is more likely to be seen in the evening than during the day. Even in nature the collector searches for them back in caves or under ledges where the light intensity is very low.
SIZE: Reaches length of about 7 inches.

THE FILEFISHES
Family Monacanthidae

The filefishes are similar to triggerfishes but lack the "trigger" mechanism of that family. They have instead a single, long, sharp dorsal spine, sometimes armed with small, downwardly directed spinules. The gill openings are restricted and the pelvic fins are absent. The common name "filefish" comes from the use of the skin as an abrasive. The scales are modified, giving the skin a shagreen-like texture similar to that of sharks.

Filefishes are inoffensive little fishes some species of which are easy to keep, others difficult. They are omnivorous and should receive a mixture of animal and vegetable food.

SCIENTIFIC NAME: *Alutera schoepfii* (Walbaum).
POPULAR NAME: Orange Filefish.
RANGE: Atlantic coast of the United States to Bermuda.
REMARKS: The body of the Orange Filefish is grayish with numerous orange spots. The lips are black. They can usually be found in grass beds or sand. Orange Filefish feed on the algae or grasses found there. In the aquarium brine shrimp fed along with cooked spinach is advisable.
SIZE: Reaches a length of 20 inches.

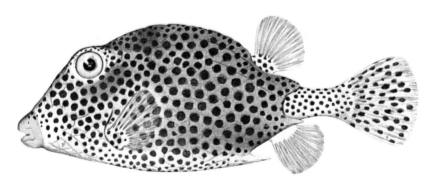

Lactophrys bicaudalis, one of the smooth trunkfishes.

The trunkfish *Lactophrys trigonus* is numerous in Florida waters.

Because of the horns and bovine expression, *Acanthostracion quadricornis* is known as Cowfish, along with other related species.

These cowfish, *Lactoria cornuta*, soon become tame enough to accept tidbits from their owner's hand and make fascinating acquisitions for the marine tank, especially with their very pleasing color pattern.

SCIENTIFIC NAME: *Alutera scripta* (Osbeck).

POPULAR NAME: Scrawled Filefish; Scribbled Filefish.

RANGE: Tropical seas of the world.

REMARKS: The Scrawled Filefish is elongate and has a large fan-like tail. It often hangs head down among *Sargassum* or floating blades of grass ready to make its escape downwards if danger threatens. The color pattern bears a resemblance to the *Sargassum* and it acts like part of the weed itself by swaying back and forth with the gentle motion of the current. Small fishes or shrimps that approach this floating "weed" are quickly dispatched.

SIZE: Grows to about 2 feet in length.

SCIENTIFIC NAME: *Cantherhines pardalis* (Rüppell).

POPULAR NAME: Reticulated Filefish.

Illustrated on pages 85, 160-161.

RANGE: Tropical Indo-Pacific and Red Sea.

REMARKS: This species is easily recognized by the bright white spots on the upper and lower edges of the caudal peduncle, and reticulated pattern. Similar species can be found in the Hawaiian Islands and Caribbean Sea.

SIZE: Attains a length of over 6 inches.

SCIENTIFIC NAME: *Cantherhines verecundus* E. K. Jordan.

POPULAR NAME: Mottled Filefish.

RANGE: Apparently endemic to the Hawaiian Islands.

REMARKS: The mottled pattern of this fish can be changed to an almost solid brownish. Its food consists mainly of small crustaceans.

SIZE: A small species of about 5 inches.

SCIENTIFIC NAME: *Monacanthus hispidus* (Linnaeus).

POPULAR NAME: Common Filefish.

Illustrated on page 84.

RANGE: Nova Scotia to Brazil.

REMARKS: This species is closely related to *Monacanthus setifer* Bennett. It differs from that species in having more dorsal and anal rays and more gill rakers.

SIZE: About 8 or 9 inches.

SCIENTIFIC NAME: *Oxymonacanthus longirostris* (Bloch & Schneider).

POPULAR NAME: Longnosed Filefish.

For the lovers of odd and bizarre fishes, what could be more odd and bizarre than *Ostracion cubicus*, a trunkfish?

To push about such an ungainly, hard body must require a considerable effort and results in slow swimming, but the trunkfish is well protected by its hard shell. Both photos by Gerhard Budich.

Another of the smooth trunkfishes, *Ostracion cubicus.*

Acanthostracion quadricornis has a habit of keeping its caudal fin folded, which adds to its already odd appearance. Photo by Wilhelm Hoppe.

These two little trunkfishes are juvenile specimens of *Ostracion cubicus.* Photo by Robert P. L. Straughan.

There is no mistaking the distinctive markings of *Ostracion cubicus* as an adult. Photo by Dr. Herbert R. Axelrod.

Illustrated on pages 84, 326.

RANGE: East Indies through the Pacific Islands (excluding Hawaii).

REMARKS: The Longnosed Filefish is one of the most brightly colored of filefishes. Its green body with orange spots is easily recognized. This species is found on the reef hiding among the branches of coral. They are adept at using the coral to advantage when chased and are difficult to collect.

SIZE: Attains a length of 4 inches.

SCIENTIFIC NAME: *Pervagor spilosoma* Lay & Bennett.

POPULAR NAME: Fan-tailed Filefish.

Illustrated on page 155.

RANGE: East Indies to the Hawaiian Islands.

REMARKS: The red tail of this species is very attractive making recognition of this fish easy. The Fan-tailed Filefish often becomes faded in captivity and ultimately succumbs. They are omnivorous and should be supplied with some greens.

SIZE: Reaches a length of about 6 inches.

SCIENTIFIC NAME: *Pervagor tomentosus* (Linnaeus).

POPULAR NAME: Red-tailed Filefish.

Illustrated on page 85.

RANGE: Tropical Indo-Pacific.

REMARKS: This species is closely related to the Fan-tailed Filefish but lacks the spotting on the head and body. It is omnivorous and should be given a varied diet.

SIZE: Attains a length of about 5 inches.

THE TRUNKFISHES
Family Ostraciidae

The scales of trunkfishes are fused together to form a solid shell which covers almost the entire body. This shell is provided with openings for the various fins, the eyes, gill openings, and snout. In some species there are sharp spines projecting from the corners providing a rather unpleasant mouthful for any fish. The small fins and bulky body make rapid swimming an impossibility. Trunkfishes can easily be run down and caught by hand.

Trunkfishes are found in shallow water, often over grass flats. They feed on various small crabs and shrimps by "blowing" into the sand and scaring up the prey like a hydraulic miner. In an aquarium they will sometimes swim near the surface with snout protruding above water and "squirt" water into the air like a small fountain.

When "unhappy" some species of trunkfishes exude a poisonous substance into the water killing all their tankmates and ultimately themselves.

SCIENTIFIC NAME: *Acanthostracion quadricornis* (Linnaeus).
POPULAR NAME: Scrawled Cowfish.
Illustrated on pages 88, 92.
RANGE: Tropical Atlantic.
REMARKS: The Scrawled Cowfish is a common Florida species which can usually be collected by seining through grass flats. It comes into shallow water and crosses areas where its back ridge breaks water and is exposed. It feeds on various invertebrates including such unusual animals as sponges, sea squirts, and gorgonids, as well as the usual crustaceans.
SIZE: Reaches a length of a foot and a half.

SCIENTIFIC NAME: *Lactophrys bicaudalis* (Linnaeus).
POPULAR NAME: Spotted Trunkfish.
Illustrated on page 88.
RANGE: Brazil to Florida.
REMARKS: Easily distinguished from other Caribbean Trunkfishes by the spotted pattern, *Lactophrys bicaudalis* has a rather odd diet. It dines on such things as echinoderms (starfish, sea cucumbers, sea urchins, etc.), crabs, sea squirts, and a variety of grasses and algae.
SIZE: Reaches a length of over 1 foot.

SCIENTIFIC NAME: *Lactophrys triqueter* (Linnaeus).
POPULAR NAME: Smooth Trunkfish.
RANGE: Florida and the West Indies, straggling north to Massachusetts.
REMARKS: The Smooth Trunkfish lacks the sharp spines over the eyes of *Acanthostracion*. The bases of the dorsal and pectoral fins are black as is a ring about the lips. It eats a wide variety of foods and will probably do well on most fish foods.
SIZE: To about 1 foot.

Ostracion meleagris, adult male from Ceylon.

Ostracion meleagris, adult male. Photo by Gene Wolfsheimer.

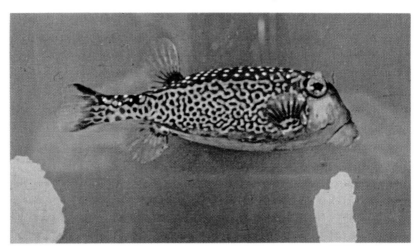

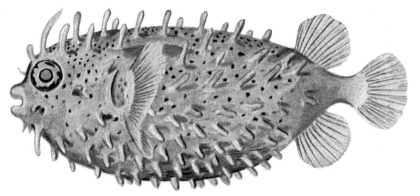

One of the Spiny Boxfishes, *Chilomycterus antennatus.*

Imagine how a larger fish feels when he tries to swallow a *Diodon hystrix* which has puffed itself up. Photo by Dr. Herbert R. Axelrod.

SCIENTIFIC NAME: *Lactophrys trigonus* (Linnaeus).

POPULAR NAME: Buffalo Trunkfish; Common Trunkfish.

Illustrated on page 88.

RANGE: Common in Florida waters.

REMARKS: The Buffalo Trunkfish differs from *L. triqueter* by having a slight concavity in the shell behind the head. It is found in the grass beds near reefs feeding on the usual crustaceans, molluscs, worms, and other invertebrates as well as algae and marine plants.

SIZE: A little over one foot in length.

SCIENTIFIC NAME: *Lactoria cornuta* (Linnaeus).

POPULAR NAME: Long-horned Cowfish.

Illustrated on page 89.

RANGE: Tropical Indo-Pacific.

REMARKS: The Long-horned Cowfish is well deserving of its name. The spines above the eyes are balanced by similar spines projecting from the ventral edge of the carapace. Long-horned Cowfish thus present a very disagreeable mouthful. Rearing these fishes involves promoting an algal bloom (green) and frequent feedings of natural plankton. They grow rapidly and soon are able to handle newly hatched brine shrimp.

SIZE: Grows to a length of about 20 inches.

SCIENTIFIC NAME: *Lactoria fornasini* Bianconi.

POPULAR NAME: Cowfish.

RANGE: Tropical Indo-Pacific (including the Hawaiian Islands).

REMARKS: The armament of this species is formidable. It has a spine over each eye, a strong spine on its back, and a pair of spines just anterior to the anal fin. This does not appear to provide perfect protection since it occasionally is found in the stomachs of tuna fish.

SIZE: Grows to a size of about 5 inches.

SCIENTIFIC NAME: *Ostracion cubicus* Linnaeus.

POPULAR NAME: Spotted Boxfish; Spotted Trunkfish.

Illustrated on pages 91, 92, 93.

RANGE: Throughout the tropical Indo-Pacific.

REMARKS: The Spotted Boxfish is easily recognized by the small spots on the body which change drastically with age. The juvenile of this species is unspotted, but is checkered with the intersections of the checkers being heavy, dark spots which continue throughout the change to become the spots characteristic of the adults.

When the fish is lifted from the water in a net, it has a strange, not unpleasant odor. Could this possibly be the poisonous substance it exudes when frightened?

Natural food includes crustaceans, snails and worms.

SIZE: To about 10 inches.

SCIENTIFIC NAME: *Ostracion meleagris* Bloch.
POPULAR NAME: Spotted Boxfish.
 Illustrated on page 96.
RANGE: Tropical Indo-Pacific.
REMARKS: The Spotted Boxfish is a very variable species with regards to color. The males and the females differ in pattern and the individuals vary in color. The male has orange spots on its sides, differing sharply from the small white spots on the dorsal surface. The female is covered with small white spots. The Spotted Boxfish exudes a poisonous mucus when frightened so if possible keep it separate or it may kill its tankmates.
SIZE: Grows to about 9 inches in length.

THE PORCUPINEFISHES
Family Diodontidae

Porcupinefishes are well deserving of their name, having spines protruding from all over the body. This, combined with the ability to inflate themselves, creates a living pincushion, enough protection to ward off all but the hungriest of enemies. They are eaten, however, as they have been found in the stomachs of tunas.

The porcupinefishes grow quite large but the young ones are interesting additions to an aquarium. They need plenty of room since the oxygen requirements are high. Their natural diet includes hard-shelled crustaceans so shrimp or crab meat is ideal.

SCIENTIFIC NAME: *Chilomycterus antennatus* (Cuvier).
POPULAR NAME: Bridled Burrfish.
 Illustrated on page 97.
RANGE: Tropical Western Atlantic.
REMARKS: The spines in the genus *Chilomycterus* are fixed, and the Bridled Burrfish is not as apt to inflate itself as the following species. The juveniles are "personality" fish with fleshy tabs above each eye giving them a rather bizarre appearance when seen from the front. They are inhabitants of grass beds and may be collected by seining.
SIZE: To about 10 inches.

There are many frogfishes all over the world. This one, *Antennarius bigibbus*, has a range from Hawaii to California and all the way to Madagascar. Photo by Gene Wolfsheimer.

Antennarius drombus comes from Hawaii. Photo by Gene Wolfsheimer.

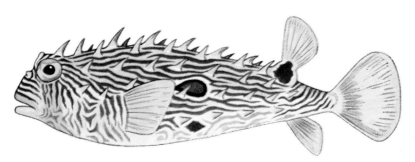

The Spiny Boxfish, *Chilomycterus schoepfi*.

Diodon hystrix, the Porcupine fish, puffs itself into a prickly ball.

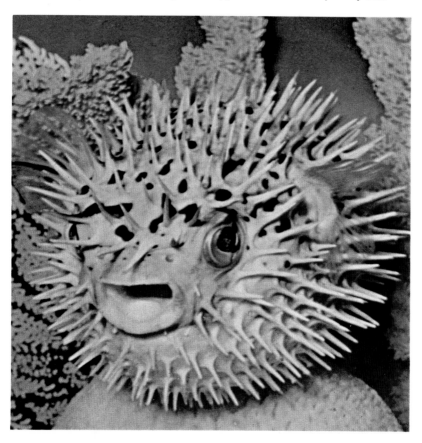

SCIENTIFIC NAME: *Chilomycterus schoepfi* (Walbaum).

POPULAR NAME: Spiny Boxfish.

Illustrated on page 101.

RANGE: Cape Cod to Florida and the Gulf of Mexico. More common in the southern portion of its range.

REMARKS: In this species the fish is apparently dark greenish with light longitudinal lines forming a pattern on the back. In *C. antillarum* dark lines join to form reticulations against a light background. Feeds mainly on crustaceans in shallow water.

SIZE: Reaches at least to 10 inches.

SCIENTIFIC NAME: *Diodon holacanthus* Linnaeus.

POPULAR NAME: Spiny Puffer.

RANGE: Found in tropical areas of the world's oceans.

REMARKS: Large brown blotches above and below each eye, on the back, surrounding the dorsal fin, and across the head distinguish this species from the closely related *Diodon hystrix*. Food includes mostly crabs and shellfish.

SIZE: Attains a length of about a foot and a half.

SCIENTIFIC NAME: *Diodon hystrix* Linnaeus.

POPULAR NAME: Porcupinefish.

Illustrated on pages 97, 101.

RANGE: Circumtropical.

REMARKS: The Porcupinefish is able to inflate itself like the puffers. Its spines, actually modified scales, are normally folded back for streamlining but stick straight out when the fish is inflated. It is the Porcupinefish that is dried when inflated and used to make lamps and lanterns. It feeds mainly on molluscs and crustacea.

SIZE: To about 2 feet.

THE FROGFISHES

Family Antennariidae

The frogfishes are one of the oddest groups ever kept in marine aquaria. They walk, crawl, go fishing with a rod and bait, and look like nondescript lumps!

Although they can swim, with the caudal fin providing the main propulsion, they normally remain close to the substrate, whether it be the bottom itself or a floating raft of *Sargassum*. The pectoral and pelvic

Puzzle: find the fish! Most of the anglerfishes lie on the bottom and imitate rocks, but the Sargassum Fish represents a remarkable adaptation by Nature to blend in the background. N.Y.Z.S. Photo.

Taken out of its surroundings, the Sargassum Fish still looks like a bundle of seaweed. N.Y.Z.S. Photo.

Antennarius chironectes is a Philippine species which can change its color to match plants or algae. Photo by Gene Wolfsheimer.

Note the "fishing rod" just behind the upper lip of *Antennarius scaber.* This is waved in front of the fish's mouth to attract smaller fishes.

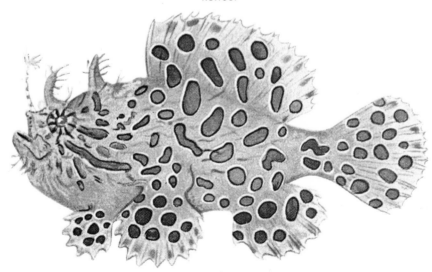

Antennarius scaber (black phase). Note how the pectoral fins are on a jointed elongation which resembles a short "leg" and permits the fish to "walk" along the bottom.

Another Sargassum Fish species, *Histrio histrio.* These fishes are very uncomfortable when taken out of their Sargassum weed hiding places. Photo by Dr. Herbert R. Axelrod.

fins are modified as "stalks" with the fins at the end, which are used almost like hands and feet, as they crawl from one branch of the weed to another or walk along the bottom of its tank. They are masters of disguise looking for the most part like a rock or a piece of weed. When danger threatens they will sit quietly, relying on this protective resemblance rather than flight.

Frogfishes are notorious for their large mouths and equally large capacity for food. Fishes almost as large as themselves have disappeared down the throat into the distensible stomach. To capture their food they remain quietly waiting for their prey confident that in their camouflage they will not be spotted. To entice the prey within striking range one of the dorsal spines has been modified into a "fishing pole" with a bait or lure at the end. The bait is wiggled as a fish approaches. If the fish is attracted to the bait and comes close, a swift movement by the frogfish is made and the fish is no longer there.

In the aquarium then, these fishes will of course prefer to feed on living fishes which they capture in a surprisingly short length of time. Other foods will be accepted and you may be able to tame these fishes to accept strips of fish dangled in front of them with a rod or pair of tweezers. Remember that they have enormous mouths and a distensible stomach so they can (and usually will) eat any fish up to their own size.

Frogfishes are hardy and will normally live in captivity for a long time.

SCIENTIFIC NAME: *Antennarius bigibbus* Lacepede.
POPULAR NAME: Pygmy Anglerfish.
　Illustrated on page 100.
RANGE: Tropical Indo-Pacific to the Gulf of California.
REMARKS: The "fishing rod" of this species is a bit longer than in other species, reaching almost to the third dorsal spine. Its small size and availability make it a popular aquarium fish. In the Hawaiian Islands they are found in and under rocks blending closely to them.
SIZE: Reaches a length of only 3 inches.

SCIENTIFIC NAME: *Antennarius chironectes* (Lacepede).
POPULAR NAMES: Toadfish; Fishing Frog.
　Illustrated on page 104.
RANGE: Tropical Indo-Pacific.
REMARKS: The Fishing Frog is another species which relies on its protective coloration to avoid capture. It is best to keep it by itself or with fishes considerably larger than itself. Any small fishes placed in the aquarium will serve as food.
SIZE: Attains a length of 5 inches or more.

Antennarius scaber, a Florida species, has a really odd wormlike attachment on its "fishing rod." Here we see it in action. N.Y.Z.S. Photo.

Here *Antennarius* has grabbed its prey. From the bulge of its belly, it looks as if many more have preceded it. Photo by Kurt Severin.

The *Heniochus* species are very popular because of their attractive colors, their perky behavior and hardiness in the aquarium. Shown is *Heniochus acuminatus*. Photo by Dr. Herbert R. Axelrod.

The fabulous Moorish Idol, *Zanclus canescens*. Unfortunately, they are a bit delicate and shipping them, as well as keeping them alive in an aquarium, is difficult. Photo by Dr. Herbert R. Axelrod.

SCIENTIFIC NAME: *Antennarius drombus* Jordan & Evermann.

POPULAR NAME: Spotted Angler.

Illustrated on page 100.

RANGE: Central Pacific Islands, including Hawaii.

REMARKS: The dark brown spots and lack of an ocellate spot in the soft portion of the dorsal fin aid in the identification of this species. Care and feeding are similar to other members of this genus.

SIZE: Attains about 4 inches in length.

SCIENTIFIC NAME: *Antennarius nummifer* Cuvier.

POPULAR NAME: Scarlet Angler.

RANGE: Red Sea, tropical Indo-Pacific, including the Hawaiian Islands.

REMARKS: The Scarlet Anglerfish should be provided with sand and rocks. It has been reported partially buried in mud "fishing" for small passing fishes. They will eat as much as they can catch and the abdomen will become greatly distended due to its catch.

SIZE: Attains a length of 6 inches or more.

SCIENTIFIC NAME: *Antennarius phymatodes* Bleeker.

POPULAR NAME: Wartskin Frogfish.

RANGE: Indian Ocean to East Indies and the Philippines.

REMARKS: The Wartskin Frogfish is a very oddly shaped frogfish. One must look carefully to be able to distinguish the various parts of the body. In nature this species blends closely with its environment not only for its protection but also to hide from its prey. The wiggly bait resembles a worm on a rock. Small fishes are almost mandatory as food for this species.

SIZE: Attains a length of 4-5 inches.

SCIENTIFIC NAME: *Antennarius scaber* (Cuvier).

POPULAR NAME: Splitlure Frogfish.

Illustrated on pages 104, 105, 107.

RANGE: Widespread from New Jersey to Brazil.

REMARKS: This species can be very confusing since it is able to change color from black to tan with black spots. It blends in well with its surroundings and its food, usually passing fishes, apparently sees nothing except the "bait" waving near some rock.

SIZE: Reaches about 6 inches in length.

110

SCIENTIFIC NAME: *Histrio histrio* Linnaeus.
POPULAR NAME: Sargassumfish.
Illustrated on pages 103, 105.
RANGE: Tropical seas of the world.
REMARKS: The color of this fish can vary somewhat through shades of yellow to brown to suit their surroundings. The Sargassumfish is found almost exclusively in the floating *Sargassum* and takes its name from that alga, which it closely resembles. As noted above the fins are modified for such an existence and the fish is able to climb around its floating home without much difficulty. This slow moving fish gets its wide distribution from the floating weed, the currents carrying it across the oceans.

The small fishes or shrimps that seek refuge in the *Sargassum* may find they have made a terrible mistake if they encounter one of these Sargassumfishes. This fish will also cannibalize its own kind and this must be taken into account when setting up an aquarium.
SIZE: Attains a length of about 8 inches.

THE MOORISH IDOL

Family Zanclidae

The Moorish Idol is a favorite everywhere. Its distinctive color pattern and pleasingly artistic shaped body have prompted its use as a design in many aspects of our life, surpassed only by the sea horses.

The Moorish Idol has a projecting snout, deep, compressed body, and elongate dorsal and anal fins. The dorsal fin has a filament that, intact, is longer than the body length itself.

This fish spends its larval life in the open ocean waters, returning to shore when about two to three inches in length. It usually thrives on live, cleaned mussels on the half-shell.

The Moorish Idol is closely related to the Surgeonfishes.

SCIENTIFIC NAME: *Zanclus canescens* Linnaeus.
POPULAR NAMES: Moorish Idol; Kihikihi Laulau (Hawaiian).
Illustrated on pages 109, 124, 144.
RANGE: Red Sea and East African coast to the Hawaiian Islands and eastward to the Mexican coast.
REMARKS: There has been a great deal of controversy as to whether there is but one or two species in this family. The names *Zanclus cornutus* and *Z. canescens* have been used at one time or another (or simultaneously when two species were recognized) for the Moorish Idol. The preorbital spikes or horns were cited as the distinguishing

111

Pygoplites diacanthus. This beauty comes from the tropical Indo-Pacific region. Photo by Hans and Klaus Paysan.

The Copperband Butterflyfish, *Chelmon rostratus*, is a favorite among marine aquarists. Photo by Roger Steene.

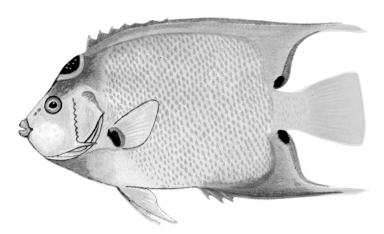

The Queen Angelfish is a beautiful and highly prized
aquarium fish when young.

This fish, considerably different from the one represented above,
may be a hybrid between the Queen and Blue Angelfish. This
hybrid cross has been referred to at times as *Holacanthus
townsendi.*

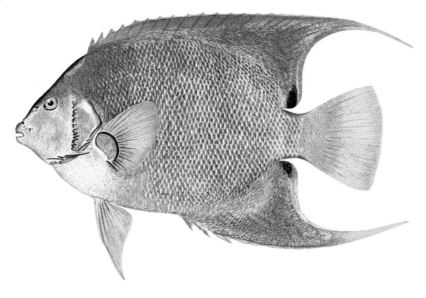

characteristic. Dr. Randall in 1958 looked into the problem and came to the conclusion that there were not two species but a single one.

SIZE: About 12 inches.

THE BUTTERFLYFISHES
Family Chaetodontidae

The angelfishes, usually classified with the butterflyfishes, are listed separately due to the recent work of one of the authors (WEB). The butterflyfishes lack the large spine on the preopercle or cheek bone that is present on that of the angelfishes. They are compressed, deep bodied, and have very pleasing color patterns. Some have long snouts, others elongate fin rays or filaments trailing from the fins. The family is a large one, containing over one hundred species.

Butterflyfishes are strictly marine although reports of adaptations to brackish or even fresh-water have been received. Most butterflyfishes can be found on the coral reefs of the world's oceans. The corals not only provide shelter but food also. The small mouths and brush-like teeth are adapted for nipping at the coral polyps as well as the small creatures that live in and around the corals themselves. In the aquarium they are apt to be a bit temperamental as far as food is concerned, and may insist on live shrimp, live coral, or other small invertebrate animals. They may be carefully weaned to other foods more readily accessible such as live brine shrimp, white worms or small earthworms.

Spawning of butterflyfishes in nature has never been observed, or at least, never reported. It is known that for the first few months the young butterflyfishes live in the open ocean (though relatively close to some land mass).

SCIENTIFIC NAME: *Chaetodon auriga* Forskål.
POPULAR NAME: Thread-fin Butterflyfish.
   Illustrated on page 117.
RANGE: Widely distributed from the Red Sea and East African coast to the Hawaiian Islands.
REMARKS: In Red Sea specimens the black dorsal spot is often missing. In young specimens the dorsal filament is missing, but as the fish grows it soon makes its appearance. The Thread-fin Butterflyfish is one of the most common of the butterflyfishes and almost always is available from the Pacific collectors.
SIZE: Attains a length of 8 inches.

SCIENTIFIC NAME: *Chaetodon bennetti* Cuvier.

POPULAR NAME: Bennett's Butterflyfish.

Illustrated on page 121.

RANGE: East African coast to the East Indies and Japan, across the Pacific Islands to Tahiti but not reaching the Hawaiian Islands.

REMARKS: The black spot on its side encircled with a bright blue ring may be obscured by a larger black blotch superimposed on it. The "V"-shaped blue lines are found only in this species.

SIZE: Attains a length of 9 inches.

SCIENTIFIC NAME: *Chaetodon capistratus* Linnaeus.

POPULAR NAME: Four-eyed Butterflyfish.

Illustrated on page 120.

RANGE: West Indies to Florida, straggling northward in the summer months.

REMARKS: The popular name refers to the two eyes plus the two black spots, one on each side of the body near the tail region. They are called false eyes and are reported to attract the attention of a predator away from the true eyes.

SIZE: Reaches 6 inches in length.

SCIENTIFIC NAME: *Chaetodon citrinellus* Broussonet.

POPULAR NAME: Citron Butterflyfish.

Illustrated on page 125.

RANGE: Hawaiian Islands and tropical Indo-Pacific.

REMARKS: This species is usually confused with other spotted butterfly-fishes. It can easily be recognized by the black edge to the anal fin and lack of black band on the caudal peduncle.

SIZE: Attains a length of about 5 to 6 inches.

SCIENTIFIC NAME: *Chaetodon collaris* Day.

POPULAR NAME: Pakistani Butterflyfish.

Illustrated on page 121.

RANGE: Southeast Asia and East Indies to Japan.

DISCUSSION: The species illustrated was photographed by the author (HRA) in Karachi, Pakistan after having been collected by the local fisheries department for a collection of their fishes to be displayed in the new aquarium erected in 1961. The director of the aquarium, Maqsood-ul-Hasan, has designed and constructed one of the most beautiful aquariums in the Middle East.

The juvenile Queen Angelfish. Photo by Dr. Herbert R. Axelrod.

This adult Queen Angelfish shows a color pattern different from that represented above, but both are *Holacanthus ciliaris* nevertheless. Photo by Robert P. L. Straughan.

Centropyge potteri, from the Indo-Pacific. Photo by Gene Wolfsheimer.

Chaetodon auriga has an unusual pattern of lines, and is a very beautiful aquarium fish. Photo by Dr. Herbert R. Axelrod.

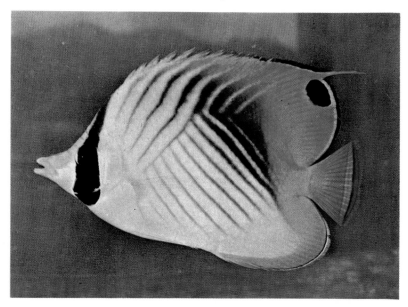

SCIENTIFIC NAME: *Chaetodon ephippium* Cuvier.

POPULAR NAME: Saddle Butterflyfish.

Illustrated on pages 128, 206.

RANGE: Pacific Ocean from East Indies and Japan to the Hawaiian Islands.

REMARKS: The dorsal filament is present in adult animals only. The eye band, present in small Saddle Butterflyfishes, disappears with age.

SIZE: Reaches about 9 inches at maturity.

SCIENTIFIC NAME: *Chaetodon falcula* Bloch.

POPULAR NAME: Double-saddle Butterflyfish.

RANGE: Pacific and Indian Oceans from East Africa to the Society Islands.

REMARKS: The two black saddles on this fish are distinctive. The Double-saddle Butterflyfish are usually found in pairs on the reef.

SIZE: Up to $7\frac{1}{2}$ inches.

SCIENTIFIC NAME: *Chaetodon fremblii* Bennett.

POPULAR NAME: Bluestripe Butterflyfish.

Illustrated on page 128.

RANGE: Known only from the Hawaiian Islands.

REMARKS: The Bluestripe Butterflyfish is common around the Hawaiian Islands but found nowhere else in the world. It has a very wide depth range, extending from shallow tide-pools to over 600 feet deep.

SIZE: Reaches a length of about 6 inches.

SCIENTIFIC NAME: *Chaetodon octofasciatus* Bloch.

POPULAR NAME: Eight-banded Butterflyfish.

Illustrated on page 137.

RANGE: Western tropical Pacific including the Philippine Islands and East Indies to Ceylon.

REMARKS: The four pairs of stripes make this butterflyfish easy to recognize. The Eight-banded butterflyfish is usually difficult to maintain in captivity.

SIZE: Reaches a length of about 5-6 inches.

SCIENTIFIC NAME: *Chaetodon lineolatus* Cuvier.

POPULAR NAME: Lined Butterflyfish.

Illustrated on page 129.

RANGE: The same wide distribution as the preceding species.

REMARKS: The Lined Butterflyfish is the largest of the species of the genus *Chaetodon*, reaching over a foot in length. They are not very common and when found are usually paired.

SIZE: Attains a length of at least 13 inches.

SCIENTIFIC NAME: *Chaetodon lunula* Lacepede.

POPULAR NAMES: Raccoon Butterflyfish; Masked Butterflyfish; Red-lined Butterflyfish.

Illustrated on page 129.

RANGE: From the east African coast to the Hawaiian Islands.

REMARKS: The Raccoon Butterflyfish undergoes a change from its juvenile coloration to the adult. A black spot in the dorsal fin eventually disappears and the large black blotches behind the head become more apparent and well defined with age.

SIZE: Reaches a length of 9 inches at maturity.

SCIENTIFIC NAME: *Chaetodon melannotus* Bloch & Schneider.

POPULAR NAME: Black-backed Butterflyfish.

Illustrated on page 132.

RANGE: Widespread in the tropical Indo-Pacific; Red Sea.

REMARKS: When frightened or sick this fish will become very dark along its back except for two light spots. This is also its nighttime coloration.

SIZE: Reaches a maximum length of about 5 inches.

SCIENTIFIC NAME: *Chaetodon mertensii* Cuvier.

POPULAR NAME: Merten's Butterflyfish.

RANGE: Pacific Ocean to Japan and Australia. Not reaching the Hawaiian Islands.

REMARKS: Merten's Butterflyfish is very often confused with the closely related *Chaetodon xanthurus* or *C. chrysurus*. In this species, however, the dark nuchal spot is not well defined and lacks the white border present in the other two species.

SIZE: Reaches a length of 7 inches.

SCIENTIFIC NAME: *Chaetodon meyeri* Bloch & Schneider.

POPULAR NAME: Meyer's Butterflyfish.

Illustrated on pages 124, 133.

RANGE: Pacific and Indian Oceans.

REMARKS: This beautiful butterflyfish is very distinctly marked with curved black lines. Although the range is extensive Meyer's Butterflyfish is not very common.

SIZE: To 10 inches in length.

The Four-Eyed Butterfly Fish, *Chaetodon capistratus*, is one of the most common of the Florida coralfishes. This is a young specimen. Photo by Dr. Herbert R. Axelrod.

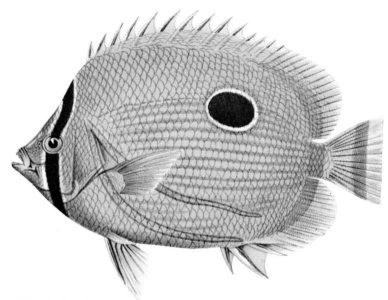

Chaetodon bennetti is a handsome, easily-recognized fish.

A great many butterfly fishes run to yellows and browns, but *Chaetodon collaris* is a beautiful exception, and a hardy aquarium fish as well. Photo by Dr. Herbert R. Axelrod.

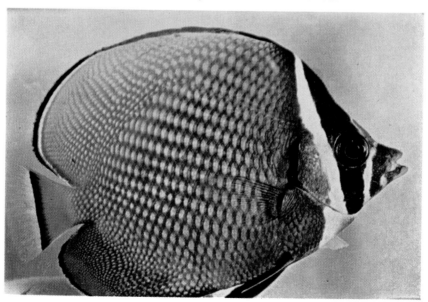

SCIENTIFIC NAME: *Chaetodon miliaris* Quoy & Gaimard.

POPULAR NAMES: Lemon Butterflyfish; Milletseed Butterflyfish.

RANGE: Known only from the Hawaiian Islands.

REMARKS: The Lemon Butterflyfish is hardier than most other species of butterflyfish. It is very common in the Hawaiian Islands, being found in schools of over 100 individuals at times. The young enter tide pools in Oahu in the spring.

SIZE: Reaches a length of 7 inches.

SCIENTIFIC NAME: *Chaetodon ocellatus* Bloch.

POPULAR NAME: Spotfin Butterflyfish.

Illustrated on page 136.

RANGE: West Indies north to Florida. Straggles further northward in the summer months.

REMARKS: The large black spot in the rayed portion of the dorsal fin sometimes fades out but the one at the angle of the fin is always there. The Spotfin Butterflyfish often is contained in the Florida shipments.

SIZE: To 8 inches.

SCIENTIFIC NAME: *Chaetodon ornatissimus* Cuvier.

POPULAR NAMES: Clown Butterflyfish; Orange-striped Butterflyfish; Ornate Butterflyfish.

Illustrated on page 141.

RANGE: East Coast of Africa to the East Indies and across the Pacific Ocean to the Hawaiian Islands.

REMARKS: The Clown Butterflyfish is one of the most beautiful of all the butterflyfishes. The orange stripes on a white background and black trimmings make this a very popular fish for the marine aquarium. In nature it is almost always paired.

SIZE: Attains a length of about 10 inches.

SCIENTIFIC NAME: *Chaetodon plebeius* Broussonet.

POPULAR NAME: Longspot Butterflyfish.

Illustrated on pages 203, 206.

RANGE: Tropical Indo-Pacific.

REMARKS: The elongate blue spot on the side and the large black ocellated spot on the caudal peduncle make this butterflyfish easily identifiable. It is an odd species in that it possesses four anal spines instead of the normal three.

SIZE: Reaches a length of about 5 inches.

SCIENTIFIC NAME: *Chaetodon punctatofasciatus* Cuvier.

POPULAR NAME: Spot-banded Butterflyfish.

RANGE: East Indies, Philippine Islands, Japan, and nearby Pacific Islands to the Marshall Islands.

REMARKS: This species will undoubtedly be confused with the closely related *Chaetodon pelewensis*. The bands in the Spot-banded Butterflyfish are almost vertical, those in *C. pelewensis* are slanting posteriorly. This species is not common but is almost always found in pairs.

SIZE: Reaches a length of about 5 inches.

SCIENTIFIC NAME: *Chaetodon quadrimaculatus* Gray.

POPULAR NAMES: Four-spotted Butterflyfish; Neon-banded Butterflyfish.

Illustrated on page 124.

RANGE: Polynesia, including the Hawaiian Islands.

REMARKS: The Four-spotted Butterflyfish will appear from time to time in dealers' tanks. Although it is not very common where it is found it is not especially rare either.

SIZE: To 6 inches.

SCIENTIFIC NAME: *Chaetodon rafflesi* Bennett.

POPULAR NAME: Raffles Butterflyfish.

Illustrated on pages 204, 205.

RANGE: Tropical Indo-Pacific.

REMARKS: The basic color of this fish varies from yellowish to greenish with each scale outlined in orange or grayish. The dark color inside the margin of the dorsal fin is distinctive for this species.

SIZE: About 5 to 6 inches.

SCIENTIFIC NAME: *Chaetodon reticulatus* Cuvier.

POPULAR NAME: Reticulated Butterflyfish.

RANGE: Pacific Ocean from Hawaii to Japan and the East Indies.

REMARKS: The Reticulated Butterflyfish is closely related to the Clown Butterflyfish. Although the basic colors are black, gray and white, it is a very beautiful species. The little red or orange spot at the end of the anal fin adds a touch of color that can easily be seen in nature.

SIZE: Reaches a length of 11 inches.

Chaetodon quadrimaculatus, the Four-spot Butterflyfish. Photo by Dr. Herbert R. Axelrod.

Underwater photograph of an Indo-Pacific coral reef. Photo by Rodney Jonklaas.

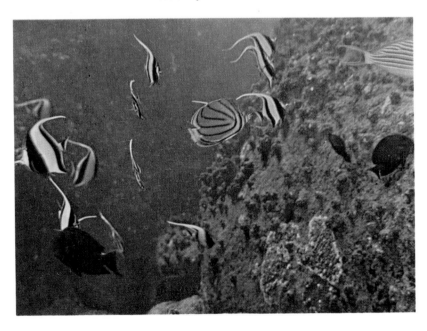

Chaetodon citrinellus. Photo by Wilhelm Hoppe.

The circular ocellated spot in the rayed portion of the dorsal fin is a mark of *Coradion chrysozonus.*

SCIENTIFIC NAME: *Chaetodon speculum* Kuhl & Van Hasselt.

POPULAR NAME: Blackspot Butterflyfish.

Illustrated on pages 203, 204.

RANGE: Southern Japan to northern Australia.

REMARKS: This species differs from *Chaetodon unimaculatus* by having a rounded to oval spot and being entirely yellow instead of a teardrop-shaped spot and a body colored white below and yellow dorsally.

SIZE: Reaches 6 inches in length.

SCIENTIFIC NAME: *Chaetodon striatus* Linnaeus.

POPULAR NAME: Banded Butterflyfish.

Illustrated on page 202.

RANGE: West Indies to Florida.

REMARKS: The Banded Butterflyfish is moderately common in the Florida area and occasionally is shipped from there with other West Indian fishes. It is closely related to the Four-eyed Butterflyfish from the same area.

SIZE: To 7 inches when mature.

SCIENTIFIC NAME: *Chaetodon triangulum* (Kuhl & Van Hasselt).

POPULAR NAME: Triangle Butterflyfish.

Illustrated on pages 132, 202.

RANGE: East Indies and vicinity to Africa.

REMARKS: This fish has been called *Gonochaetodon triangulum* but apparently is not different enough to have a genus of its own. It is a very deep-bodied but narrow fish and has a reputation of being very difficult to keep in an aquarium.

SIZE: Reaches a length of $5\frac{1}{2}$ inches.

SCIENTIFIC NAME: *Chaetodon trifasciatus* Park.

POPULAR NAME: Redfin Butterflyfish.

Illustrated on pages 256-257.

RANGE: Widely distributed from the east African coast to the Hawaiian Islands.

REMARKS: The Redfin Butterflyfish is another very widely distributed and very common butterflyfish. It is beautiful but quite delicate. In many instances, if it does not have access to live coral to feed upon, it rapidly declines and eventually dies.

SIZE: Only about 5 inches.

SCIENTIFIC NAME: *Chaetodon unimaculatus* Bloch.
POPULAR NAMES: One-Spot Butterflyfish; Tear-drop Butterflyfish.
RANGE: Widespread throughout tropical areas of the Pacific and Indian Oceans.
REMARKS: The Tear-drop Butterflyfish is relatively common and does well in marine aquaria. The black spot on the side of its body has an extension from the bottom making it more tear-drop shaped. This extension will fade at times leaving a round spot.
SIZE: Attains a length of about 6 inches at maturity.

SCIENTIFIC NAME: *Chaetodon vagabundus* Linnaeus.
POPULAR NAME: Vagabond Butterflyfish.
RANGE: East coast of Africa to the Pacific Islands (not including the Hawaiian Islands).
REMARKS: This species is almost always paired. The young resemble the adults although they have a black spot in the dorsal fin. The Vagabond Butterflyfish does well in marine aquaria and is readily available.
SIZE: About 6 inches at maturity.

SCIENTIFIC NAME: *Chaetodon xanthurus* Bleeker.
POPULAR NAME: Yellow-tailed Butterflyfish.
Illustrated on page 205.
RANGE: East Indies and Philippine Islands.
REMARKS: Each scale in this species appears to be outlined with black. It thus differs from *Chaetodon mertensii* which has more or less distinct chevrons on the body.
SIZE: Attains a length of about 6 inches.

SCIENTIFIC NAME: *Chelmon rostratus* (Linnaeus).
POPULAR NAME: Copperband Butterflyfish.
Illustrated on pages Frontispiece, 112, 201.
RANGE: Japan to Australia and East Indies to the east coast of Africa.
REMARKS: The Copperband Butterflyfish is one of the most popular of butterflyfishes. It is not hardy but well worth the attempt to keep it alive. The long snout is used to probe into holes and crevices for small bits of food. This species is almost always included in shipments from the Philippine Islands. It sometimes thrives on live mussels on the half-shell.
SIZE: To about 7 inches.

Chaetodon tremblii, a young specimen. Photo by Dr. Herbert R. Axelrod.

Chaetodon ephippium is easily identified by the large black marking in the rear dorsal area. Photo by Earl Kennedy.

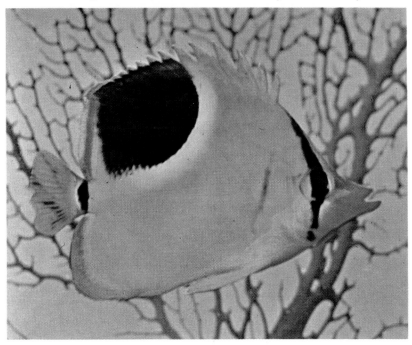

One of the most beautiful of the butterflyfishes is *Chaetodon lunula*. Photo by Dr. Herbert R. Axelrod.

Chaetodon lineolatus, in addition to the fine vertical bars, has a "mark" that covers most of its face.

SCIENTIFIC NAME: *Coradion chrysozonus* (Kuhl & Van Hasselt).

POPULAR NAME: Golden-barred Butterflyfish.

Illustrated on page 125.

RANGE: From southern Japan through the East Indies to Australia.

REMARKS: This species is not common and seldom appears in the markets. It is distinguished from butterflyfishes in general by a lateral line which continues onto the caudal peduncle, not ending near the end of the dorsal fin.

SIZE: Reaches a length of up to 6 inches.

SCIENTIFIC NAME: *Coradion melanopus* Bleeker.

POPULAR NAME: Two-spot Butterflyfish.

Illustrated on page 133.

RANGE: East Indies, Philippines, and New Guinea.

REMARKS: This is a very poorly known species that probably will never be seen in the pet stores. Only a dozen or so specimens are presently known. It is easily recognized by the two spots in the dorsal and anal fins and the split anterior band. Very rare.

SIZE: Largest known about 5 inches.

SCIENTIFIC NAME: *Forcipiger flavissimus* Jordan & McGregor.

POPULAR NAMES: Long-nosed Butterflyfish; Lauwiliwili Nukunuku Oeoe (Hawaiian).

Illustrated on page 201.

RANGE: From the Red Sea and east coast of Africa across the Indian and Pacific Oceans to the west coast of North America.

REMARKS: The Long-nosed Butterflyfish has the widest distribution of all the butterflyfishes. Even so it is not common anywhere throughout its range.

Due to a recent discovery of the original specimen the species commonly known as *Forcipiger longirostris* has a new name. There still is a *F. longirostris* but it is a different species, quite rare, and not expected to appear very often, if at all, in the shipments from the Pacific. The rare species has fewer dorsal spines and a longer snout. It also has a dark brown color phase.

SIZE: Reaches a length of 10 inches.

SCIENTIFIC NAME: *Heniochus acuminatus* Linnaeus.

POPULAR NAME: Pennant Butterflyfish.

Illustrated on pages 4, 108.

RANGE: From the Hawaiian Islands to the Red Sea.

REMARKS: The elongate fourth dorsal fin spine is not only characteristic of this species but of the entire genus as well. In large specimens characteristic "horns" appear above the eyes. These "horns" never become as well developed as in other species of *Heniochus*. Thrives on live mussels on the half-shell.

SIZE: To 12 inches, largest of the species of genus *Heniochus*.

SCIENTIFIC NAME: *Megaprotodon strigangulus* Gmelin.
POPULAR NAME: Triangulate Butterflyfish.
Illustrated on page 141.
RANGE: A wide ranging species extending from the Red Sea and east coast of Africa to the Hawaiian Islands.
REMARKS: The Triangulate Butterflyfish is common throughout its range. It almost always lives alone under the flat, outstretched branches of the coral, *Acropora*. Juveniles have a posterior black band which decreases in size with growth and eventually disappears in the adult.
SIZE: To 7 inches.

SCIENTIFIC NAME: *Parachaetodon ocellatus* Bloch.
POPULAR NAME: Ocellated Butterflyfish.
Illustrated on page 207.
RANGE: Southeast Asia to Australia and Ceylon.
REMARKS: *Parachaetodon ocellatus* should not be confused with *Chaetodon ocellatus* of the West Indies. The Ocellated Butterflyfish has a high dorsal fin and several dark bars crossing the body.
SIZE: About 5 inches at maturity.

THE ANGELFISHES
Family Pomacanthidae

The angelfishes are among the most beautiful marine fishes of the world. Not only are the colors vivid and the patterns esthetically pleasing but they are graceful in form and motion.

Some of the species grow quite large with long, flowing fins, others are small, quick, and act somewhat like the damselfishes.

Many of the juveniles bear no resemblance whatever to the adults in color pattern, giving ichthyologists a puzzle when trying to discover which juvenile belongs to which adult. Each stage usually has a different scientific name causing a great deal of confusion. To add to the confusion

Chaetodon melannotus has diagonal stripes that cross the body. Photo by Dr. Herbert R. Axelrod.

Very similar is *Chaetodon triangulum*, but this fish has a herringbone pattern on its sides. Photo by Dr. Herbert R. Axelrod.

Coradion melanopus resembles *C. chrysozonus* but has an extra ocellated black spot in its anal fin.

Chaetodon meyeri in its juvenile colors. Photo by Earl Kennedy.

several species have crossed and produced hybrids which, of course, were named. A good example of this is *Holacanthus townsendi*, a cross between the Queen and the Blue Angelfish.

The angelfishes all have a strong spine at the angle of the cheek-bone which may be used in fighting. It is well known that they are scrappy fishes, particularly with members of their own species. Individuals seem to get along better with each other when there is a fairly good size difference between them. When two angelfishes of similar size are placed together a fight may ensue which could end in the death of one or both of the combatants.

The natural food of angelfishes includes such odd items as sponges, coral, algae, and sea anemones, as well as the usual crustaceans and worms.

More than 60 species of angelfishes have been discovered.

SCIENTIFIC NAME: *Centropyge bicolor* Bloch.
POPULAR NAMES: Oriole Angelfish; Two-colored Angelfish; Vaqueta de Dos Colores.
RANGE: East Indies; Philippines; New Guinea, north to southern Japan, south to northern Australia.
REMARKS: The Oriole Angelfish is half blue and half yellow, a very attractive combination. It appears in the shipments from the Philippines from time to time. Unfortunately it has proven difficult to maintain.
SIZE: About 4 inches.

SCIENTIFIC NAME: *Centropyge bispinosus* Günther.
POPULAR NAMES: Dusky Angelfish; Red and Blue Angelfish.
RANGE: Pacific Ocean to East Indies, Japan and Australia. Not found in the Hawaiian Islands.
REMARKS: Almost every striped angelfish has been referred to by this name. This red-orange and blue beauty is easily recognized, however, once properly identified.
SIZE: Reaches a length of 6 inches.

SCIENTIFIC NAME: *Centropyge ferrugatus* Randall & Burgess.
POPULAR NAME: Rusty Angelfish.
Illustrated on page 145.
RANGE: Known only from the Ryukyu Islands.
REMARKS: The Rusty Angelfish is known from only a few specimens

captured around the Ryukyu Islands. Very little is known about it yet. Similar treatment as for the other species of the genus *Centropyge* should be given.

SCIENTIFIC NAME: *Centropyge potteri* Jordan & Metz.
POPULAR NAMES: Russet Angelfish; Potter's Angelfish.
Illustrated on page 117.
RANGE: Found only in the Hawaiian Islands.
REMARKS: Potter's Angelfish is another Hawaiian endemic (found only in Hawaiian waters). It is commonly found in relatively shallow water. It shows a great deal of distress when brought to the surface too rapidly, suffering undoubtedly from a form of the bends.
SIZE: Reaches a size of 4 inches.

SCIENTIFIC NAME: *Centropyge tibicen* Cuvier.
POPULAR NAME: Keyhole Angelfish.
Illustrated on page 211.
RANGE: East Indies, Philippines to Japan.
REMARKS: The Keyhole Angelfish is an attractive little species but unfortunately not too common. It should not be confused with the all black *Centropyge nox*, which is solid black, lacking the white lateral spot.
SIZE: To 4 inches.

SCIENTIFIC NAME: *Chaetodontoplus mesoleucus* (Bloch).
POPULAR NAME: Singapore Angelfish.
Illustrated on page 21.
RANGE: Southeast Asia, East Indies, Philippines, to Australia and Ceylon.
REMARKS: This angelfish may turn up in shipments from the Philippines or Ceylon, but most likely will arrive from Singapore where it is common.
SIZE: Reaches a length of 10 inches or so.

SCIENTIFIC NAME: *Pomacanthus annularis* Bleeker.
POPULAR NAME: Blue-ring Angelfish.
Illustrated on pages 138, 147, 149.
RANGE: Indian Ocean to East Indies. Common about Ceylon.
REMARKS: This fish is easily identified by its color pattern. The juveniles are quite different, with vertical light stripes against a dark background.
SIZE: Reaches a length of 18 inches.

Chaetodon ocellatus is a well-known Butterflyfish from Florida.
Photo by Robert P. L. Straughan.

An old painting of the juvenile form of *Pomacanthus imperator*, a highly prized angelfish.

This *Chaetodon octofasciatus* came from the Philippines. Photo by Earl Kennedy.

A young specimen of *Pomacanthus annularis*. Photo by Wilhelm Hoppe.

Note how the pattern changes as the fish get older. Photo by Gerhard Budich.

The Gray Angelfish, *Pomacanthus arcuatus*. N.Y.Z.S. photo.

SCIENTIFIC NAME: *Pomacanthus arcuatus* Linnaeus.
POPULAR NAME: Gray Angelfish.
Illustrated on page 139.
RANGE: Brazil to Florida.
REMARKS: This species also changes color with age, the juveniles being prized specimens for the marine aquarist. They have yellow stripes when young which disappear with age. The Gray Angelfish is often confused with the French Angelfish. The juvenile Gray has a clear edge to the caudal fin compared to the yellow edge of the French Angelfish. The adult color patterns are more different and they can easily be identified.
SIZE: Reaches 18 or more inches in length.

SCIENTIFIC NAME: *Pomacanthus imperator* Bloch.
POPULAR NAME: Emperor Angelfish.

The dusky beauty of *Holacanthus xanthurus* is well illustrated in this Gene Wolfsheimer photo.

Chaetodon ornatissimus. Photo by Dr. Herbert R. Axelrod.

A young specimen of *Megaprotodon strigangulus.* Photo by Earl Kennedy.

Illustrated on pages 137, 144, 147, 148.

RANGE: Pacific Islands (except the Hawaiian Islands) to Japan and the East Indies, across the Indian Ocean to East Africa and the Red Sea.

REMARKS: The Emperor Angelfish is very beautiful both in its juvenile and its adult color phases. The photos of this beauty speak for themselves. There is a small filament extending from the dorsal fin in some adults possibly denoting the male.

SIZE: About 15 inches when mature.

SCIENTIFIC NAME: *Holacanthus arcuatus* Gray.

POPULAR NAMES: Arcuate Angelfish; Striped Angelfish.

Illustrated on page 207.

RANGE: Hawaiian Islands.

REMARKS: This Hawaiian angelfish is sometimes caught in traps. It does not do well in aquaria, perhaps requiring a specialized diet not normally available to the marine aquarist. One of the authors (WEB) examined stomach contents of this species and found remains of sponges along with algal debris.

SIZE: To about 10 inches.

SCIENTIFIC NAME: *Holacanthus bermudensis* Jordan & Rutter.

POPULAR NAMES: Blue Angelfish; Common Angelfish.

RANGE: Brazil to Florida.

REMARKS: See remarks on *H. ciliaris* below.

SIZE: About 18 inches at maturity

SCIENTIFIC NAME: *Holacanthus ciliaris* Linnaeus.

POPULAR NAME: Queen Angelfish.

Illustrated on pages 113, 116.

RANGE: Brazil to Florida.

REMARKS: The Queen and the Blue Angelfish are often confused and justifiably so. They are very close and will crossbreed to produce hybrids which are a blend of the characteristics of both parent species. The pure Queen Angelfish has a solid yellow tail (body color in the Blue Angelfish), a blue trailing edge for the dorsal and anal fins (yellow in the Blue), and a definite "crown" on the nape (incomplete or obscure in the Blue).

SIZE: Attains a length of 18 inches to 2 feet in nature.

SCIENTIFIC NAME: *Holacanthus tricolor* Bloch.

POPULAR NAME: Rock Beauty.

Illustrated on pages 150, 252.

RANGE: Brazil to Florida.

REMARKS: The Rock Beauty is common in Florida and the Bahama Islands. It is more often found on the outer reef in clear water than on the inner reefs where silting may occur. The juvenile has a black spot ringed with blue. As the fish grows the ring and spot become obscured by the larger black area of the adult.

SIZE: About 18 inches at maturity.

SCIENTIFIC NAME: *Holacanthus xanthurus.*
POPULAR NAME: Yellow-tailed Angelfish.
Illustrated on page 140.
RANGE: Tropical Indian Ocean.

REMARKS: This angelfish is uncommon and rarely is offered in pet shops. The dark posterior portion of the body and abruptly bright yellow tail fin are characteristic.

SIZE: Attains a length of about one foot.

SCIENTIFIC NAME: *Pomacanthus maculosus* Forskål.
POPULAR NAME: Half-moon Angelfish.
Illustrated on page 146.
RANGE: East Africa to the Red Sea.

REMARKS: This species is confined to the western part of the Indian Ocean and the Red Sea. It does not appear often in the aquarium shops although the juveniles are as colorful as those of other species of *Pomacanthus.* It is often seen in European aquaria.

SIZE: To about 18 inches in length.

SCIENTIFIC NAME: *Pomacanthus paru* Bloch.
POPULAR NAME: French Angelfish.
Illustrated on pages 146, 151.
RANGE: Brazil to Florida.

REMARKS: See remarks under *P. arcuatus,* the Gray Angelfish, above.

SIZE: About 15 inches when fully grown.

SCIENTIFIC NAME: *Pomacanthus semicirculatus* (Cuvier & Valenciennes).
POPULAR NAME: Blue Koran.
Illustrated on pages 148, 150.
RANGE: Japan, East Indies, Philippines, to India and the west coast of Africa.

REMARKS: The Blue Koran is one of the most popular of the Philippine angelfishes. The juveniles are deep blue with semicircular white lines

143

A *Pomacanthus imperator* guards its chosen spot in a coral reef.
Photo by Rodney Jonklaas.

A lively spot in an Indo-Pacific coral reef, with a small school of
Moorish Idols and some surgeonfishes. Photo by Rodney Jonklaas.

Centropyge ferrugatus Randall & Burgess. 73 mm standard length. Photo of the type by Dr. John E. Randall.

crossing the body. It is hardy, colorful, relatively common, and within the range of the average marine aquarist. Unfortunately the adult is not as colorful as some of the other pomacanthids.

SIZE: Attains a length of 20 inches.

SCIENTIFIC NAME: *Pygoplites diacanthus* Boddaert.

POPULAR NAME: Regal Angelfish.

Illustrated on page 112.

RANGE: Tropical Pacific Islands (excluding the Hawaiian Islands) to the Red Sea.

REMARKS: This beautiful angelfish does not undergo a great change with growth. The juveniles are similar to the adults except for a dark spot in the dorsal fin which is eventually obscured by the general color of that fin. The Regal Angelfish adapts fairly well to captivity.

SIZE: About 14 inches at maturity.

Pomacanthus paru, the French Angelfish from the Caribbean. Sub-adult form. Photo by Wilhelm Hoppe.

Pomacanthus maculosus, the Half-Moon Angelfish, is found in the Western Indian Ocean and Red Sea. Photo by Wilhelm Hoppe.

Pomacanthus annularis. Photo by Dr. Herbert R. Axelrod.

Here is what the Germans call the "Kaiserfisch" (Emperor Fish), as suggested by the specific name *imperator*. Photo by Dr. Herbert R. Axelrod.

Pomacanthus imperator undergoes considerable changes from the young form before it gets the adult coloration shown on the preceding page.

Pomacanthus semicirculatus, juvenile form. Photo by Gene Wolfsheimer.

A pair of *Pomacanthus annularis*, guarding a coral cleft. Photo by Rodney Jonklaas.

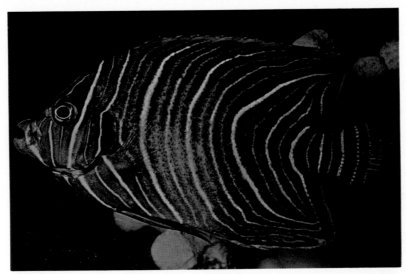

Pomacanthus semicirculatus, young form. Photo by Rodney Jonklaas.

The coloration of the very young Rock Beauty, *Holacanthus tricolor*. Photo by Dr. Herbert R. Axelrod.

The yellow bars of the French Angelfish, *Pomacanthus paru*, disappear as the fish grows. Photo by Dr. Herbert R. Axelrod.

THE TRIGGERFISHES
Family Balistidae

The first dorsal fin of the triggerfishes is reduced to two or three spines connected with a small membrane. The spines are so constructed and arranged that they form a locking mechanism where the first and longest spine cannot be depressed without "releasing" it by moving the third spine first. This long spine is used to hold the fish in place when it jams itself into a hole when escaping danger or coming to rest at night. In addition this spine erected makes the triggerfish a very difficult fish to swallow.

Aside from the general shape of the body being unusual, the head in relation to the body is large. The eyes are set high in the head, the gill openings are restricted to a small slit, and the pelvic fins are absent. As in the case of the filefishes the scales are modified giving the body a rough texture.

Triggerfishes are often colorful and hardy making them good aquarium fishes. They tend to be quite aggressive and, though they can be taught to take foods from one's fingers they might just nip the finger as well. The triggerfishes quickly dominate the aquarium and will kill the other inhabitants that prove weaker than itself. Triggerfishes will eat almost anything.

SCIENTIFIC NAME: *Balistes bursa* Bloch & Schneider.
POPULAR NAME: White-lined Triggerfish.
Illustrated on page 155.
RANGE: Red Sea, east African coast to the East Indies and the Hawaiian Islands.
REMARKS: The White-lined triggerfish is similar in aspect to *Rhinecanthus aculeatus* and probably should be included in the same genus as that fish. It is quite common and regularly available. Like the other triggerfishes it is hardy and will eat almost anything.
SIZE: Reaches a length of at least 8 inches.

SCIENTIFIC NAME: *Balistes capriscus* Gmelin.
POPULAR NAME: Gray Triggerfish.
RANGE: Temperate and tropical waters of the Atlantic.
REMARKS: The gray triggerfish is a hardy species for the aquarium. It eats well and survives a great deal of conditions which would quickly dispose of more delicate fishes. It is not colorful, however, and tends to be a bully in the tank.
SIZE: Reaches a foot in length.

The famous Hawaiian "Humuhumunukunuku-a-puaa", known scientifically as *Rhinecanthus aculeatus*. Photo by Dr. Herbert R. Axelrod.

SCIENTIFIC NAME: *Balistes vetula* Linnaeus.
POPULAR NAMES: Queen Triggerfish; Old Wench; Peje Puerco; Cochino.
Illustrated on pages 159, 162, 163.
RANGE: Brazil to Florida.
REMARKS: The bright color of the Queen Triggerfish makes it a popular fish with marine aquarists. The extensions of the dorsal, anal, and caudal fins of the adult are absent in the juveniles.
SIZE: Attains a length of 16 inches.

SCIENTIFIC NAME: *Balistapus undulatus* (Park).
POPULAR NAMES: Orange-striped Triggerfish; Undulate Triggerfish.
Illustrated on pages 154, 156-157.
RANGE: Red Sea and east African coast to the East Indies, Philippines, Japan, and Australia to the Hawaiian Islands.
REMARKS: The Undulate Triggerfish is often imported from the Philippine Islands. It is easily recognized by the undulating lines of orange and the three stripes extending from the mouth to the ventral area. They are aggressive and should be kept by themselves. Any delicate decoration may be attacked as well. Their diet is quite varied and they will eat almost anything in the aquarium.
SIZE: Attains a length of 10 inches.

SCIENTIFIC NAME: *Melichthys niger* (Bloch).

POPULAR NAME: Black Durgeon.

Illustrated on page 167.

RANGE: Circumtropical.

REMARKS: The Black Durgeon is a very interesting fish to keep in an aquarium. Normally it inhabits open waters eating floating algae or animals from the plankton. It differs from *Melichthys ringens* only slightly in color and is often confused with that species.

SIZE: Reaches a length of one foot or more.

The Orange-Striped Triggerfish, *Balistapus undulatus*. Photo by Gene Wolfsheimer.

SCIENTIFIC NAME: *Melichthys ringens* Osbeck.

POPULAR NAME: Black Triggerfish.

Illustrated on page 166.

RANGE: Every warm ocean contains this species.

REMARKS: The Black Triggerfish is a scrappy fish when caught on a hook and line. They are very aggressive and have been referred to as the "Piranhas of the Sea" by one author. Black Triggerfish often travel in schools, the black bodies with blue lines at the base of the dorsal and anal fins creating an impressive sight.

Balistes bursa is a triggerfish from the Philippines. Photo by Dr. Herbert R. Axelrod.

Pervagor spilosoma, the Fantail Filefish, is an odd-looking but beautiful species · Photo by Gene Wolfsheimer.

This magnificent photo of *Balistapus undulatus* was made by Hans and Klaus Paysan and shows the fantastic color pattern.

Like most triggerfishes they sleep on their sides, just lying on the bottom as though they were dead.

SIZE: To about 20 inches long.

SCIENTIFIC NAME: *Melichthys vidua* (Solander).

POPULAR NAMES: Pink-tailed Triggerfish; Humuhumu Hiokole; Humuhumu Uli (Hawaiian).

Illustrated on page 158.

RANGE: East Indies to the Hawaiian Islands.

REMARKS: This black colored triggerfish's claim to fame is the bright pink tail and white dorsal and anal fins. Its natural food consists of crustaceans, molluscs, and some algae.

SIZE: To 12 inches.

SCIENTIFIC NAME: *Odonus niger* Rüppell.

POPULAR NAMES: Black Triggerfish; Green Triggerfish.

Illustrated on page 167.

RANGE: Throughout the tropical Indo-Pacific.

REMARKS: The Green Triggerfish is easily identified with its light to dark green coloration and red teeth. Its disposition and care are similar to that of other triggerfishes.

SIZE: Reaches a length of about 20 inches.

SCIENTIFIC NAME: *Rhinecanthus aculeatus* (Linnaeus).

POPULAR NAME: Humuhumunukunuku-a-puaa. This is the famous name from the Hawaiian song. Freely translated it means a fish which

The Pink-Tailed triggerfish, *Melichthys vidua*, is often shipped to the United States from the Philippine Islands. Photo by Earl Kennedy.

The Queen Triggerfish is common in Florida waters. Photo by Dr. Herbert R. Axelrod.

carries a needle (the dorsal spine) and has a snout or grunts like a pig.

Illustrated on page 153.

RANGE: Red Sea and the east African coast to the East Indies, Japan, Australia, and Pacific Islands (including the Hawaiian Islands).

REMARKS: This is one of the more common triggerfishes imported from the Pacific Ocean. It is commonly found in shallow water and is very easy to catch. They usually rely on the trigger mechanism to securely wedge themselves into small holes. By moving the rock or releasing the trigger they can be netted.

SIZE: Grows to a length of 10 inches.

SCIENTIFIC NAME: *Rhinecanthus rectangulus* (Bloch & Schneider).

POPULAR NAME: Humuhumunukunuku-a-puaa. (See above.)

Illustrated on page 163.

RANGE: Similar to the above species.

REMARKS: This triggerfish is very much like the above species but differs in color. They are often found together in same habitat, shallow water with rocks or coral. Also like the above species the Humuhumu can behave very aggressively towards other fishes in the aquarium.

SIZE: To 9 inches.

Cantherhines pardalis, the Mottled Filefish, Photo by Dr. Herbert R. Axelrod.

Head of *Balistes vetula*. Note the beautiful green eye. Photo by Dr. Herbert R. Axelrod.

A young specimen of the Queen Triggerfish, *Balistes vetula*. Photo by Dr. Herbert R. Axelrod.

Rhinecanthus rectangulus can be very aggressive in an aquarium. Photo by Earl Kennedy.

One of Rodney Jonklaas' helpers with an expensive handful, *Balistoides niger.* Photo by Rodney Jonklaas.

SCIENTIFIC NAME: *Balistoides niger* (Bonnaterre).

POPULAR NAME: Clown Triggerfish.

Illustrated on pages 164, 165, 166.

RANGE: Tropical Indo-Pacific as far as South Africa.

REMARKS: If there is such a thing as "the most beautiful fish in the world" then this fish would be high among the contenders. It is certainly one of the most expensive and probably the most universally desired marine fish. Clown Triggerfish always draw a lot of attention when kept in public aquaria. Rodney Jonklaas, who captured the first live fish in the Maldive Islands, initially received $250, shipped from Ceylon at the purchaser's expense and risk, for each fish. At that time half died before they reached their destination, primarily because of the rough handling they received.

Its fantastic color and markings make *Balistoides niger* one of the most prized fishes in the world. Photo by Hans and Klaus Paysan.

The Clown Triggerfish, *Balistoides niger*, is often a drawing attraction in public aquaria. Photo by Hans Peter.

Most of the Clown Triggerfish are rather large when shipped. The juveniles have not been found, possibly because of an undiscovered color change.

SIZE: Reaches over a foot in length.

Although the fins of this *Melichthys ringens* are a bit tattered, they will quickly grow back again. Photo by Dr. Herbert R. Axelrod.

Melichthys niger is almost identical with *M. ringens.* Photo by Dr. Herbert R. Axelrod.

Odonus niger. Photo by Peter Irtz.

THE WRASSES
Family Labridae

The wrasses are a large group of fishes primarily occurring in tropical waters. They are moderate to large sized with a variety of body forms and special adaptations. Most wrasses are elongate with a slightly flattened body and long, continuous dorsal and anal fins. They have small mouths with separate, non-coalesced teeth.

The wrasse family has members which are among the most brilliantly colored of fishes. They often undergo changes when growing from juvenile to adult so that a single species may be brightly colored as a juvenile and change into a magnificently colored adult.

Rodney Jonklaas leaves the water with a colorful Ceylonese fish in his net.

Spawning is accomplished in two ways: group spawning where males and females are mixed together all releasing eggs and sperm at approximately the same time; and individual spawning where a male and female separate from the group and spawn by themselves. These males that spawn separately are often called "supermales" or "dominant males" and have a color pattern distinct from the other males and females of the species. The Bluehead Wrasse is an example, the normal males and females being yellow, white and black, the supermales with the blue head and green body.

These fishes have the habit of nibbling constantly at bits of coral and always looking for food in the form of small crustaceans or worms. In the aquarium they usually take food readily and are not difficult to keep. Aside from the usual animal foods some plant material must be added.

Many species of wrasses have a habit of diving into the sand and disappearing for hours on end. This does not hurt them at all. Many wrasses have escaped capture by suddenly disappearing from view into a sandy patch. Other wrasses often assume odd positions in repose, sometimes partially burying themselves in the sand, or lying on their sides. Similar to some parrotfishes there are wrasses that manufacture a mucus cocoon within which they spend the night.

SCIENTIFIC NAME: *Anampses cuvieri* Quoy & Gaimard.
POPULAR NAMES: Spotted Wrasse; White-spotted Wrasse: Opule (Hawaiian).
RANGE: Hawaiian Islands.
REMARKS: In the Hawaiian Islands the White-spotted Wrasse occurs in shallow water. The juvenile is quite different from the adult. It is light green, without spots, and with a black ocellated spot in the dorsal fin.
SIZE: Attains a length of 15 inches.

SCIENTIFIC NAME: *Bodianus rufus* Linnaeus.
POPULAR NAME: Spanish Hogfish.
Illustrated on page 170.
RANGE: West Indies to the Florida Keys.
REMARKS: The Spanish Hogfish is a beautiful fish in which the young have the habit of swimming in attendance with larger fishes in the aquarium, nibbling at their sides. This "cleaning" service is well known in this family, particularly in the genus *Labroides*.
SIZE: Attains a length of 2 feet.

The Spanish Hogfish, *Bodianus rufus*, gets to be quite large, and only small specimens are suitable for home aquaria.

SCIENTIFIC NAME: *Bodianus bilunulatus* Lacepede.
POPULAR NAMES: Spot Wrasse; Aawa (Hawaiian).
RANGE: East coast of Africa to the Hawaiian Islands.
REMARKS: There is a considerable change in color pattern in this species as it grows from juvenile to adult. The young fishes are purple posteriorly, yellow and white anteriorly. They are usually captured in water exceeding 25 feet in depth on the reef.
SIZE: Adult specimens attain a length of 14 inches.

SCIENTIFIC NAME: *Cheilinus bimaculatus* Valenciennes.
POPULAR NAMES: Poou; Pilikoa Liilii ((Hawaiian).
RANGE: East Indies to the Hawaiian Islands.
REMARKS: According to the Hawaiian legend this fish was the last to be created. It has a dark spot behind the eye and another on its side, thus the name *bimaculatus* meaning two spots.
SIZE: Attains a length of 6 inches.

SCIENTIFIC NAME: *Cheilio inermis* Forskål.
POPULAR NAMES: Cigar Wrasse; Kupoupou (Hawaiian).
Illustrated on page 171.
RANGE: East Indies to the Hawaiian Islands.
REMARKS: This is the only known species of the genus *Cheilio*. It is easily recognized by the long, slender, cigar-shaped body. It is suggested that in Hawaii the green-colored individuals are males, the brown ones are females. In other areas females may be yellow, males blue-green. In most instances these colors blend well into the general colors of its habitat. The Cigar Wrasse lives in grass beds.
SIZE: Attains a length of a foot and a half.

SCIENTIFIC NAME: *Coris flavovittata* Bennett.

POPULAR NAME: Black-and-White Wrasse.

RANGE: Hawaiian Islands to Guam.

REMARKS: The juvenile of this species is white with black stripes, a very pleasing pattern. As it grows the lower body stripes disappear, and the upper part of the body becomes yellowish with black markings.

SIZE: Reaches 16 inches in length.

Cheilio inermis, because of its shape, is known as the Cigar Wrasse. Photo by Gene Wolfsheimer.

SCIENTIFIC NAME: *Coris formosa* (Bennett)

POPULAR NAME: Clown Wrasse.

Illustrated on page 172.

RANGE: Tropical Indian Ocean.

REMARKS: Although the adult color pattern is quite distinct from its close relative, *Coris gaimard*, the juveniles are very close. *Coris formosa* has a dark spot in the dorsal fin that is absent in *C. gaimard* which will help identify this species.

SIZE: Reaches a length of a foot and a half.

SCIENTIFIC NAME: *Coris gaimard* Quoy and Gaimard.

POPULAR NAMES: Clown Wrasse; Red Wrasse.

Illustrated on page 172.

Coris formosa juveniles can be distinguished from those of *Coris gaimard* by the black spot in the dorsal fin. Photo by Wilhelm Hoppe.

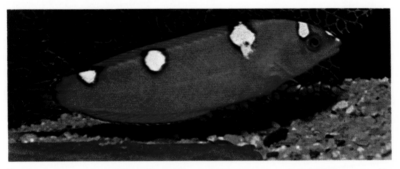

Coris gaimard juvenile. The Clown Wrasse completely changes its color pattern with age. Photo by Klaus Paysan.

RANGE: Micronesia, and Polynesia, including the Hawaiian Islands.

REMARKS: This is a species that is very beautiful as a juvenile and changes dramatically to a different, but similarly beautiful, adult. The juvenile is highly prized in marine aquaria with its bright orange color crossed by white bands edged with black. *Coris* species elude their enemies by diving into the sand.

SIZE: Reaches a length of about 6 inches.

SCIENTIFIC NAME: *Coris julis* (Linnaeus).

POPULAR NAME: Mediterranean Wrasse.

RANGE: Mediterranean Sea.

REMARKS: This wrasse is one of the few temperate water species accepted by marine aquarists. A deep layer of sand should be provided for it since it burrows in the sand, remaining submerged except for its head. The natural diet includes various invertebrates, such as crustaceans, molluscs, echinoderms, and fishes. Spawning is accomplished in the spring when they release small, spherical eggs that float.

SIZE: Attains a length of 8 inches.

SCIENTIFIC NAME: *Doratonotus megalepis* Günther.

POPULAR NAME: Dwarf Wrasse.

Illustrated on page 174.

RANGE: Brazil to Florida.

REMARKS: The Dwarf Wrasse is one of the smallest of the wrasses. It is commonly found among the green grasses near rocks or coral. The green color of this fish makes it difficult to see in that habitat. Drawing a seine through the grass may produce one or more of these fishes.

SIZE: Usually less than 3 inches long.

Hemigymnus melapterus (Bloch). Photo by Dr. Herbert R. Axelrod.

Dwarf Wrasse, *Doratonotus megalepis.*

SCIENTIFIC NAME: *Epibulus insidiator* (Pallas).
POPULAR NAME: Long-jawed Wrasse.
RANGE: Tropical Indo-Pacific.
REMARKS: The common name of this wrasse refers to the highly protractile jaws. They open remarkably wide forming a distinctive feeding apparatus. As in the case of other wrasses there is a color change with growth. Juveniles are brownish-violet with white markings, adults usually plain brown or plain yellow.
SIZE: Reaches 15 inches at maturity.

SCIENTIFIC NAME: *Gomphosus varius* Lacepede.
POPULAR NAMES: Longface; Beakfish; Bird Wrasse.
Illustrated on pages 175, 176.
RANGE: Central Indo-Pacific as far as the Hawaiian Islands.
REMARKS: The green variety of this species appears to be the male, the brown form being female. The elongate snout identifies the species immediately and accounts for the various common names. The Longface Wrasse can be seen swimming over the reefs usings its pectoral fins for locomotion.
SIZE: Grows to a length of 10 or more inches.

SCIENTIFIC NAME: *Halichoeres bivittatus* (Bloch).
POPULAR NAME: Slippery Dick.
Illustrated on page 189.
RANGE: Brazil to the Carolinas and Bermuda.

Hawaiians call *Gomphosus varius* "Birdfish." Photo by Gene Wolfsheimer.

REMARKS: The Slippery Dick is very common around reefs and rocky areas of Florida and the Caribbean. Shipments from Florida will often contain one or several of these fishes. Normally it feeds on a variety of invertebrate animals and will take to substitutes quite readily.

SIZE: Attains a length of over 8 inches.

SCIENTIFIC NAME: *Halichoeres radiatus* (Linnaeus).

POPULAR NAME: Pudding-wife.

Illustrated on page 179.

RANGE: North Carolina to Brazil.

REMARKS: Very small individuals of this wrasse are bright orange-yellow with a neon blue stripe from nose to tail. Slightly larger specimens have the yellow portion more subdued, tan to orange, and it is broken up by vertical whitish lines. The neon blue fades to the color of these lines.

SIZE: Attains a length of up to a foot and a half.

SCIENTIFIC NAME: *Hemigymnus melapterus* (Bloch).

POPULAR NAME: Half-and-half Wrasse.

Illustrated on page 173.

RANGE: Tropical Indo-Pacific.

REMARKS: The juveniles of this species have the half-and-half coloration, with a white anterior and dark brown posterior separated by a brilliant white band. The tail fin is yellow. The Half-and-half Wrasse is one exception to the sand burrowing habit. They normally sit

175

Another view of *Gomphosus varius.* Photo by Gene Wolfsheimer.

among the branches of coral as solitary individuals. The diet is the usual small invertebrates.

SIZE: Grows to about 1 foot in length.

SCIENTIFIC NAME: *Hemigymnus fasciatus* (Bloch).
POPULAR NAME: Banded Wrasse.
   Illustrated on page 178.
RANGE: Tropical Indo-Pacific.
REMARKS: The Banded Wrasse is a hardy fish, doing very well in home aquaria. It eats chopped clam and fish, a diet very close to its natural one, but can be coaxed onto some of the dry flake foods.
SIZE: Reaches a length of about 4 feet.

SCIENTIFIC NAME: *Hemipteronotus pentadactylus* (Linnaeus).
POPULAR NAME: Pastel Razorfish.

Hemipteronotus pentadactylus, commonly known as Razorfish.
Photo by Dr. Herbert R. Axelrod.

Illustrated on page 177.

RANGE: Tropical Indo-Pacific.

REMARKS: The razorfish are known to dive into the sand when frightened. A deep sand layer is therefore a necessity for this fish. It eats hard-shelled animals such as clams, snails, etc.

SIZE: Reaches a length of one foot.

SCIENTIFIC NAME: *Hemipteronotus taeniurus* (Lacepede)

POPULAR NAME: Indian Wrasse.

Illustrated on page 326.

RANGE: Tropical Indo-Pacific.

REMARKS: This fish is one of the more interesting fishes for the home aquarium. It dives into the sand when frightened or can imitate floating or attached algae remarkably well. The Indian Wrasse will also build a stone wall around a patch of sand which it treats as home. This is the spot which is most used when doing his disappearing act.

SIZE: Reaches a length of just under one foot.

SCIENTIFIC NAME: *Iniistius niger* Steindachner.

POPULAR NAMES: Black Razorfish; Laenihi Eleele (Hawaiian).

RANGE: Hawaiian Islands.

REMARKS: Although this species is predominantly brown or black in color it is a popular species. The elongate anterior dorsal ray makes this fish appear like it sports an antenna . Small sections of tubing are used as hiding places by the Black Razorfish.

SIZE: To 8 inches.

SCIENTIFIC NAME: *Labroides phthirophagus* Randall.

POPULAR NAME: Hawaiian Cleaning Wrasse.

RANGE: Hawaiian Islands.

REMARKS: The genus *Labroides* includes the now famous cleaning wrasses. This species is found exclusively in the Hawaiian Islands but resembles its close relatives from nearby Pacific islands. The Hawaiian Cleaning Wrasse changes color from juvenile to adult. The young form is mostly black but has neon purple bands running from one end

Hemigymnus fasciatus. Photo by Dr. Herbert R. Axelrod.

Halichoeres radiatus, a wrasse from Puerto Rico. Photo by Gene Wolfsheimer.

of the fish to the other. The adult fish resembles that of the other species of *Labroides* but contains more yellow on the head. These cleaners are not sand burrowers but build cocoons of mucus for the evening or when frightened.

SIZE: About 3 inches at maturity.

SCIENTIFIC NAME: *Labroides dimidiatus* Bleeker.
POPULAR NAME: Cleaning Wrasse.
RANGE: Tropical Indo-Pacific.
REMARKS: This is the common cleaning wrasse that is often seen in photos with other fishes as it performs its "chores." It pokes into the gill chambers and mouths of fishes searching for parasites apparently oblivious to the potential danger of being eaten. Some are eaten!
SIZE: To about 4 inches.

SCIENTIFIC NAME: *Lachnolaimus maximus* (Walbaum).
POPULAR NAMES: Hogfish, Hog Snapper.
RANGE: Tropical Western Atlantic.

REMARKS: The Hogfish has the first three dorsal spines elongate in individuals over two inches in length. In addition the body depth is greater than in most wrasses. The Hogfish is a real chameleon in the sea changing from a barred pattern to a blotched pattern to a plain color apparently with ease. Its diet consists of molluscs, crustaceans, and sea urchins. It is easily speared and very good tasting.

SIZE: Reaches 3 feet in length.

SCIENTIFIC NAME: *Macropharyngodon pardalis* (Kner).

POPULAR NAME: Leopard Wrasse.

RANGE: East Indies and Pacific Islands (excluding the Hawaiian Islands).

REMARKS: This wrasse is common in the Philippine Islands and is often imported from that country. It normally occurs in shallow water in association with reef areas. The Leopard Wrasse readily eats chopped shrimp and fish, brine shrimp, and Norwegian brine shrimp. It is recommended that some greens should be added.

SIZE: Attains a length of 6 inches.

Thalassoma ballieui has an interesting pattern. Photo by Gene Wolfsheimer.

A very young *Thalassoma bifasciatum* known in the West Indies and Florida as Bluehead.

SCIENTIFIC NAME: *Stethojulis axillaris* Quoy & Gaimard.

POPULAR NAME: Tahitian Wrasse.

RANGE: Red Sea and east coast of Africa to the East Indies, Queensland, Melanesia, Micronesia, and Polynesia.

REMARKS: There are two distinct color phases in the Tahitian Wrasse. Females and juveniles of both sexes are a drab green with some orange markings. The adult male, however, is more colorful with bright red markings and white spots. The red above the pectoral fin and the two black spots at the base of the tail will identify this wrasse.

SIZE: Reaches a length of 5 inches.

SCIENTIFIC NAME: *Thalassoma ballieui* (Vaillant & Sauvage).

POPULAR NAME: Hinalea Luahine (Hawaiian).

Illustrated on page 180.

RANGE: Hawaiian Islands and Johnston Atoll.

REMARKS: This large wrasse is found in the Hawaiian Islands and Johnston Atoll and nowhere else. This strange distribution is shared by very few species. *Thalassoma ballieui* does not undergo much change from juvenile to adult although some very old individuals turn

When the Bluehead gets older, the after end of his body changes color Photo by Wilhelm Hoppe.

blackish. A dark vertical line on each scale makes this species easy to recognize.

SIZE: Reaches a length of about 2 feet.

SCIENTIFIC NAME: *Thalassoma bifasciatum* (Bloch).

POPULAR NAME: Bluehead Wrasse.

Illustrated on pages 181, 182, 183.

RANGE: Brazil to Florida.

REMARKS: The Bluehead Wrasse is common in Florida waters. It is easily attracted by breaking open a sea urchin. In a few seconds wrasses, particularly the Bluehead, will appear for their share of the unexpected feast. The Bluehead phase is only the "supermale," the females and juveniles having more of a yellow and white pattern.

SIZE: Reaches a length of 6 inches or more.

SCIENTIFIC NAME: *Thalassoma duperreyi* Quoy & Gaimard.

POPULAR NAME: Saddle Wrasse; Aalaihi (Hawaiian).

RANGE: Hawaiian Islands.

REMARKS: The Saddle Wrasse is the most abundant wrasse in the Hawaiian Islands. One of the authors (WEB) witnessed the actual spawning sequence (given under the family discussion) in nature.

SIZE: Attains a length of 10 inches.

Thalassoma bifasciatum is the fish with the white belly and yellow
back. The other fish are Neon Gobies, *Gobiosoma oceanops.*
Photo by Robert P. L. Straughan.

SCIENTIFIC NAME: *Thalassoma lucasanum* (Gill).

POPULAR NAME: Mexican rock wrasse.

Illustrated on page 184.

RANGE: Pacific coast of Mexico to the Gulf of California.

REMARKS: This wrasse is found commonly in rocky tide pools. It feeds
on various crustaceans in nature and should be supplied with chopped
shrimp or crab meat, although some substitutes are acceptable. Larger
adults have the black edging of the tail fin extended to form a lunate-
shaped tail.

SIZE: Reaches a length of 5 inches.

These handsome wrasses are *Thalassoma lucasanum.* Photo by Gene Wolfsheimer.

SCIENTIFIC NAME: *Thalassoma lunare* (Linnaeus).

POPULAR NAME: Lyretail Wrasse.

Illustrated on page 185.

RANGE: Red Sea to Tropical Indo-Pacific (including the Hawaiian Islands).

REMARKS: The dark outer rays of the tail fin gives this species its common name. They are similar in general shape to the two preceding species but differing in color. The dark lines on the scales are present, as well as the lines on the head. Spawning is similar to the other species.

SIZE: Attains a length of about 6 inches.

SCIENTIFIC NAME: *Thalassoma lutescens* Lay & Bennett.

POPULAR NAME: Orange-lined Wrasse; Aalaihi (Hawaiian).

This *Thalassoma lunare* was a bit shy about posing for his picture and had to be pushed toward the front glass.
Photo by Dr. Herbert R. Axelrod.

Thalassoma vitidum. Photo by Dr. Herbert R. Axelrod.

This close-up view of *Thalassoma vitidum* shows the teeth, which are perfectly adapted to nibbling and tearing at the coral growths. Photo by Dr. Herbert R. Axelrod.

RANGE: East Indies to Japan, Australia, and across the Pacific to the Hawaiian Islands.

REMARKS: The Orange-lined Wrasse is similar in aspect to the Saddle Wrasse but is yellow in color. The vertical marks on the scales are very faint. The orange lines which gives this wrasse its common name are on the head.

SIZE: Reaches a length of about 6 inches.

SCIENTIFIC NAME: *Thalassoma vitidum* (Bleeker).

POPULAR NAME: Dusky-finned wrasse.

Illustrated on pages 185, 186.

RANGE: Tropical Indo-Pacific.

REMARKS: The ear-spot and pattern of purple or violet lines characterize this species. Care and feeding are similar to that for other members of the genus.

SIZE: Reaches a size of about 6 inches.

Serranus tigrinus, from Bimini. Photo by Dr. Herbert R. Axelrod.

Native Ceylonese fishermen with a catch of Green Parrotfish.
Photo by Rodney Jonklaas.

THE PARROTFISHES
Family Scaridae

Parrotfishes are a large and colorful family of fishes, some of which grow to over four feet in length. In some areas of the world they are sold in fish markets, in others they are discarded as "trash" fish.

The Parrotfishes get their common name from the fact that their teeth are fused into a structure resembling a parrot's beak. This strong beak is used to munch on corals, clams, crabs, and other crustaceans or molluscs. The well-developed pharyngeal teeth aid in the crushing of this material. They can bite the hand that feeds them so care should be exercised when handling them.

Parrotfishes resemble the wrasses and at times it is difficult to tell them apart. The habit of sleeping inside a cocoon of mucus is common to both families but more prevalent in the parrotfishes. Spawning methods are likewise similar and there is no doubt that these two families are closely related.

Parrotfishes normally have two color patterns per species, a supermale being present.

Scarus vetula, the Queen Parrotfish.

Halichoeres bivittatus, a wrasse. Photo by Robert P. L. Straughan.

Sparisoma viride.

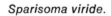

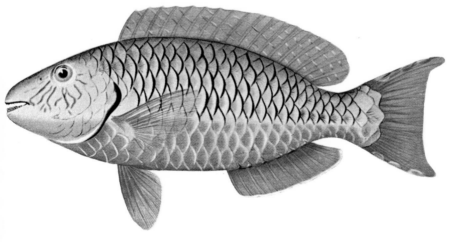

SCIENTIFIC NAME: *Bolbometopon bicolor* (Rüppell).

POPULAR NAME: Bi-color Parrotfish.

Illustrated on page 351.

RANGE: Tropical Indo-Pacific to the Red Sea.

REMARKS: Contrary to most parrotfishes there is little color change with age in this species. The spot in the dorsal fin disappears with growth. The contrasting white and yellow colors and the large black dorsal spot make this species easily recognizable. Individuals will occasionally appear in shipments from the Philippine Islands or Ceylon.

SIZE: Reaches a length of about 2 feet.

SCIENTIFIC NAME: *Scarus coeruleus* (Bloch).

POPULAR NAME: Blue Parrotfish.

RANGE: Brazil to Maryland.

REMARKS: Throughout most of their lives the Blue Parrotfishes remain blue. The adults are darker. There are some pinkish bands under the chin. The large adult males have a much-enlarged nose, and a true lyretail shaped caudal fin.

SIZE: Attains a length of 3 feet.

A Sharp-nosed Puffer, *Canthigaster valentini*. Photo courtesy of Alimenta-Brussels.

SCIENTIFIC NAME: *Scarus taeniopterus* Desmarest.

POPULAR NAME: Princess Parrotfish.

RANGE: Brazil to southern Florida and Bermuda.

REMARKS: The Princess Parrotfish has a beautiful adult male color phase in contrast to the dull, brown-striped females and juveniles. The young are suitable for the home aquarium but by the time they assume the full colors of the adult they are too large to keep.

SIZE: Attains a length of about 1 foot.

Canthigaster cinctus, from Israel. We thought when this fish came in that it was very sick, but later found that the tail is usually folded like this. Photo by Dr. Herbert R. Axelrod.

SCIENTIFIC NAME: *Scarus vetula* Bloch & Schneider.

POPULAR NAME: Queen Parrotfish.

Illustrated on page 189.

RANGE: Caribbean Sea, Florida and Bahama Islands.

REMARKS: Similar to other parrotfishes the males and females have different color phases. The males are brightly colored but the females are rather drab reddish brown with a light stripe along the side.

SIZE: Grows to a length of almost two feet.

SCIENTIFIC NAME: *Sparisoma viride* (Bonnaterre)

POPULAR NAME: Stoplight Parrotfish.

Illustrated on page 189.

RANGE: Tropical western Atlantic Ocean.

REMARKS: The stoplight referred to in the popular name is a cluster of bright yellow colored scales at the base of the tail of the male fish. Females, although having a drab colored head and upper body, have a bright red lower body.

SIZE: Reaches a length of less than two feet.

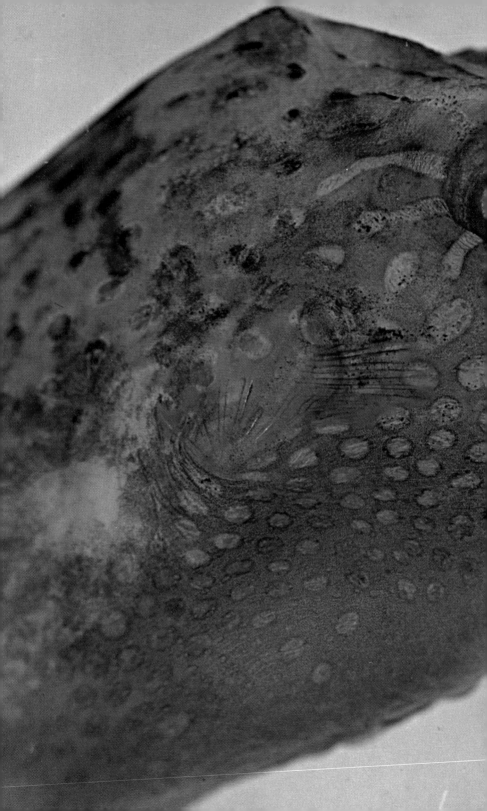

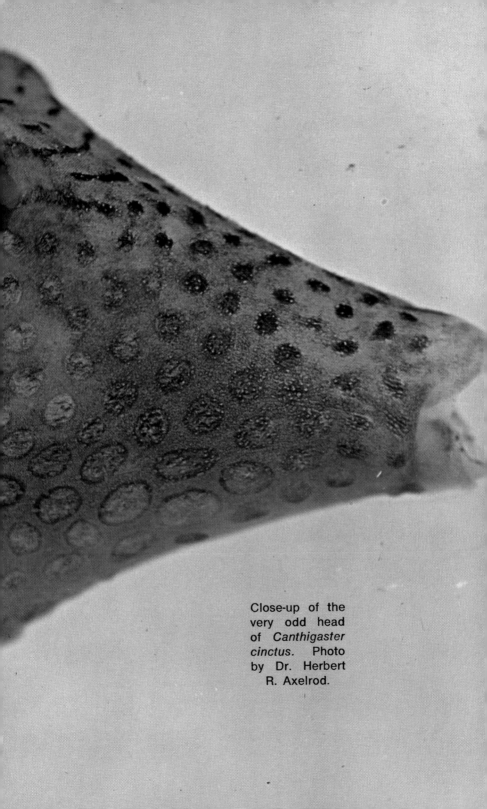

Close-up of the very odd head of *Canthigaster cinctus*. Photo by Dr. Herbert R. Axelrod.

THE SHARP-NOSED PUFFERS
Family Canthigasteridae

The Sharp-nosed Puffers are closely related to the family Tetraodontidae and they have the same ability to inflate themselves. The snouts are pointed, thus the common name of sharp-nosed puffers. Some ichthyologists do not place them in a separate family but combine them with the tetraodontids.

Sharp-nosed puffers are native to the tropical waters of the world's oceans. They usually are found grubbing around on sandy or grass bottoms rather than around coral or rock. Their principal food consists of crustaceans and molluscs so feed them things like chopped shrimp, crab meat, clams, oysters, or even chopped fish. Brine shrimp will be readily accepted.

In the aquarium their oxygen requirements are rather high so they should be provided with plenty of room or lots of aeration.

Canthigaster rostratus is native to the West Indies, but sometimes reaches Florida waters. Photo by Dr. Herbert R. Axelrod.

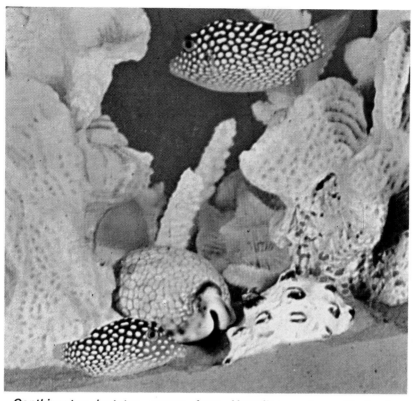

Canthigaster jactator comes from Hawaiian waters. Photo by Gene Wolfsheimer.

Canthigaster valentini has bright blue lines radiating from its eyes. Photo by Klaus Paysan.

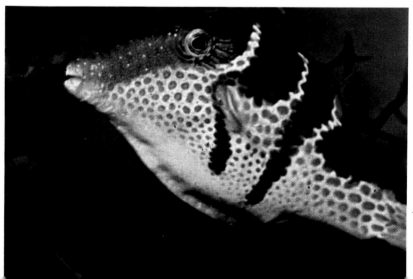

SCIENTIFIC NAME: *Canthigaster cinctus* (Richardson).
POPULAR NAME: Israeli Puffer.
Illustrated on pages 191, 192-193.
RANGE: Tropical Indo-Pacific to Hawaii, Red Sea.
REMARKS: *Canthigaster cinctus* has three black triangular saddles across its back. It is a very popular fish and common enough to be available from time to time at the retail outlets.
SIZE: Reaches a length of 5 inches.

SCIENTIFIC NAME: *Canthigaster jactator* (Jenkins).
POPULAR NAME: Hawaiian Sharp-nosed Puffer.
Illustrated on page 195.
RANGE: Hawaiian Islands.
REMARKS: The Hawaiian Sharp-nosed Puffer has white spots covering its body, making it easy to identify. A closely related puffer, *C. solandri*, also spotted, has lines radiating from the eyes, a character which seems to distinguish these two species. The Hawaiian Sharp-nosed Puffer is a small species and will adapt well to captivity. Feed it live shrimp, Norwegian brine shrimp and freeze-dried foods of all types.
SIZE: About $3\frac{1}{2}$ inches.

SCIENTIFIC NAME: *Canthigaster rostratus* (Bloch).
POPULAR NAME: Atlantic Sharp-nosed Puffer.
Illustrated on page 194.
RANGE: West Indies, rarely to Florida, West Africa.
REMARKS: This puffer is very hardy though its brown and white coloration is not spectacular. They eat a wide variety of foods, feeding on the grasses and algae as well as many types of invertebrates including sponges. Seining through grass flats is apt to produce some of these animals.
SIZE: Reaches a length of 5 inches.

SCIENTIFIC NAME: *Canthigaster valentini* (Bleeker).
POPULAR NAME: Valentyn's Sharp-nosed Puffer.
Illustrated on pages 190, 195.
RANGE: Tropical Indo-Pacific.
REMARKS: The Valentyn Puffer has black triangular patches resembling those of *Canthigaster cinctus* but there are four of these instead of three. The rest of the color pattern bears little resemblance to that species. The Valentyn Puffer will probably be confused with *Paraluteres prionurus* to which it bears a startling resemblance. Since *Paraluteres* is a filefish, the presence of a dorsal spine will quickly contrast the two.
SIZE: Reaches a length of 8 inches.

THE PUFFERS
Family Tetraodontidae

When frightened the puffers have the ability to "puff" up into a round ball, making themselves larger and more difficult to swallow. Under

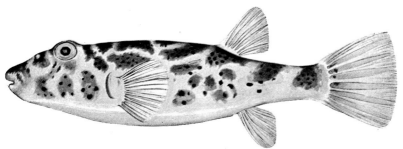

Sphaeroides testudineus, in its normal state.

normal circumstances they accomplish this by swallowing water. When netted and removed from the water they inflate themselves with air. After being replaced in the water they expel the air and swim away.

Puffers are eaten, especially in Japan where they are considered a delicacy, but it is a risky business. If they are not properly cleaned the meat can become poisonous, causing sickness or even death to the person who eats it.

SCIENTIFIC NAME: *Arothron meleagris* (Schneider).
POPULAR NAME: White-spotted Puffer.
RANGE: Micronesia and Polynesia (including Hawaii).
REMARKS: The small white spots covering this puffer and the black ocellated spot at the base of the pectoral fin are diagnostic. The natural diet of the White-spotted Puffer includes gastropods (snails). At certain times of the year some internal organs take on a poisonous nature.
SIZE: Attains a length of 10 inches.

SCIENTIFIC NAME: *Arothron reticularis* (Bloch).
POPULAR NAME: Reticulated Blowfish.
Illustrated on page 198.
RANGE: Tropical Indo-Pacific.
REMARKS: The Reticulated Blowfish is very similar to the above species except for color pattern. In this species, as the name implies, there is a reticulated pattern. The poisoning associated with puffers has been

attributed to this species as well. It is a delicacy in Japan but reportedly takes several lives annually.

SIZE: Reaches a length of 17 inches.

SCIENTIFIC NAME: *Sphaeroides spengleri* (Bloch).

POPULAR NAME: Southern Swellfish.

RANGE: Massachusetts to Brazil.

REMARKS: The line of dark spots along the ventral edge of the body is diagnostic. The Southern Swellfish is common in Florida and a seine pulled through grass flats will often produce some of these fishes. They feed on a host of invertebrates including crustaceans, molluscs, polychaete worms, sea urchins, brittle starfish, and algae.

SIZE: Reaches 8 inches in length.

Arothron reticularis is one of the puffers having a complex pattern of markings. Photo by H. Hansen.

Sphaeroides testudineus, the Turtle Puffer, occurs in the western Atlantic Ocean. Photo by R. Zukal.

SCIENTIFIC NAME: *Sphaeroides testudineus* (Bloch).

POPULAR NAME: Turtle Puffer.

Illustrated on pages 197, 199.

RANGE: Temperate and tropical western Atlantic.

REMARKS: The pattern of light markings on the dorsal surface of this fish are distinctive. They are usually confined to the back, the sides having black spots. Normal food in nature consists of small invertebrates.

SIZE: Grows to about 7 or 8 inches in length.

SCIENTIFIC NAME: *Tetraodon hispidus* Linnaeus.

POPULAR NAME: Oopuhue; Maki Maki; Keke; Akeke (Hawaiian).

RANGE: Red Sea, east Africa to the Hawaiian Islands.

REMARKS: This puffer can stand brackish or even fresh water. It was regarded by old Hawaiians as highly poisonous and it is said that the gall was once used to poison arrows. In China and Japan it is used as a soup base and highly regarded as a food fish.

SIZE: To 14 inches.

Amphiprion clarkii. Photo by Dr. Herbert R. Axelrod.

Amphiprion clarkii, dark phase. Photo by Dr. Herbert R. Axelrod.

Forcipiger flavissimus, the Long-nosed Butterflyfish, is well known in the Hawaiian Islands.

The Copperband Butterflyfish, *Chelmon rostratus*, also has an extended snout. Photo by G. Marcuse.

Chaetodon striatus is found in Puerto Rico. Photo by
Gene Wolfsheimer.

Chaetodon (Gonochaetodon) triangulum is found, among other
places, in the coral reefs of the Philippines. Photo by Earl Kennedy.

The disruptive coloration of *Chaetodon plebeius* includes the dark bar running through the eye and the ocellus at the caudal peduncle. Photo by Dr. Herbert R. Axelrod.

This specimen of *Chaetodon speculum* is scarcely more than a baby. Photo by Earl Kennedy.

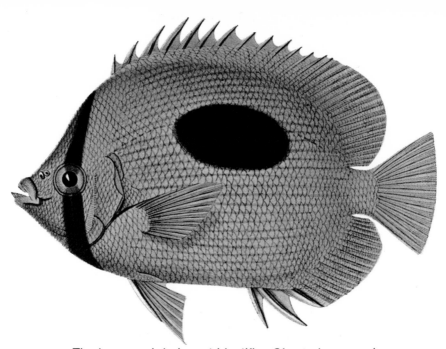

The large oval dark spot identifies *Chaetodon speculum.*

Chaetodon rafflesi has a long snout and criss-crossed markings.

Chaetodon rafflesi. Photo by Dr. Herbert R. Axelrod.

This old painting of *Chaetodon xanthurus* does not indicate the true colors of this fish.

This *Chaetodon plebeius* shows heavy yellow in its coloration. Photo by Dr. Herbert R. Axelrod.

As *Chaetodon ephippium* matures the bar running through the eyes becomes more obscure.

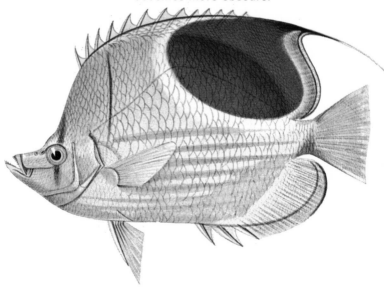

Holacanthus arcuatus is occasionally caught in fish traps in the Hawaiian Islands. Photo by Dr. Herbert R. Axelrod.

Parachaetodon ocellatus, from the Philippines. Photo by Earl Kennedy.

THE ANEMONEFISHES AND DAMSELFISHES
Family Pomacentridae

Pomacentrids are among the most popular of marine aquarium fishes. Besides being small, colorful, lively, hardy, and plentiful, they are usually priced well within the means of the average aquarist. Their only drawback seems to be an aggressive nature. They choose a territory and defend it with vigor against anything or anyone that appears to threaten it.

Damselfishes are found in almost all tropical waters of the world. They are common in shallow water around the coral and rocks. In some instances (*Dascyllus, Amphiprion*) they become closely associated with corals and sea anemones, even to the extent of forming a commensal relationship with them.

Pomacentrids were among the first marine fishes to be spawned and raised in captivity. They are nest builders and guarders, a behavioral trait similar to the fresh-water cichlids. The male damselfish will prepare the nest site by cleaning a rock surface, making sure it is ready for the deposit of the eggs. He will change color at this time and do a looping action signaling a nearby female that all is ready. If the female is also ready to spawn she will accept the invitation and deposit her eggs on the selected spot. The male follows close behind, fertilizing them. The female is then driven off and the male stands guard until hatching. Several females may contribute eggs to the nest.

The natural food of the damselfishes varies with the species. Some species are herbivores, others are carnivores. Most of the damselfishes are omnivores, however, feeding on such items as algae, worms, small crustaceans, detrital material, and various small benthic or planktonic animals.

SCIENTIFIC NAME: *Abudefduf abdominalis* Quoy & Gaimard.
POPULAR NAME: Mao Mao (Hawaiian).
RANGE: Southern Polynesia to the Hawaiian Islands.
REMARKS: The Mao Mao is a very common species of damselfish in Pacific waters. In Hawaii it can be found at various depths. Spawning has been observed in nature and appears to follow the classic pomacentrid pattern outlined above. This fish accepted flat plates set out on the reef as spawning sites. The plates were brought back to the laboratory with the eggs attached and hatching was accomplished in aquaria. This species is one that has been successfully reared this way.
SIZE: Attains a length of 9 inches but usually much less in an aquarium.

SCIENTIFIC NAME: *Abudefduf curacao* (Bloch).

POPULAR NAME: Three-barred Damselfish.

Illustrated on page 214.

RANGE: East Indies and vicinity to the Ryukyu Islands.

REMARKS: The common name indicates this fish has three stripes. Usually there is a connection between the anterior stripes giving the appearance of only three stripes crossing the body.

SIZE: About 3½ inches.

SCIENTIFIC NAME: *Abudefduf dickii* Lienard.

POPULAR NAME: Black-Bar Devil.

Illustrated on page 231.

RANGE: East Indies, Melanesia, Micronesia, Polynesia.

REMARKS: The dark vertical band in the posterior end of the body is distinctive for the species. In an aquarium they tend to be aggressive. Feeding is easily accomplished with prepared foods, live brine shrimp, and *Tubifex* with *Chlorella* algae.

SIZE: To about 5 inches.

SCIENTIFIC NAME: *Abudefduf leucozona* (Bleeker).

POPULAR NAME: Single-barred Devil.

Illustrated on page 210.

RANGE: Tropical Pacific and East Indies.

Abudefduf sordidus. Photo by Gene Wolfsheimer.

REMARKS: The white stripe crossing the body, the black spot at the end of the dorsal fin and the large dark spot on the last spines of the dorsal fin are characteristic of this species.

SIZE: Attains a length of about 4 inches.

SCIENTIFIC NAME: *Abudefduf saxatilis* (Linnaeus).

POPULAR NAME: Sergeant Major.

Illustrated on pages 212, 213.

RANGE: Both tropical coasts of the Americas.

REMARKS: This fish is a hearty eater and likely to get the lion's share of the food at mealtimes. It is extremely common in South Florida, very easy to catch, and usually is one of the first aquarium inhabitants of the beginning marine hobbyist.

SIZE: Reaches a length of 6 inches at maturity.

SCIENTIFIC NAME: *Abudefduf septemfasciatus* (Cuv. & Val.).

POPULAR NAME: Seven-striped Damselfish.

Illustrated on page 215.

RANGE: Tropical Indo-Pacific to Red Sea.

REMARKS: The scientific name refers to the seven stripes crossing the body. This species occasionally is imported in shipments from the Philippines.

SIZE: About 6 inches.

The Single-barred Devil, *Abudefduf leucozona*, is easily recognized. Photo by H. Hansen.

On the reef, species of the genus *Centropyge*, like this *C. tibicen*, are often mistaken for damselfishes. Photo by Earl Kennedy.

SCIENTIFIC NAME: *Abudefduf sordidus* (Forskål).

POPULAR NAME: Kupipi (Hawaii).

Illustrated on pages 209, 214.

RANGE: Widespread in the tropical Indo-Pacific, Red Sea, and Hawaiian Islands.

REMARKS: Although not very colorful this species is a very hardy aquarium fish, and usually welcome in a marine aquarium. Like other damselfishes it tends to be a bit scrappy at times.

SIZE: Reaches a length of $2\frac{1}{2}$ to 3 inches.

SCIENTIFIC NAME: *Chromis coeruleus* (Cuvier & Valenciennes).
POPULAR NAME: Blue-Reef Fish
   Illustrated on page 230.
RANGE: Tropical Indo-Pacific and Red Sea.
REMARKS: This *Chromis* species is very abundant around reefs. They hover over the coral in large numbers and disappear into it at the approach of danger. They spawn on pieces of filamentous algae

The Sergeant Major, *Abudefduf saxatilis*, is frequently found along the Florida coast. Photo by Dr. Herbert R. Axelrod.

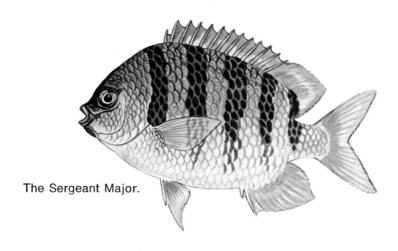

The Sergeant Major.

which become entwined in the coral. The male guards the eggs which hatch in 3-4 days.

SIZE: Attains a length of 4 inches.

SCIENTIFIC NAME: *Chromis multilineata* (Guichenot).
POPULAR NAME: Yellow-edge Chromis.
RANGE: Tropical Western Atlantic.
REMARKS: The Yellow-edge Chromis does well in an aquarium if provided with live food and plenty of aeration. Their disposition is peaceful. In nature they are what is known as particulate plankton feeders. That is, they hover over the reef and select the animals in the plankton that they desire, in contrast to other plankton feeders which strain everything out of the plankton.
SIZE: Mature specimens attain a length of 6 inches.

SCIENTIFIC NAME: *Dascyllus albisella* Gill.
POPULAR NAME: Aloiloi-Paapaa (Hawaiian).
RANGE: Hawaiian Islands.
REMARKS: This species is closely related to *D. trimaculatus* though it has a much larger lateral white spot than that species. In the Hawaiian Islands it is very common and hides among the branches of coral when frightened. The Aloiloi-Paapaa goes through the typical pomacentrid spawning sequence though at about 30 feet or more in depth. The young are very pretty with a neon blue spot across their forehead. They are very hardy and easy to keep but quite aggressive.
SIZE: To about 5 inches.

213

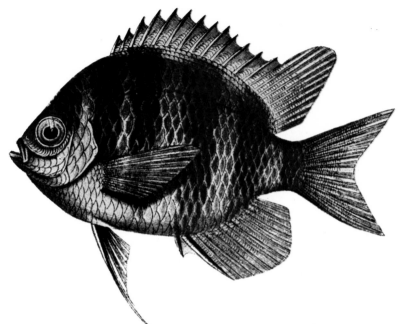

Abudefduf curacao usually has the anterior bars joined, giving a three-barred effect.

Abudefduf sordidus is dusky and does not show the bars plainly.

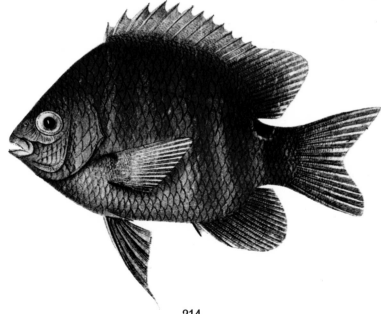

SCIENTIFIC NAME: *Dascyllus aruanus* (Linnaeus).
POPULAR NAME: White-tailed Damselfish.
Illustrated on pages 219, 220, 221.
RANGE: From the Red Sea and East African coast to India, the East Indies, China and Queensland, through Melanesia, Micronesia, and Polynesia. (Not to the Hawaiian Islands).
REMARKS: The White-tailed Damselfish is often confused with the Black-tailed Humbug, *Dascyllus melanurus*. They are easily distinguishable when seen together. The position of the anterior black bars and the lack of black on the caudal fin will serve to identify the White-tailed Damselfish.
SIZE: Grows to a length of 6 inches.

SCIENTIFIC NAME: *Dascyllus marginatus* Rüppell.
POPULAR NAME: Marginate Damselfish.
Illustrated on pages 216-217.
RANGE: Red Sea.
REMARKS: The Marginate Damselfish is closely related to the Reticulate Damselfish (*D. reticulatus*) of the Indian and Pacific Oceans. The black of the ventral region including the anal fin is characteristic of *D. marginatus*.
SIZE: Reaches a length of 8 inches.

Abudefduf septemfasciatus has the seven bars that its name indicates.

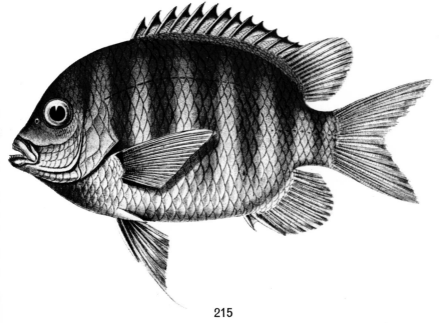

215

*Dascyllus mar-
ginatus*, from
the Red Sea.
Photo by Dr.
Herbert R. Axel-
rod.

SCIENTIFIC NAME: *Dascyllus melanurus* Bleeker.

POPULAR NAME: Black-tailed Humbug.

Illustrated on page 221.

RANGE: East Indies, Melanesia, Micronesia, and Polynesia (not including the Hawaiian Islands).

REMARKS: Similar to the White-tailed Damselfish but differs from that species by the anterior black bands and the presence of black on the caudal fin. Like other species of the genus *Dascyllus,* it eats small crustaceans, and will take to other foods, living or prepared, very readily.

SIZE: Reaches a length of about 4 inches.

SCIENTIFIC NAME: *Dascyllus reticulatus* Bleeker.

POPULAR NAME: Reticulated Damselfish.

Illustrated on page 231.

RANGE: East Indies, Melanesia, Micronesia, and Polynesia.

REMARKS: The Reticulated Damselfish is found in the same habitat as the other species of *Dascyllus.* They are found in shallow water among coral and rocks. They frequently spawn on a cleared section of Staghorn Coral. The male guards the eggs. There are reports that this species has a life span of up to 4 or 5 years.

SIZE: Reaches a length of 4-5 inches.

SCIENTIFIC NAME: *Dascyllus trimaculatus* Rüppell.

POPULAR NAME: Three-Spotted Damselfish.

Illustrated on page 223.

RANGE: The same wide distribution as *D. aruanus.*

REMARKS: The small white spot on the jet black background is very striking. This is the most common species of the genus *Dascyllus* and is a good beginner's fish. When conditions are not proper the black of the body will become quite pale.

SIZE: To about 3 inches.

SCIENTIFIC NAME: *Hypsypops rubicunda* (Girard).

POPULAR NAME: Garibaldi.

Illustrated on page 245.

RANGE: California to Mexico.

REMARKS: The Garibaldi is bright orange as an adult but in addition has many neon blue spots when a juvenile. It is one of the few aquarium fishes from the west coast of the United States. The Garibaldi can stand lower temperatures than most other pomacentrids.

SIZE: Attains a length of about one foot.

This color phase of *Dascyllus aruanus* occurs when the fish is young. Photo by Dr. Herbert R. Axelrod.

It is not surprising that these clownfish, *Amphiprion clarkii*, have body markings similar to those of some of the damsels of the genus *Dascyllus* when it is considered that both belong to the same family. Photo by Earl Kennedy.

A mature specimen of *Dascyllus aruanus*. Photo by Dr. Herbert R. Axelrod.

SCIENTIFIC NAME: *Microspathodon chrysurus* Cuvier & Valenciennes.

POPULAR NAMES: Marine Jewelfish.

Illustrated on page 232.

RANGE: West Indies to southern Florida.

REMARKS: In young specimens the velvet blue body is covered with brilliant blue spots resembling jewels. As the fish ages the spots fade but the tail turns from transparent to a bright yellow. One of its favorite hiding places is among the branches of the common stinging coral making it very difficult to capture.

SIZE: Reaches a length of 6 inches at maturity.

SCIENTIFIC NAME: *Pomacentrus coelestis* (Jordan & Starks).

POPULAR NAME: Blue Damselfish.

RANGE: Tropical Indo-Pacific.

REMARKS: The contrasting colors of blue and yellow make this a popular fish. In nature they are found in groups of up to 50 individuals in the shallow rubble areas of the reef.

SIZE: To 3 inches.

Dascyllus melanurus is on the left, *Dascyllus aruanus* on the right.
Photo by Gene Wolfsheimer.

Dascyllus melanurus. Photo by Dr. Herbert R. Axelrod.

SCIENTIFIC NAME: *Abudefduf uniocellatus* Quoy & Gaimard.

POPULAR NAME: Blue Devil.

Illustrated on pages 226, 240.

RANGE: Tropical Indo-Pacific.

REMARKS: There are many bright blue pomacentrids on the reef that can easily be confused. This one has no yellow on the body but has a black stripe through the eye and one or two black spots at the base of the soft dorsal fin.

SIZE: About 4 inches at maturity.

SCIENTIFIC NAME: *Pomacentrus fuscus* (Cuvier & Valenciennes).

POPULAR NAMES: Dusky Damselfish; Flame-back Damselfish; Orange-back Damselfish.

Illustrated on pages 227, 229.

RANGE: West Indies to Florida.

REMARKS: The Flame-back Damselfish is very colorful when young but eventually changes into a dark gray to blackish adult. Juveniles are a pretty gray and have a red-orange back. They often have neon blue spots on the body and head. A combination of young damselfishes of different species in a large tank is an excellent combination of compatibility, color, and hardiness.

SIZE: Reaches a length of about 6 inches.

SCIENTIFIC NAME: *Pomacentrus leucostictus* Müller & Troschel.

POPULAR NAME: Beau Gregory.

Illustrated on page 228.

RANGE: West Indies north to Florida, where it is abundant.

REMARKS: The Beau Gregory is a very beautiful fish. In nature, with the sun striking on its blue back and the contrasting yellow below, it is a sight to behold. It is very common in Florida and has become a standby for marine aquarists despite its aggressiveness. The Beau Gregory is recommended as a beginner's fish.

SIZE: Grows to a length of 4 inches.

SCIENTIFIC NAME: *Pomacentrus melanochir* Bleeker.

POPULAR NAME: Yellow-tailed Damselfish.

Illustrated on page 230.

RANGE: East Indies and vicinity.

REMARKS: This fish is very colorful and usually available from the Philippine Islands. A dark spot at the upper corner of the gill cover and a dark base to the pectoral fins are additional characteristics that may be used to identify this fish.

SIZE: Reaches 3 inches in length.

The startling contrast between the white spots and velvety-black background makes *Dascyllus trimaculatus* one of the favorites among marine aquarists. Photo by Dr. Herbert R. Axelrod.

SCIENTIFIC NAME: *Pomacentrus planifrons* (Cuvier & Valenciennes).
POPULAR NAMES: Orange Demoiselle; Yellow Damselfish.
    Illustrated on pages 224, 225.
RANGE: West Indies to Florida.
REMARKS: The Orange Demoiselle is sometimes confused with the Honey Gregory. The Orange Demoiselle, however, lacks the violet streaks on the head and back of that species but has a black spot or saddle on top of the caudal peduncle that the Honey Gregory does not.
SIZE: To about 5 inches.

SCIENTIFIC NAME: *Pomacentrus partitus* (Poey).
POPULAR NAME: Black and White Demoiselle.
    Illustrated on page 229.
RANGE: West Indies to Florida.

Pomacentrus sp. is known as the Honey Gregory. This is a mature specimen. Photo by Robert P. L. Straughan.

REMARKS: This fish is found in Florida in the clear waters of the outer reef. It is easily recognized by the black anterior portion of the body and white posterior. It is sometimes called the Bicolor Damselfish. Because of its habitat this species should do better in very clean, highly oxygenated water.

SIZE: Attains a length of 4 inches.

The black mark on the caudal peduncle in the Orange Demoiselle *Pomacentrus planifrons*, is not present in the Honey Gregory. Photo by Dr. Herbert R. Axelrod.

This picture shows the two damselfishes together, the Orange Demoiselle on top and the Honey Gregory below. Photo by Dr. Herbert R. Axelrod.

Abudefduf uniocellatus, one of the more common reef damselfishes. Photo by Dr. Herbert R. Axelrod.

SCIENTIFIC NAME: *Pomacentrus vaiuli* Jordan & Seale.

POPULAR NAME: Ocellate Damselfish.

RANGE: Tropical Indo-Pacific.

REMARKS: This species is very common on the reefs of the Indo-Pacific. It is very colorful and hardy as are most of the damselfishes. The Ocellate Damselfish likes to browse on plants so be sure to add some vegetable matter to its diet. Brine shrimp, *Daphnia,* and *Tubifex* are excellent foods. The common name refers to the large blue-bordered black spot at the base of the latter part of the dorsal fin.

SIZE: Attains a length of 4 inches.

SCIENTIFIC NAME: *Pomacentrus* sp.

POPULAR NAME: Honey Gregory.

Illustrated on pages 224, 225.

RANGE: Southern Florida and the Bahama Islands, probably further south.

REMARKS: The Honey Gregory was discovered by one of the authors (WEB) while diving on Long Reef in the Florida Keys. Looking down upon this fish it appeared to have the colors of the Royal Gramma, reddish-violet anteriorly, yellow posteriorly. It was captured and brought back alive to be identified. It turned out to be a new species and has not been named yet.

SIZE: Reaches a length of 3 inches.

Pomacentrus fuscus, from the West Indies. Photo by Dr. Herbert R. Axelrod.

An older specimen of *Pomacentrus fuscus*.

The Beau Gregory, *Pomacentrus leucostictus.*

A young Beau Gregory. Photo by Dr. Herbert R. Axelrod.

Pomacentrus partitus. Photo by Dr. Herbert R. Axelrod.

The juvenile color phase of *Pomacentrus fuscus.* Photo by Dr. Herbert R. Axelrod.

The Yellow-Tailed Damsels, *Pomacentrus melanochir*, are popular because of the contrast between the blue body and the yellow tail. Photo by Wilhelm Hoppe.

SCIENTIFIC NAME: *Abudefduf xanthonotus* (Bleeker).
POPULAR NAME: Yellow-banded Damselfish.
    Illustrated on page 232.
RANGE: East Indies, Melanesia, Micronesia, and Polynesia.
REMARKS: The Yellow-banded Damselfish is an excellent addition to an aquarium when a change of color is desired, that is, to get away from the predominant blue usually found in these pomacentrids. It takes similar food and conditions as the other members of this family.
SIZE: Attains a length of about 4 inches.

Chromis caeruleus, the blue reef-fish. Photo by Klaus Paysan.

Abudefduf dickii, like many other damselfishes, is very aggressive in an aquarium. Photo by Dr. Herbert R. Axelrod.

Dascyllus reticulatus can be found in shallow, reef-type or rocky habitats. Photo by U. Erich Friese.

Microspathodon chrysurus, the Marine Jewelfish.

A mature pair of *Abudefduf xanthonotus*, which came from the Philippines. Photo by Gene Wolfsheimer.

Amphiprion frenatus loses the body stripe with age. Photo by Gene Wolfsheimer.

THE ANEMONEFISHES

Anemonefishes are specialized pomacentrids that have entered a commensal relationship with sea anemones. They are perhaps the best known of all marine aquarium fishes. Every one of the 26 currently recognized clownfishes are colorful and readily accepted as aquarium fishes.

Anemonefishes are not usually particular in an aquarium as to which species of anemone they will inhabit. It seems that if their own species is not at hand the clownfish will live among the tentacles of other species that are placed with it. There are many records of sea anemones from the Florida coast acting as hosts to several species of *Amphiprion*. In nature they are more apt to be living in a specific type of anemone, however.

The anemone and fish have become adapted to each other through physiological and behavioral means. They maintain a delicate relationship with each other that at times can be broken, the anemonefish becoming just another morsel of food.

233

A fish of most other genera would be stung, killed and eaten, but the clownfishes enjoy immunity. Photo by Dick Boyd.

Clownfishes are small and hardy. They are common enough to be available most of the time at moderate to low prices.

At the time of this writing some species of anemonefishes have been bred and raised in captivity. The techniques are not standardized yet but it is hoped that tank-raised clownfishes will be available in the near future.

Lee Chin Eng was one of the first persons to repeatedly spawn the clownfishes of his area. He used his "natural system" aquarium which was "purified" by living corals and anemones. Unfortunately, he was unable to raise the fry past the ½-inch mark for unknown reasons. Dr. Gerald Allen in his book *Anemonefishes*, reports how he has successfully raised some species of anemonefishes by collecting eggs in the field, placing them in open sea-water systems, and feeding them initially on blenderized flake food and sea water. After three days newly-hatched brine shrimp were eaten. Dr. Allen discusses the methods of other successes with clownfishes (Neugebauer; Hackinger). Anyone interested in clownfishes should read Allen's book.

There must be a good reason for this partnership, but nobody can
do more than advance a theory. Photo by Dick Boyd.

Sometimes *Amphiprion sebae* assumes a chocolate brown color, like this one. Photo by Herbert R. Axelrod.

Anemonefishes are found in tropical areas of the Pacific and Indian Oceans (Red Sea included) but are completely absent from the Atlantic Ocean.

The one disadvantage of keeping these fishes is that they are not really "happy" unless provided with an anemone. The aquarist is then faced with keeping both animals alive.

The variety of excellent photographs will help you in identifying the anemonefishes presented here.

Amphiprion sandaracinos is a handsome yellow-orange anemone-fish with a white stripe down its back. Photo by Dr. Herbert R. Axelrod.

Amphiprion polymnus is an attractive, hardy species. Photo by Earl Kennedy.

Amphiprion polymnus or Saddle Clownfish used to be called *A. laticlavius.* Photo by Gene Wolfsheimer.

Red clownfish, *Amphiprion frenatus*. Photo by Gaylord Davis.

Amphiprion frenatus is a very hardy species. Photo by Dr. Herbert R. Axelrod.

We seldom see *Amphiprion frenatus* small enough so that it still has remnants of the body stripe. Photo by Dr. Herbert R. Axelrod.

Amphiprion perideraion has a more modest coloration than most of the Clownfishes. Photo by Dr. Herbert R. Axelrod.

Three clownfish, *Amphiprion ocellaris,* with a blue damselfish, *Abudefduf uniocellatus.* Photo by Robert P. L. Straughan.

Amphiprion biaculeatus was previously known as *Premnas biaculea-tus.* Photo by Dr. Herbert R. Axelrod.

Amphiprion clarkii. Photo by Dr. Herbert R. Axelrod.

SCIENTIFIC NAME: *Amphiprion biaculeatus* (Bloch).

POPULAR NAME: Spine-cheeked Anemonefish.

Illustrated on page 241.

RANGE: Solomon Islands, New Guinea, Queensland, Philippines, Malayan-Indonesian Archipelago, eastern Indian Ocean, Mauritius, Madagascar.

REMARKS: This species has been known under the name *Premnas biaculeatus*. It has been found however that the differences between this species and the other anemonefish are not enough to warrant keeping them separated under the genus *Premnas*. The name *biaculeatus* translated means two-spined referring to the sharp spines on the cheek.

SIZE: Reaches a length of 5 inches.

SCIENTIFIC NAME: *Amphiprion clarkii* Cuvier.

POPULAR NAME: Clark's Anemonefish.

Illustrated on pages 200, 219, 241, 243.

RANGE: Caroline Islands, Marianas Islands, Melanesia, except Fiji, Philippines, South China Sea, Ryukyu Islands, southern Japan, Malay-Indonesian Archipelago, Western Australia and Northern Territory, eastern and northern Indian Ocean to the Persian Gulf.

REMARKS: This species was commonly known under several other names like *A. xanthurus* or *A. sebae*. Although the pattern remains fairly constant the basic color can change from light tan to dark brown.

SIZE: Reaches a length of about 4 inches.

SCIENTIFIC NAME: *Amphiprion frenatus* (Brevoort).

POPULAR NAME: Red Clownfish.

Illustrated on pages 233, 238, 239.

RANGE: Borneo, Singapore, Philippines, South China Sea, Ryukyus, southern Japan.

REMARKS: The single white bar across the back of the head that is outlined with black is typical of this species. It is commonly imported from Singapore and the Philippine Islands. When young this species has a second white bar across the center of the body but this fades with growth.

SIZE: Attains a length of 4 inches.

SCIENTIFIC NAME: *Amphiprion ocellaris* Cuvier.

POPULAR NAME: Clown Anemonefish.

Illustrated on pages 234, 235, 240.

A handsome clown is *Amphiprion clarkii*. Photo by Gene Wolfsheimer.

RANGE: Northern Australia, Malayan-Indonesian Region, eastern Indian Ocean, Philippine Islands, South China Sea, Ryukyu Islands, southern Japan.

REMARKS: The ichthyologists have done it again! One of the best known clownfish has a new name. Although the name *Amphiprion percula* is still around, the species that has been known by that name for such a long time now sports a new one. The true *A. percula* comes from Melanesia and Queensland. Aside from some technical differences it has a darker (blackish) color between the white bars than *A. ocellaris* does.

SIZE: Reaches a length of 4 inches.

SCIENTIFIC NAME: *Amphiprion perideraion* Bleeker.

POPULAR NAME: Skunk Clownfish.

Illustrated on page 240.

RANGE: Micronesia, New Hebrides, Indo-Australian Archipelago, Thailand, Philippines, South China Sea, Ryukyu Islands, southern Japan.

REMARKS: This species is similar to other Skunk Clownfish but is easily recognized by the white streak across the gill cover. In addition the general color is more pinkish when compared to the more orange-hued *Amphiprion sandaracinos* or *A. akallopisos*.

SIZE: Does not quite reach a length of 3 inches.

SCIENTIFIC NAME: *Amphiprion polymnus* (Linnaeus).

POPULAR NAME: Saddle-back Clownfish.

Illustrated on page 237.

RANGE: Northern Australia, New Guinea, Philippine Islands, South China Sea, Ryukyu Islands, southern Japan.

REMARKS: The Saddle-back Clown is easily recognized by the white saddle-shaped marking on the back which reaches only to the lateral line. The edges of the tail are white, the dark portion tapering towards the end of the tail.

SIZE: About $3\frac{1}{2}$ inches at maturity.

SCIENTIFIC NAME: *Amphiprion sandaracinos* Allen.

POPULAR NAME: Skunk Clown.

Illustrated on page 236.

RANGE: Philippine Islands.

REMARKS: All the Philippine specimens that were called *Amphiprion akallopisos* are in reality this new species. The true *A. akallopisos* is restricted to the Indian Ocean and can only be distinguished from *A. sandaracinos* by technical measurements. If an aquarist has exceptional eyes he may be able to spot the conical teeth of *Amphiprion sandaracinos* as compared to the incisiform teeth of *A. akallopisos*.

SIZE: Reaches a length of 3 inches.

SCIENTIFIC NAME: *Amphiprion sebae* Bleeker.
POPULAR NAME: Seba's Anemonefish.
Illustrated on page 236.
RANGE: East Indies to central Indian Ocean.
REMARKS: This fish is reportedly closely related to *Amphiprion polymnus*, but has the middle band extending down to the ventral side whereas *A. polymnus* has it extending only partway down.
SIZE: Reaches a length of about 4 inches.

A young pair of *Hypsypops rubicunda*, known in California as the Garibaldi Perch. Photo by Gene Wolfsheimer.

Pterois lunulatus, one of the lionfishes.

THE SCORPIONFISHES

Family Scorpaenidae

Scorpions have a poisonous sting. These fishes are named after them for that reason. Most, if not all of the scorpionfishes, also have a poisonous sting, being equipped with poisonous sacs at the base of their dorsal spines. The sting varies from something similar to a bee sting to a very powerful jolt which can cause excruciating pain or even death. Most of the scorpionfishes are too large or too ugly for the marine aquarist. The latter category includes the deadly stonefishes, the most feared of the scorpionfishes. Collectors in the field have learned to step carefully around the reefs where they are found lest they step on one.

Members of the genus *Pterois*, perhaps second in line of dangerous scorpionfish, are very popular aquarium fish. These lionfish or turkey-fish, as they are sometimes called, are brightly colored and have outstanding fin development as can be seen by the accompanying photographs. Most of the comments will be applicable to these species.

Scorpionfishes are hardy aquarium fishes which can live for a considerable time and grow to a large size. Lionfishes prefer live food such as small fishes or shrimps, but can be coaxed into taking strips of fish or other food such as hamburger.

Due to their poisonous nature these fishes are easy to catch. When approached they make no real effort to escape but spread their fins and wait.

Dendrochirus zebra. Photo by Gene Wolfsheimer.

Pterois volitans. Photo by Dr. Herbert R. Axelrod.

*Pterois lunulatus.*The species of *Pterois* are just as poisonous as they are beautiful. Photo by Dr. Herbert R. Axelrod.

SCIENTIFIC NAME: *Dendrochirus zebra* Quoy & Gaimard.

POPULAR NAME: Zebra Lionfish.

Illustrated on pages 247, 249.

RANGE: Red Sea and east Africa to Polynesia.

REMARKS: The sting of this species is not as toxic as some species but there is a bit of pain involved. This genus is different from the various lionfishes of the genus *Pterois* by having the pectoral rays connected to each other almost to the tips. In *Pterois* they are separated for most of their lengths.

SIZE: Attains a length of 8 inches.

SCIENTIFIC NAME: *Pterois lunulatus* Bleeker.

POPULAR NAME: Zebrafish; Zebra Lionfish.

Illustrated on pages 246, 248.

RANGE: Red Sea and east Africa to Polynesia.

Dendrochirus zebra. Photo by Dick Boyd.

Pterois radiata. The first dorsal spines are hollow and carry poison sacs.

REMARKS: The Zebrafish is very similar to the very popular *Pterois volitans* and may often be confused with it. Unfortunately the differences are minor and technical with no easy way to distinguish them.

SIZE: Attains a length of 10 inches.

SCIENTIFIC NAME: *Pterois radiata* Cuvier & Valenciennes.

POPULAR NAME: Whitefin Lionfish.

Illustrated on page 249.

RANGE: Tropical Indo-Pacific and Red Sea.

REMARKS: The Whitefin Lionfish is easily recognized by the pair of horizontal white lines along the caudal peduncle. It is colorful and hardy, but may hide in caves or corners until coaxed out at mealtimes or until it becomes adjusted to aquarium life.

SIZE: Grows to about 10 inches.

SCIENTIFIC NAME: *Pterois russelli* Bennett.

POPULAR NAME: Fireworks Lionfish.

Illustrated on page 250.

RANGE: Tropical Indo-Pacific.

REMARKS: This species is close to *Pterois volitans* but differs in number of lateral scales as well as color pattern. It prefers live foods as small fish and shrimp but will eat prepared foods.

SIZE: Attains 12 inches.

Pterois russelli,
Russell's Lionfish.

Pterois sphex, the most commonly imported of the group. Photo by Dr. Herbert R. Axelrod.

SCIENTIFIC NAME: *Pterois sphex* (Jordan & Evermann).
POPULAR NAME: Hawaiian Lionfish.
   Illustrated on page 251.
RANGE: Hawaiian Islands.
REMARKS: This lionfish is found only in the Hawaiian Islands. One of the authors (WEB) saw a friend stung by an adult of this species in the finger. He was in moderate pain for about an hour, after which it subsided. There were no ill after-effects.
SIZE: Reaches a length of 7 inches or so.

SCIENTIFIC NAME: *Pterois volitans* (Linnaeus).
POPULAR NAME: Turkeyfish; Lionfish; Butterfly Cod.
   Illustrated on page 247.
RANGE: Red Sea and east Africa to Polynesia.
REMARKS: This Lionfish is the species most prized by aquarists but, unfortunately, also the most venomous. The accompanying photographs give only a small idea of the unusual beauty of the Lionfish. It does well on guppies and other small fishes as well as shrimps and fish meat. The Lionfish, like its namesake, can be trained but caution should be exercised. Aquarists have been stung by their fishes while caring for the tank.
SIZE: One of the largest of the lionfishes, it reaches a length of a foot or more in nature.

THE SURGEONFISHES
Family Acanthuridae

There are many common names applied to this family, Surgeonfish, Doctorfish, Tangs, Lancetfish, and Unicornfish are some of them. Many of these names are based on the outstanding characteristic of this group, namely one or more sharp spines on each side of the caudal peduncle.

Top to bottom: *Naso lituratus, Holacanthus tricolor* and *Acanthurus lineatus.* Photo by Hans and Klaus Paysan.

A young specimen of *Naso brevirostris*. Photo by Dr. Herbert R. Axelrod.

These spines are formidable weapons being sharp and directed forwards. They are often marked with contrasting colors, making them quite conspicuous, perhaps as a warning to other fishes.

The body is flat and disc-shaped. Both dorsal and anal fins are continuous, that is, without a broken outline. There are many species in the family containing several variations on the basic shape. The genus *Naso* develops a long "nose" in the adult, and species in the genus *Zebrasoma* have very high dorsal and anal fins.

Surgeonfishes are tropical marine fishes found on coral reefs along with the butterflyfishes and angelfishes. Their chief food is algae and they should be offered small pieces of partially cooked spinach or lettuce leaves.

In some areas of the world (Hawaii, Philippines) species of surgeonfishes are used for food. In other places they are shunned, the people fearing their sometimes poisonous nature. It is known that the tail spines are poisonous in some species and it is suspected that the spines of the dorsal fin may also contain a toxin of sorts, including the larval forms. Whatever the case may be, care should be taken when handling these fishes for a wound from one of the spines is definitely painful and infection may result.

SCIENTIFIC NAME: *Acanthurus achilles* Shaw.
POPULAR NAME: Red-tailed Surgeonfish; Achilles Tang.
RANGE: Southeast Asia; Micronesia, and Polynesia including the Hawaiian Islands.

REMARKS: The Red-tailed Surgeonfish is a handsome fish with the red area contrasting sharply with the dark brown background. The caudal spine is located in the red area, possibly directing attention to it.

SIZE: Attains a length of 10 inches.

SCIENTIFIC NAME: *Acanthurus coeruleus* Bloch & Schneider.
POPULAR NAME: Blue Tang.
 Illustrated on pages 254, 263.
RANGE: West Indies to Florida.
REMARKS: It may be strange to keep a bright yellow surgeonfish and have to tell your friends it is called the *blue* tang but in this case it is appropriate. In a short time you may find that your fish has really turned a blue color.

SIZE: Reaches a foot or more in length.

SCIENTIFIC NAME: *Acanthurus dussumieri* Cuvier & Valenciennes.
POPULAR NAME: Hawaiian Surgeonfish; Palani (Hawaiian).
 Illustrated on page 255.
RANGE: East coast of Africa to South Africa, across the Indian Ocean to the East Indies, Japan, Australia, the Philippines, and the Pacific Islands including Hawaii.

Acanthurus coeruleus.

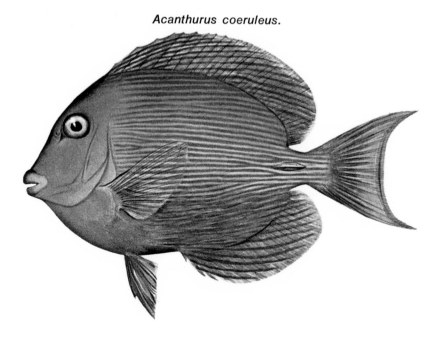

Acanthurus dussumieri becomes large when mature, and it is practical to keep only young ones. Photo by Dr. Herbert R. Axelrod.

REMARKS: Juvenile Palani are somewhat more colorful than the adults. This species is common in the Hawaiian Islands and often captured in traps. The juveniles turn up in tide pools. The Palani has narrow blue lines on the body; the tail is bright blue with black spots.
SIZE: To 18 inches in length.

SCIENTIFIC NAME: *Acanthurus guttatus* Bloch & Schneider.
POPULAR NAME: Mustard Surgeon.
RANGE: East coast of Africa to the Hawaiian Islands.
REMARKS: The Mustard Surgeonfish does much better with a high degree of aeration. In Hawaii it frequents the zone behind the reef where the surf breaks and the water is highly oxygenated. It eats vegetable matter and some algae, or as a substitute, lettuce could be supplied.
SIZE: Up to 12 inches in length.

SCIENTIFIC NAME: *Acanthurus leucosternon* Bennett.
POPULAR NAME: Powder-blue Surgeonfish.
Illustrated on pages 144, 258, 259.
RANGE: Tropical waters of the Indo-Pacific.
REMARKS: The Powder-blue Surgeonfish has a wide range but is not common. It is a popular species mainly due to its pleasing color pat-

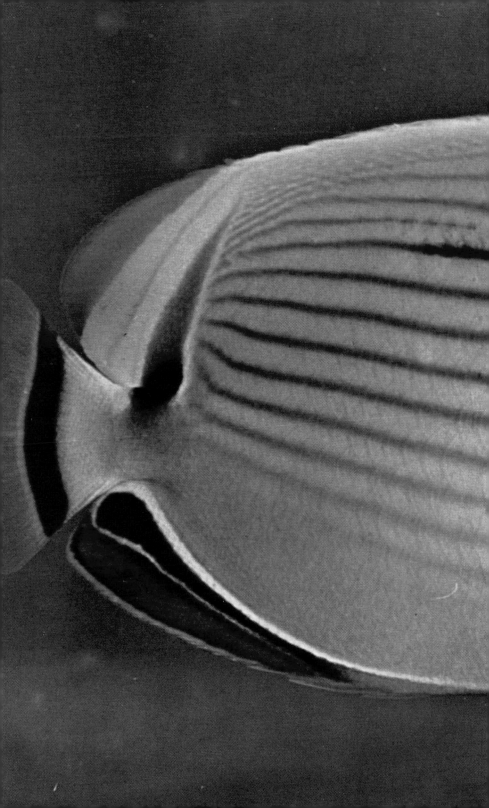

The gorgeous
*Chaetodon
trifasciatus*.
Photo by
Dr. Herbert R.
Axelrod.

tern. This species sometimes turns up in the local fishermen's traps in the Hawaiian Islands.

SIZE: Attains a length of at least 8 inches.

SCIENTIFIC NAME: *Acanthurus lineatus* (Linnaeus).

POPULAR NAME: Clown Surgeonfish.

Illustrated on page 252.

RANGE: Tropical Indo-Pacific.

REMARKS: This beautifully marked surgeonfish is always welcome in a home aquarium and almost always can be found in public aquaria. It will accept most prepared foods and will do very well as long as some vegetable matter is added.

SIZE: Reaches a length of about 8 inches.

SCIENTIFIC NAME: *Acanthurus nigrofuscus* (Linnaeus).

POPULAR NAME: Gray Surgeonfish.

Illustrated on page 261.

RANGE: Central Indo-Pacific.

Acanthurus leucosternon in its natural surroundings. Underwater Photo by Dr. Wolfgang Klausewitz.

A closer look at *Acanthurus leucosternon*. Photo by Dr. Herbert R. Axelrod.

REMARKS: The Gray Surgeonfish is a rather rare species and does not get trapped as easily as the other species. It is more apt to be found in the deeper lagoons than close to the shallow coral reefs. However it takes a baited hook readily. The young specimens of the Gray Surgeonfish show a barred pattern.

SIZE: Usually about 8 inches long.

SCIENTIFIC NAME: *Acanthurus olivaceous* Bloch & Schneider.

POPULAR NAME: Olive Surgeonfish.

Illustrated on page 351.

RANGE: East Indies to the Hawaiian Islands, and to Australia.

REMARKS: The Olive Surgeonfish is easily recognized by its red "ear" or long, red-orange band below the eye. Perhaps a better common name would be Red-eared Surgeonfish. This species is territorial and requires heavy aeration. An aquarium of no less than 50 gallons size is recommended.

SIZE: Attains a length of 12 inches.

The Convict Tang, *Acanthurus triostegus.* Photo by Dr. Herbert R. Axelrod.

Acanthurus nigrofuscus. Photo by Dr. Herbert R. Axelrod.

SCIENTIFIC NAME: *Acanthurus triostegus* (Linnaeus).
POPULAR NAME: Convict Tang.
    Illustrated on page 260.
RANGE: Widely distributed from the east African coast to the Hawaiian Islands, Japan, and Australia.
REMARKS: The Convict Tang is a very common species in the Hawaiian Islands. It arrives inshore from a pelagic larval existence as a silvery and transparent fish. Within a short time it transforms to a silvery-white color with black vertical stripes like that of the adult.
SIZE: Reaches a length of 9 inches.

SCIENTIFIC NAME: *Ctenochaetus strigosus* Quoy & Gaimard.
POPULAR NAME: Kala (Hawaiian Islands).
    Illustrated on page 263.
RANGE: Widely distributed from the Red Sea to the Hawaiian Islands.
REMARKS: In Hawaii the Kala was once tabu (kapu in Hawaiian) as food to all but the king, and the death penalty was imposed upon anyone else who ate it.
SIZE: Grows to about one foot in length.

SCIENTIFIC NAME: *Naso lituratus* (Bloch & Schneider).

POPULAR NAME: Smoothhead Unicornfish.

Illustrated on page 252.

RANGE: Widespread in the Indo-Pacific from the Hawaiian Islands to the Red Sea.

REMARKS: Although generally shaped like the other species of genus *Naso*, the Smoothhead Unicornfish lacks the prominent projection above the mouth. The beautiful colors of this fish are assumed as adults, the juveniles having a spotted or mottled pattern.

SIZE: Reaches a length of about a foot and a half.

SCIENTIFIC NAME: *Naso brevirostris* (Valenciennes).

POPULAR NAME: Short-nosed Unicornfish.

Illustrated on page 253.

RANGE: Tropical Indo-Pacific.

REMARKS: Juveniles of this species do well in the aquarium. They lack the projection of the adult. They will eat prepared foods as well as live brine shrimp. Adults in nature are particulate plankton feeders, selecting individual tidbits from the open water.

SIZE: Reaches a length of a foot and a half.

Outstanding in its color contrasts is *Zebrasoma xanthurum*.

The Blue Tang from Florida waters, *Acanthurus coeruleus*.

Ctenochaetus strigosus Photo by Dr. Herbert R. Axelrod.

The Yellow Tang, *Zebrasoma flavescens*, is a stand-out in any aquarium. Photo by Dr. Herbert R. Axelrod.

SCIENTIFIC NAME: *Zebrasoma flavescens* (Bennett).
POPULAR NAME: Yellow Tang.
    Illustrated on page 264.
RANGE: East Indies to the Hawaiian Islands.
REMARKS: The Yellow Tang is easily recognized by its bright yellow color. In different parts of its range the yellow may be of various shades, tending towards brownish in some areas but brilliant chrome yellow in individuals from Hawaii.

    In the genus *Zebrasoma* the fins are high, particularly as juveniles, and the snout is projecting.
SIZE: Reaches about 7 inches in length.

SCIENTIFIC NAME: *Zebrasoma scopas* (Cuvier).
POPULAR NAME: Brown Tang.
    Illustrated on page 265.
RANGE: Tropical Indo-Pacific.
REMARKS: This species is often confused with the Yellow Tang in areas where the Yellow Tang is darker in color than the bright lemon yellow fishes found in the Hawaiian Islands. The Brown Tang is spotted on

Zebrasoma scopas. Photo by Dr. Herbert R. Axelrod.

The Sailfin Tang, *Zebrasoma veliferum.* Photo by Dr. Herbert R. Axelrod.

the head, the spots joined on the body to form irregular wavy, narrow lines on the body.

SIZE: Reaches a length of about 7 inches.

SCIENTIFIC NAME: *Zebrasoma veliferum* (Bloch).
POPULAR NAME: Sailfin Tang.
   Illustrated on page 265.
RANGE: East African coast to the Hawaiian Islands.
REMARKS: The distinctive color pattern is well illustrated in the accompanying photograph. The color is changeable, at least with respect to the lightness or darkness.
SIZE: May reach a length of 16 inches although fishes greater than 10 inches are rare.

SCIENTIFIC NAME: *Zebrasoma xanthurum* Valenciennes.
POPULAR NAME: Purple Surgeonfish.
   Illustrated on page 262.
RANGE: Pacific coast of North America to the east coast of Africa.
REMARKS: The juvenile Purple Surgeonfish is very colorful with its yellow tail contrasting with the purple of the body. The outer portion of the pectoral fin is also yellow.
SIZE: Attains a length of about two feet.

THE SEA HORSES AND PIPEFISHES
Family Syngnathidae

Sea horses and pipefishes are very distinctive creatures with their scales modified into plates that fit closely together forming a flexible armor. The pipefishes are more eel- or snake-like, being stretched out into a straight line from the tip of the snout to the tip of the tail. Sea horses on the other hand have heads bent at an angle to the body and swim "upright" in the water. Both groups have a small dorsal fin in the middle of the back. Their small, tubular mouths are adapted for feeding on the drifting organisms called plankton.

THE SEA HORSES

Sea horses are fascinating, readily available, and reasonably priced little fishes and therefore have gained considerable popularity as an aquarium fish. They are excellent fishes for the beginner and are always welcome in the more advanced aquarist's tanks.

Sea Horse, holding on with its prehensile tail.
Photo courtesy of Marine Studios, Marine-
    land, Florida.

The head is the most conspicuous character, shaped somewhat like that of a horse and set at an angle to the body. The tail is prehensile, similar to that of a monkey, and is used to hang on to some feature of the bottom such as blades of grass. Sea horses have small fins and their locomotion is accomplished mainly through use of the dorsal and pectoral fins. These latter fins, attached just behind the gill openings, appear like tiny ears.

In many fishes the male will take part, even the dominant part, in caring for the eggs and young. This is carried to the extreme in sea horses. The male and *not* the female gives birth to the young! When the fishes are ready for spawning a courtship takes place which climaxes with the female inserting her ovipositor into a specially constructed "brood pouch" on the ventral side of the male. Here the female deposits the eggs which are fertilized inside by the male, and where they undergo a period of incubation. The male's "pregnancy" becomes more and more apparent until the time for birth when he goes into violent contortions as the young are popped out one or several at a time until all are expelled. These young are tiny replicas of their parents complete with prehensile tail. It is not uncommon to find one or more of these young firmly holding on to the elongate snout of the parent. The female does not take part in the proceeding and should be removed. After the birth of the young the male can also be removed. Although Sea Horses have been bred in captivity, those who want the pleasure of raising them might do best at first to obtain a pregnant male.

Sea horses have hearty appetites and there should be some food available in their tanks almost continuously. It is easy to feed Sea Horses. Live brine shrimp, some of which may also live in the same tank with them for a couple of days, is the most popular food. Baby guppies and occasional white worms can be used to vary the diet. In some instances sea horses have been coaxed to accept the Wardley's flake foods but preference is still for live foods. Some sea horses have been calculated to consume 3,600 brine shrimp in a ten-hour feeding period. It is said that even when satiated the sea horse will continue to kill brine shrimp without eating them.

Sea horses are generally found in places where there is a current. They anchor themselves to the bottom by curling their tails around some object and await food that the current brings to them. The aeration or filtration necessary for marine aquaria usually provides enough water motion. Care should be taken not to have too swift a current that would prevent the sea horses from catching their food.

Hippocampus male with the brood pouch fully inflated
with young. Photo courtesy Marine Studios, Marineland, Florida.

Phycodurus eques

Photo Courtesy American Museum
of Natural History.

With a constant food supply there is always the danger of polluting the tank with bits of uneaten food. Besides a constantly operating filter (which should be cleaned often) frequent siphoning of the bottom proves beneficial. Particular care should also be taken to prevent brine shrimp egg shells from getting into the tank. They are indigestible and can cause all sorts of problems if eaten.

Tank mates for sea horses are not recommended. Since they are poor swimmers other fishes with better swimming ability get most of the food.

The most frequent trouble with sea horses is gas bubbles. Though not fatal in itself it disturbs the animal's equilibrium and prevents it from feeding properly. In some cases the sea horse ultimately starves to death. To correct the condition all that is necessary is to puncture the bubble with a sharp, sterile instrument and press or squeeze out the gas.

Sea horses, like other fishes, can regenerate fins that are torn off by tank aggressors. Be sure not to confuse torn fins with fin rot disease although ripped fins can develop fungus or become infected if not treated. Fins may regenerate as quickly as two to three weeks.

There are many different kinds of sea horses, but because of limitations of space, only the two most common species are fully reported here. Significant among the exclusions is the Sea Dragon (*Phycodurus*) (Illustrated on page 270) from Australia. This species has fleshy tabs over the body, giving it a startling resemblance to the weeds in which it lives.

SCIENTIFIC NAME: *Hippocampus erectus* Perry.
POPULAR NAME: Lined Sea Horse.
Illustrated on pages 267, 269, 272, 274.
RANGE: Maine to Cuba.
REMARKS: The Lined Sea Horse is a temperate to sub-tropical species which is often collected in the New York area. It is highly unpredictable where found, being common one year and almost nonexistent the next. This is one of the larger species, and appears in a variety of colors.

As mentioned above large amounts of food are needed. If one lives near the sea shore and can supply small shrimp, baby minnows, and the like, his Lined Sea Horse will thrive beautifully. An inland aquarist will have to resort to raising baby guppies or other small fish, brine shrimp, and trying to supplant these with *Tubifex,* white worms, and freeze-dried *Calanus finmarchicus* (if the sea horse can be persuaded to eat the latter non-living food). Other foods found acceptable by this species are salt marsh mosquito larvae, marine crustaceans, insects, or adult brine shrimp. Unfortunately not all of these are readily available.

These three sea horses are all the same species and show some of the color phases encountered. Photo by Stan Wayman and Rapho Guillemette.

The spawning sequence has already been presented above. It has been reported that the incubation period extends to one and a half months. Large sea horses are prone to generation of gas within the pouches usually due to stillborn young.

These sea horses are susceptible to white spot disease. It initially appears on the fins, tips of the cirri, etc. Those spots beneath the skin then proliferate, causing loss of pigment, and appear as white areas. This fatal disease is caused by a microsporidian related to *Glugea* and may be a specific disease of sea horses and pipefishes as no other fish has been seen afflicted by it. Isolation helps to prevent spreading to other sea horses, but no known cure has been reported.

Lined Sea Horses probably have life expectancies of two to three years.

SIZE: Up to 10 inches.

SCIENTIFIC NAME: *Hippocampus zosterae* Jordan & Gilbert.

POPULAR NAME: Dwarf Sea Horse.

RANGE: Southeast coast of the United States, around Florida to the Gulf Coast; common in Pensacola Bay.

REMARKS: This is the smaller of the two species of sea horses covered in this book. It readily takes brine shrimp which constitutes the major portion of its diet. Baby guppies and other young fishes are also eagerly eaten.

The Dwarf Sea Horse is more hardy than the preceding and will breed more readily in the aquarium. Newly born Dwarfs are as big or bigger than the newborn of other species and can handle baby brine shrimp.

Dwarf Sea Horses start breeding in late February and continue on through to fall. Ten days are required from fertilization to birth of the young. After only two to three days the males are ready to breed again. The usual size of the brood is 25, with around 55 near maximum.

Male Dwarf Sea Horses are likely to take air bubbles into their pouches when pumping them in preparation for the deposit of eggs. These bubbles cause them to lose their equilibrium making breeding and eating difficult or impossible. In Dwarfs the bubbles are usually released during courtship or after birth of the young as the pouch is normally dilated.

The life span of Dwarf Sea Horses is somewhat less than the two to three years of the larger species.

Three Sea Horses waiting for their dinner to swim by. Photo courtesy Marine Studios, Marineland, Florida.

The sea horse uses its long tail to good advantage, most usually as a gripping mechanism. Photo by Earl Kennedy.

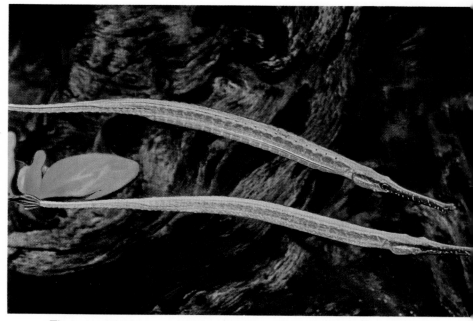

The pipefishes are closely related to the sea horses. This is a freshwater species, *Syngnathus spicifex*. Photo by A. van den Nieuwenhuizen.

THE PIPEFISHES

The pipefishes are very similar to the sea horses except that the head is in a straight line with the body. The body is slender and eel-like but encased in a semi-rigid armor of modified scales. They are found in the same habitat as sea horses and are easily collected through the use of a beach seine.

The color pattern of pipefishes varies from plain, mottled, or delicately striped to boldly barred. In addition to the small dorsal and pectoral fins, pipefishes have a caudal fin.

The male pipefish carries the eggs until hatching, much like the sea horses. Spawning is accomplished by the intertwining of the long snake-like bodies and usually occurs in the late spring or early summer.

The food is the same as that for sea horses, live brine shrimp or baby fish being best.

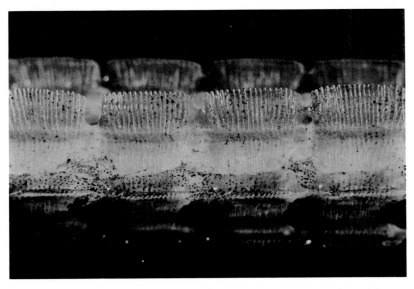

Instead of a brood pouch, the pipefish male carries a series of flaps along its belly. Photo by A. van den Nieuwenhuizen.

The distended flaps are now packed with eggs. Photo by A. van den Nieuwenhuizen.

SCIENTIFIC NAME: *Syngnathus fuscus* Storer.

POPULAR NAME: Northern Pipefish.

RANGE: Halifax to North Carolina.

REMARKS: This Northern Pipefish is more readily found in seine hauls than the sea horses during the summer months.

SIZE: 7 inches, usually much smaller.

SCIENTIFIC NAME: *Dunckerocampus dactyliophorus* (Bleeker).

POPULAR NAME: Banded Pipefish; Zebra Pipefish.

RANGE: East Indies, Philippines, Micronesia.

REMARKS: This is one of the more spectacularly patterned of the pipe-fishes. Its name is almost as long as the fish itself.

SIZE: Attains a length of 6-7 inches.

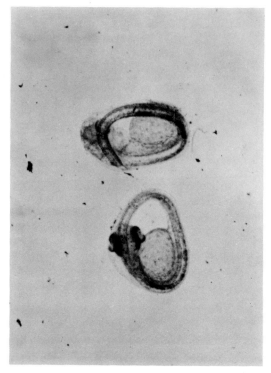

Two pipefish eggs which are about to hatch. Photo by A. van den Nieuwenhuizen.

Bathygobius fuscus. Photo by Gene Wolfsheimer.

THE GOBIES
Family Gobiidae

Gobies are small fishes well suited to the home aquarium. They are usually elongate and have one or more dorsal fins. The most distinguishing feature is the pelvic fins. They are fused along the ventral line so that they form a complete disc which acts like a suction cup to hold the fish in place. In their natural environment they usually fasten themselves onto a rock or blade of grass, but in the aquarium the side glass will do just as nicely.

The family Gobiidae is very large. There are hundreds of species occurring in all parts of the world and in a wide variety of habitats. Some have taken up a pelagic existence while others have taken on the chores of the cleaning wrasse, *Labroides.*

Gobies are usually shy and stay hidden or within quick reach of some shelter. Their size makes them ideal candidates for spawning in captivity and reports of some species being raised have already been received. They prepare a nest by cleaning the surface of a smooth object, such as a shell or rock, and deposit the eggs therein. The eggs are attached to the spawning site and are guarded by both parents until hatching. Then it's every fish for itself.

These fishes are hardy and eat a wide variety of foods. Some will exist exclusively on brine shrimp though a more varied diet is heartily recommended.

SCIENTIFIC NAME: *Bathygobius fuscus* Rüppell.

POPULAR NAME: OopuOhune (Hawaiian).

Illustrated on page 279.

RANGE: Red Sea, tropical Indo-Pacific.

REMARKS: This goby is common in Hawaiian Island tide pools. Even in this confined area it is difficult to catch as it is very fast and can disappear into small holes in the blink of an eye. Its color is variable depending upon the color of the bottom, e.g. light tan on sandy areas to almost black over dark areas.

SIZE: Attains a length of about 4 inches.

SCIENTIFIC NAME: *Gobiodon citrinus* (Rüppell).

POPULAR NAME: Citron Goby.

Illustrated on page 280.

RANGE: Tropical Indo-Pacific.

REMARKS: This goby is variable in color from almost jet black to bright yellow. It is very flattened and spends much of its time in coral branches. The pelvic fins are united into a sucking disc as most other gobies.

SIZE: Does not grow larger than 2 inches.

The dark form of *Gobiodon citrinus*, from the Philippines. Photo by Earl Kennedy.

SCIENTIFIC NAME: *Gobiosoma oceanops.*
POPULAR NAME: Neon Goby.
Illustrated on page 183.
RANGE: West Indies to the Florida Keys.
REMARKS: The Neon Goby is a cleaning fish and has apparently taken
over these duties of *Labroides,* the Indo-Pacific cleaning wrasses. The
two fishes are entirely unrelated but have a similar striped color pat-
tern along with the cleaning behavior.

Lythrypnus dalli. Photo by Gene Wolfsheimer.

The Neon Goby is very attractive, hardy, and will often set up
housekeeping in captivity. In several instances they have spawned in
home aquaria though reports of rearing have been very rare. When
keeping the Neon Goby it is best to obtain several small ones and
raise them together. Chances are one or more pairs will form. *Eleca-
tinus* has recently been relegated to a subgenus of *Gobiosoma.*
SIZE: Attains a length of 3½ inches.

SCIENTIFIC NAME: *Gobiosoma evelynae* Böhlke and Robins.
POPULAR NAME: Sharknose Goby; Yellow Neon Goby.
RANGE: Caribbean Islands including the Bahamas.
REMARKS: The Sharknose Goby is a cleaner like the blue Neon Goby.
It is very closely related to that species but can easily be distinguished
by color. As the common name implies it is a yellow neon instead of
the well known blue neon. Its habits and disposition appear to
resemble that of the blue Neon Goby. Brine shrimp will be accepted.
SIZE: To about 2½ inches.

SCIENTIFIC NAME: *Lythrypnus dalli* Gilbert.

POPULAR NAME: Catalina Goby.

Illustrated on page 281.

RANGE: Coast of southern California.

REMARKS: The Catalina Goby is a temperate water species and will do better at lower temperatures than the coral reef fishes. It is found in tide pools in California. The Catalina Goby is a beautiful goby and an excellent aquarium fish.

SIZE: Attains a length of about 1½ inches.

THE GOATFISHES
Family Mullidae

The most distinctive characteristic of the goatfishes is the presence of two barbels affixed to the tip of the chin. These barbels were likened to the whiskers of a goat, hence the common name. They are sensitive to touch, contain taste buds and, like the fresh-water catfishes, are used in searching for food. Goatfishes have two separate dorsal fins.

In Hawaii as well as other areas goatfishes are utilized as food, their capture being regulated by law.

Small goatfishes are sometimes available to the marine aquarist.

SCIENTIFIC NAME: *Mulloidichthys martinicus* (Cuvier & Valenciennes).

POPULAR NAME: Yellow Goatfish.

Illustrated on page 283.

RANGE: West Indies to the Florida Keys, tropical Western Atlantic.

The Spotted Goatfish, *Pseudupeneus maculatus.*

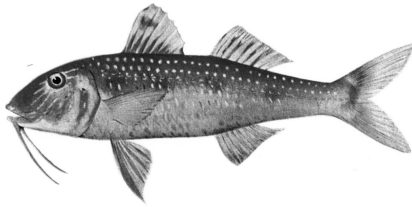

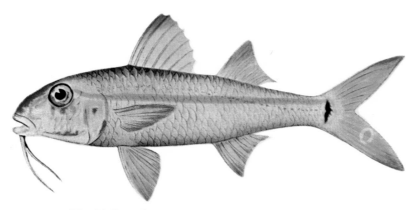

The Yellow Goatfish, *Mulloidichthys martinicus*.

REMARKS: The Yellow Goatfish is light olive on its back shading to a pale yellow ventrally. There is a yellow stripe on the side of the body and yellow fins.

SIZE: Attains a length of almost a foot and a half.

SCIENTIFIC NAME: *Mulloidichthys vanicolensis* (Cuv. & Val.).

POPULAR NAME: Red Goatfish.

Illustrated on page 283.

RANGE: East Indies, Philippine Islands, Oceania.

REMARKS: This species can usually be identified by elimination. It has no stripes, spots or other outstanding pattern. Since only small specimens are known it may be the young of a better known species.

SIZE: Less than 4 inches.

Mulloidichthys vanicolensis, the Red Goatfish.

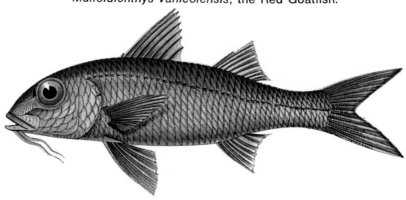

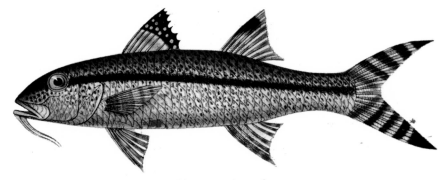

Upeneus tragula.

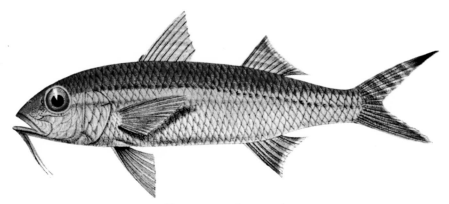

Upeneus moluccensis.

Parupeneus janseni.

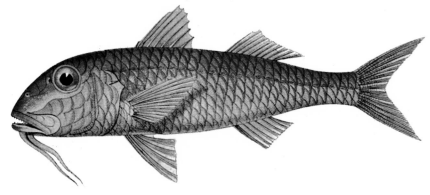

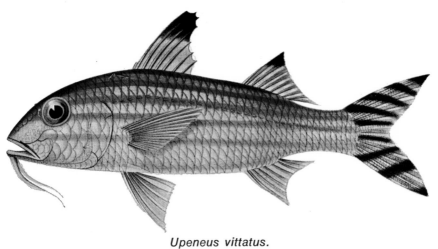

Upeneus vittatus.

Pseudupeneus macronemus. Photo by Dr. Herbert R. Axelrod.

SCIENTIFIC NAME: *Parupeneus pleurostigma* (Bennett).

POPULAR NAME: Blackspot Goatfish; Malu.

Illustrated on page 350.

RANGE: Tropical Indo-Pacific.

REMARKS: The dark lateral spot or blotch and the dark base of the second dorsal fin makes this species easily recognized. Do not be surprised when the Blackspot Goatfish takes on a blotched red and white pattern at night. In Hawaii and other areas the goatfishes are used for food.

SIZE: Reaches a length of up to a foot and a half.

SCIENTIFIC NAME: *Parupeneus janseni* (Bleeker).

POPULAR NAME: Rosy Goatfish.

Illustrated on page 284.

RANGE: Indo-Australian Archipelago, Philippines to New Guinea.

REMARKS: This uniformly colored goatfish has rather long barbels which aid in its recognition. The Rosy Goatfish occurs in shallow waters.

SIZE: Attains a length of over 7 inches.

Monodactylus argenteus is not a strictly marine species. It can be adapted to fresh water as well.

Monodactylus sebae is found along the west coast of Africa, near river mouths. Photo by Dr. Herbert R. Axelrod.

SCIENTIFIC NAME: *Pseudupeneus maculatus* (Bloch).
POPULAR NAME: Spotted Goatfish.
  Illustrated on page 282.
RANGE: Tropical West Atlantic.
REMARKS: The large blackish blotches on the side of the body are distinctive for the Caribbean species. Although usually pale in color it can change quickly assuming the pattern of large red blotches on head and body.
SIZE: Reaches a length of one foot in length.

SCIENTIFIC NAME: *Pseudupeneus macronemus* (Lacepede).
POPULAR NAME: Pink Goatfish.
  Illustrated on page 285.
RANGE: Tropical Indo-Pacific.

REMARKS: The last dorsal and anal rays of this species are quite elongate. This plus the long black bar and black spot help to identify this fish.

SIZE: Reaches a length of 14 inches.

SCIENTIFIC NAME: *Pseudupeneus multifasciatus* Quoy & Gaimard.

POPULAR NAME: Moano (Hawaiian); Red and Black Banded Goatfish.

RANGE: From India and the East Indies through Melanesia, Micronesia, and Polynesia, to the Hawaiian Islands (common).

REMARKS: The name *multifasciatus* means many stripes. This species is banded red and black, a very pretty goatfish. Its barbels are light colored and long in contrast to the short, dark ones of *P. bifasciatus,* a similarly banded goatfish. The Moano is excellent eating and always sought after on fishing trips.

SIZE: About a foot in length.

SCIENTIFIC NAME: *Upeneus moluccensis* Bleeker.

POPULAR NAME: Golden-stripe Goatfish.

Illustrated on page 284.

RANGE: India to the East Indies and Philippine Islands; Southern Japan to Northern Australia.

REMARKS: Although the lower lobe of the caudal fin is without bars the upper one has them. The lateral yellow stripe helps in the identification of this fish.

SIZE: Reaches a length of about 10 inches.

SCIENTIFIC NAME: *Upeneus tragula* Richardson.

POPULAR NAME: Barred-tail Goatfish.

Illustrated on page 284.

RANGE: Tropical Indo-Pacific.

REMARKS: This goatfish is similar to *Upeneus vittatus* but instead of the yellow lines across the body it has a single narrow black stripe.

SIZE: Reaches a length of about a foot.

SCIENTIFIC NAME: *Upeneus vittatus* (Forskål).

POPULAR NAME: Banded-tail Goatfish.

Illustrated on page 285.

RANGE: Tropical Indo-Pacific.

REMARKS: The goatfishes search for food with their long sensitive barbels. The normal diet is small fish and crustaceans but they will accept substitutes in an aquarium. The banded tail and yellow stripes on the body are characteristic of this species.

SIZE: About 15 inches.

THE MOONFISH
Family Monodactylidae

The monos, as they are sometimes called, are very compressed, deep-bodied, silver-colored fishes with tiny scales and elongated dorsal and anal fins. The first rays of these fins end in rounded, scaled tabs.

There are only two or three known species in this family, all basically silver-colored. They do well in fresh-water as well as salt-water and can be changed back and forth if the change is gradual.

One of the species, at least, has been bred and raised in captivity. It is known that *Monodactlylus sebae* has been raised in marine tanks but whether the other species have been successfully propagated in fresh-water has not been reported.

SCIENTIFIC NAME: *Monodactylus argenteus* Lacepede.
POPULAR NAME: Mono; Moonfish; Silver Batfish.
Illustrated on page 286.
RANGE: Indian Ocean through the East Indies, Philippines, to Australia and Fiji.
REMARKS: The Silver Batfish is very popular with both the fresh-water and marine aquarists. It thrives in both media. Generous feedings of brine shrimp and other small foods are recommended.

The depth of the body is less than that of *M. sebae* and it lacks the posterior black stripe of that species.
SIZE: Reaches a length of 4 inches.

SCIENTIFIC NAME: *Monodactylus sebae* (Cuvier).
POPULAR NAME: Moonfish.
Illustrated on page 287.
RANGE: West Africa in tropical waters usually close to fresh water rivers.
REMARKS: The Moonfish is a very beautiful and desirable species collected by the author (HRA) in great quantities in the rivers around Douala, Cameroons. They are found there in all sizes from two to seven inches and all do very well in fresh or salt water. For food, they prefer freeze-dried brine shrimp but also take flake foods readily.
SIZE: Reaches a length of at least 7 inches.

THE BATFISHES
Family Platacidae

This small family of fishes (only four known species) has been well accepted by the marine aquarist. The batfishes are very hardy, eat a wide variety of foods, are not shy, have an aesthetically pleasing shape, and one of the species (*Platax pinnatus*) has a fantastic color pattern.

A young batfish, *Platax orbicularis.* Photo by Earl Kennedy.

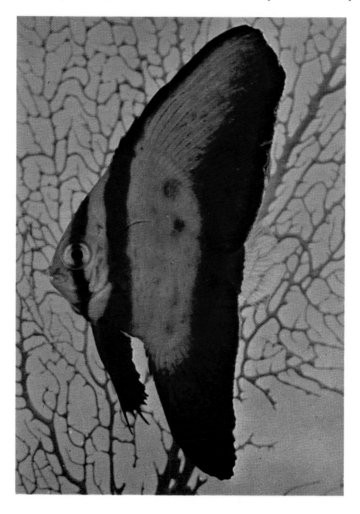

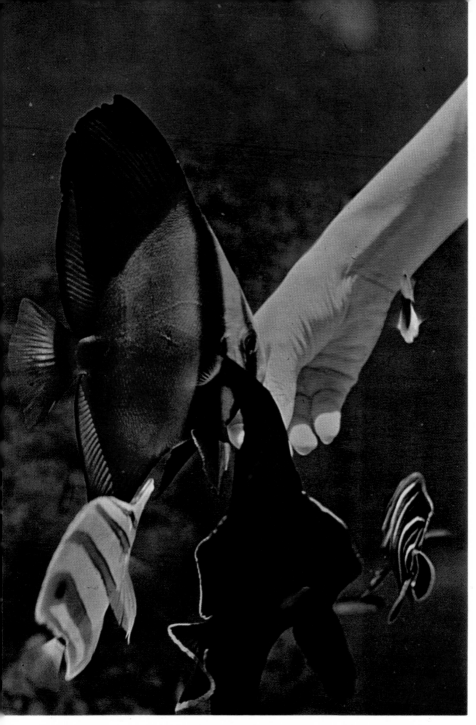

The batfishes are usually the first on hand at feeding time. Photo by
Earl Kennedy.

Platax orbicularis. Photo by Dr. Herbert R. Axelrod.

Platax pinnatus.
Photo by Earl Kennedy.

Platax teira.
Photo by Earl Kenne

The body shape changes dramatically from juvenile to adult. Juveniles of all four species have elongate dorsal, anal, and pelvic fins making them somewhat higher than long. As they grow their fins become relatively shorter when compared with body length and the fish takes on a more rounded appearance.

The adults have some characteristics of their color patterns in common. They have a band through the eye and another across the pectoral fin base. In most cases there is a darkening of the posterior end of the body and fins. Batfishes, in addition to this basic pattern, can change color by darkening the entire body, or fading the dark bands and becoming pale. They are excellent mimics, imitating fallen leaves (*Platax orbicularis* is famous for this) or other objects. Even when searching for these fishes in mangrove areas, where dead leaves are always available, it is difficult to distinguish which is which without poking it. Its "dying swan" act, where it lies on its side being swept back and forth by the surge, is very effective.

Batfishes do well on many types of food, but they appreciate a few live small fishes, such as guppies, now and then. Their growth rate is rapid and they soon reach a rather uncomfortable size for the marine aquarist who must look around for larger quarters for his pet. They are real pets too, easily trained to accept food from a person's fingers.

SCIENTIFIC NAME: *Platax batavianus* Cuvier & Valenciennes.
POPULAR NAME: Batavian Batfish.
RANGE: East Indies.
REMARKS: This species is very closely related to *Platax orbicularis* and very difficult to distinguish from that species. Differences have been found in the profile of the head and the size of the middle cusp of the teeth. Care and feeding similar to *Platax orbicularis*.
SIZE: Reaches a length of a foot or more.

SCIENTIFIC NAME: *Platax orbicularis* (Forskål).
POPULAR NAME: Orbiculate Batfish.
Illustrated on pages 290, 291, 292.
RANGE: Red Sea and east coast of Africa to the Pacific Islands as far as Tahiti (but not the Hawaiian Islands).
REMARKS: The Orbiculate Batfish is perhaps the most common of the four species of batfish. It does somewhat better in aquaria than the other three. The Orbiculate Batfish differs from the other species, besides in fin and scale counts, in having the middle cusp of the teeth conspicuously longer and stronger than the others, and the anterior profile more angular.
SIZE: Reaches a length of about a foot or more.

SCIENTIFIC NAME: *Platax pinnatus* (Linnaeus).
POPULAR NAME: Black Longfinned Batfish.
Illustrated on pages 291, 293.
RANGE: East Indies, Philippine Islands, New Guinea.
REMARKS: The Black Longfinned Batfish is very beautiful, particularly as a juvenile. The solid black of the body and fins is set off by the bright orange edgings. This fish remains dark most of its life but fades perceptibly as it grows.
SIZE: Reaches a length of a foot or more.

SCIENTIFIC NAME: *Platax teira* (Forskål).
POPULAR NAME: Long-Finned Batfish.
Illustrated on page 294.
RANGE: Red Sea and east coast of Africa to the East Indies, Philippines, to Japan, and Australia.
REMARKS: The juvenile of this species has more elongated dorsal and anal fins than those of the other species except perhaps *P. pinnatus*. Technical differences between this and other species of batfish include the shape of the teeth (the three cusps are approximately equal) and the anterior profile (evenly convex).
SIZE: Attains a length of about 20 inches.

THE TIGERFISHES
Family Theraponidae

The theraponids are perch-like fishes that are similar in general appearance to the snappers and grunts. There are fresh-water species as well as marine species, and several species able to make the change from one to the other without much difficulty. Most tigerfishes are found in tropical waters. Tigerfishes are strictly carnivorous.

The opercular bone has two noticeable spines and the preopercular bone is strongly serrated. The dorsal fin is notched and normally has about twelve to thirteen spines.

Tigerfish are usually about a foot long or less. The marine species are not valued as food but some of the fresh-water species are good tasting and turn up in the market.

There is only one species that usually finds its way into home aquaria. That is the Tigerfish or Crescent Perch, *Therapon jarbua*.

SCIENTIFIC NAME: *Therapon jarbua* (Forskål).
POPULAR NAME: Tigerfish; Crescent Perch.
Illustrated on page 297.

The Spotted Scat, *Scatophagus argus*, often ascends rivers and can be acclimated to fresh water.

The Tigerfish, *Therapon jarbua*, is distinctive with its crescent-like markings. Photo by Timmerman.

RANGE: East Coast of Africa, Red Sea, to China, East Indies, and the northern coast of Australia.

REMARKS: The common names of this species refers to the color pattern. It is white with black horizontal stripes that are curved in the center forming concentric crescents, the center of the curve directed downward.

The Crescent Perch is commonly found in coastal waters and estuaries. This is one of those species that is equally at home in fresh- or salt-water.

SIZE: Attains a length of 10 inches.

THE SCATS
Family Scatophagidae

The scats are mainly found in brackish waters but can live in either fresh-water or salt-water. These fishes are a common sight near the river mouths in some of the East Indian seaports, grubbing around the docks and boats in search of any kind of edible garbage they can find. Do not

Scatophagus argus with spots and bars is sometimes erroneously called *S. tetracanthus.*

The False Scat, *Selenotoca multifasciata.* Photo by
Gene Wolfsheimer.

Note how *Microcanthus strigatus* swims with its head down, making
the slightly diagonal stripes horizontal. Photo by Dr. Herbert R.
Axelrod.

The blennies are an interesting and comical group. This blenny is
Ophioblennius atlanticus macclurei. Photo by Dr. Herbert R. Axelrod.

Here *Ophioblennius* gives us a sly and very alert smile. Photo by
Dr. Herbert R. Axelrod.

Ever see a fish with *eyelashes*? *Ophioblennius* has them. Photo by Dr. Herbert R. Axelrod.

take this as an encouragement to feed them garbage, however. Aside from the regular menu fed to the other fishes the scats require a considerable amount of vegetable matter in their diet. They are happiest when fed an occasional meal of duckweed, with spinach or lettuce as an acceptable substitute.

Scats are closely related to the butterflyfishes but can easily be distinguished from them by their color patterns, well depicted in the accompanying photographs, and the deeply notched dorsal fin. Just like the butterflyfishes, scats have small mouths with many fine teeth, suited only for nibbling or scraping.

This is a small family containing few species.

SCIENTIFIC NAME: *Scatophagus argus* (Bloch).
POPULAR NAME: Spotted Scat.
 Illustrated on pages 297, 298.
RANGE: East Indies and Australia to East Africa.
REMARKS: There are several color variations of this species, some of

The Ribbonfish, *Equetus lanceolatus*, has an interesting finnage and color pattern. Photo by Robert P. L. Straughan.

which are still thought to be separate, valid species. The normal Spotted Scat is a light-colored fish with dark spots. The spots may be small and numerous, large and scattered, mixed, or any combination of large and small spots. A second variation has a number of vertical stripes in the front half of the body followed by some spots (*Scatophagus tetracanthus?*). A third variation has some orange-red markings about the back and head (*S. rubrifrons?*), making it a very attractive fish.

SIZE: Reaches a length of 10 inches in nature but only 4 inches or so in the home aquarium.

SCIENTIFIC NAME: *Selenotoca multifasciatus.*
POPULAR NAME: False Scat.
Illustrated on page 299.
RANGE: Australia and Melanesia.
REMARKS: The False Scat is very attractive with black bars on a silvery-white background color. It is common on the east coast of Australia and caught there by netting them in estuaries or bays where the bottom type is sandy or muddy.
SIZE: Attains a length of about 16 inches.

THE STRIPEYS

Family Scorpididae

The scorpidids are a small group of fishes, perch-like in appearance, with small mouths and a continuous or a notched dorsal fin. They have rows of small teeth in the jaws, the outermost being somewhat larger than the rest. The stripeys are apparently related to the butterflyfishes since one genus, *Microcanthus,* used to be placed in that family. It was not until 1945 that the genus was changed from the butterflyfish family to the scorpidids. There are a number of differences between these two families such as the teeth, attachment of the ribs, amount of attachment of the gill membranes to the isthmus, and the scaly sheath that covers the base of the dorsal spines.

The only species that is, at present, of interest to the marine aquarist is *Microcanthus strigatus.*

SCIENTIFIC NAME: *Microcanthus strigatus* (Cuvier & Valenciennes).
POPULAR NAME: Stripey.
Illustrated on page 299.
RANGE: From Japan through the East Indies to Queensland, and across to the Hawaiian Islands (but not on other Pacific Islands).

REMARKS: In Hawaii the young Stripeys enter tide pools early in the year. They are only about an inch in length when they arrive. The Stripey is a good aquarium fish, doing very well on a variety of foods. The striped pattern is distinctive, giving this fish its popular name.

SIZE: Reaches a length of about 6 inches.

THE PINE-CONE FISHES
Family Monocentridae

A small family of very odd-looking fishes which are spiny and enclosed in an armor-like structure composed of large, hard scales. The name Pine-cone Fish is very descriptive and quite appropriate. They are mostly deepwater fishes and bear luminescent organs.

SCIENTIFIC NAME: *Monocentris japonicus* (Houttuyn).

POPULAR NAME: Pine-cone Fish; Glowfish.

Illustrated on page 304.

As its name indicates, *Monocentris japonicus* is native to Japan.

RANGE: Widespread throughout the Indo-Pacific region.

REMARKS: This is a rather rare fish from 20 to 100 fathoms deep. It does well in large aquaria for a short time but probably will not be available to the home aquarist except at a very high price. Some specimens were recently on display at the Steinhart Aquarium in San Francisco, a gift from the Crown Prince of Japan.

On each side of the head a luminescent organ is present from which the common name "Glowfish" is derived.

SIZE: Reaches a length of up to 5 inches.

Argyrops spinifer gets large, but young specimens are quite acceptable.

THE CROAKERS AND DRUMS

Family Sciaenidae

Most of the croakers and drums are large fishes, too big to be considered for the average aquarium. There are a few species, however, that are always welcome in the aquarium being strikingly patterned, pleasingly shaped, and of the proper size. These are the ribbonfish and highhat.

Croakers and drums have molariform teeth in the oral (mouth) or pharyngeal (throat) cavities for crushing and grinding in association with a diet that includes gastropods (snails), clams, and hard-bodied crustaceans.

The Spadefish, *Tripterodon orbis.*

The common names "croaker" and "drum" originate from the sounds these fishes make. The gas bladder acts as a resonating device and is directly involved in sound production.

SCIENTIFIC NAME: *Equetus acuminatus* (Bloch & Schneider).
POPULAR NAME: Cubbyu; Highhat.
RANGE: North Carolina to Brazil.
REMARKS: This species is not distinguished by bright colors but is in fact basically black and white. Its claim to fame is an unusually elongate dorsal and ventrals. The fin rays of the dorsal fin are long and ribbon-like, the ventrals, similarly shaped, trail down gracefully. In nature they are found under rocks or ledges and quite often in the same hole as a cardinalfish. In an aquarium they tend to be shy at first but eventually move out into the open for the hobbyist to admire.
SIZE: 10 inches in length.

SCIENTIFIC NAME: *Equetus lanceolatus* (Linnaeus).
POPULAR NAMES: Ribbonfish; Jackknife; Knifefish.
Illustrated on page 302.
RANGE: West Indies northward to Pensacola, Florida.
REMARKS: The Ribbonfish is more highly prized than the Highhat but is rarer than that species. Its three black bands contrasting with the light colored background and the elongate fins make the Jackknife a very desirable acquisition to anybody's aquarium.
SIZE: Attains a length of 10 inches.

THE SNAPPERS
Family Lutjanidae

Juvenile snappers are often kept by marine aquarists. They are colorful as well as hardy although they tend to be quite aggressive. Snappers are not easily distinguishable from the grunts, porgies, or groupers. Their tapered, pointed snouts and the pair of enlarged canine teeth in each jaw are features to look for.

Snappers are good game fish and prized as food fish for humans. They are voracious feeders that require a large amount of food, live if possible. Guppies or other small fishes serve the purpose well and are able to live in salt water if adjusted slowly to it. Along with this great amount of food, snappers need large amounts of space.

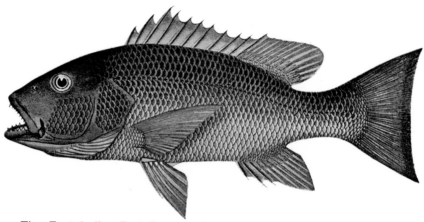

The East Indies Red Snapper is a popular food fish in its native waters. This one is *Lutjanus argentimaculatus*.

Lutjanus kasmira, from the Indo-Pacific. Photo by Rodney Jonklaas.

Lutjanus sebae, the Red Emperor. Photo by Earl Kennedy.

There is a question as to whether the spelling of the scientific name should be *Lutjanus* or *Lutianus*. The former spelling is used in this book.

Snappers are found in all the warm waters of the world.

SCIENTIFIC NAME: *Lutjanus analis* (Cuvier & Valenciennes).
POPULAR NAME: Mutton Snapper.
   Illustrated on page 313.
RANGE: Tropical western Atlantic, straying northward.
REMARKS: The Mutton Snapper is a game fish in southern Florida. It may be caught over reefs or in open water over sandy bottoms. Juveniles are often caught inshore and placed in home aquaria where they do very well. Chopped fish and shrimp are the recommended foods.
SIZE: May reach a length of over two feet.

SCIENTIFIC NAME: *Lutjanus apodus* (Walbaum).
POPULAR NAME: Schoolmaster Snapper.
   Illustrated on page 314.
RANGE: Tropical western Atlantic to Massachusetts.
REMARKS: The Schoolmaster Snapper has a series of pale bars crossing its body. It is very common in the West Indies, often in schools around large stands of coral.
SIZE: Recorded to 8 pounds.

SCIENTIFIC NAME: *Lutjanus argentimaculatus* Forskål.
POPULAR NAME: Red Snapper or Jenoar (East Indies).
   Illustrated on page 308.

RANGE: Common throughout the tropical Indo-Pacific.

REMARKS: The Red Snapper is a large fish, popular not only in the aquarium (as juveniles) but on the dinner table as well. Although blood-red in nature they tend to fade when held in captivity. When the fish approaches death it gets redder and redder until at death itself the original blood-red color returns.

This fish is said to be able to accommodate itself to fresh water if the change is made gradually.

SIZE: Grows to a length of 3 feet.

SCIENTIFIC NAME: *Lutjanus jocu* (Bloch & Schneider).

POPULAR NAME: Dog Snapper.

Illustrated on page 314.

RANGE: Tropical western Atlantic; Bermuda; straying north.

REMARKS: The pale bar below the eye which widens ventrally is characteristic of this species. Care and feeding are the same as for the other snappers.

SIZE: Attains a length of 2½ feet.

SCIENTIFIC NAME: *Lutjanus kasmira* (Forskål).

POPULAR NAME: Bluestriped Snapper.

Illustrated on page 308.

Epinephelus adscensionis is a grouper from the West Indies. Photo by Dr. Herbert R. Axelrod.

Epinephelus adscensionis.

Labracinus cyclophthalmus from the Philippines. Photo by Earl Kennedy.

Epinephelus morio.

RANGE: Throughout Middle Eastern coral reefs to the central Indo-Pacific.

REMARKS: The Bluestriped Snapper was originally described by Forskål in 1775 as coming from Arabia, the name "*kasmira*" being a latinized Arabic name. The usual color is light blue streaks bordered above and below by a brown line. The body and fins are yellow.

SIZE: Attains a length of about 1 foot.

SCIENTIFIC NAME: *Lutjanus sebae* (Cuvier & Valenciennes).

POPULAR NAME: Red Emperor.

Illustrated on page 309.

RANGE: Tropical Indo-Pacific as far south as South Africa.

REMARKS: The Red Emperor is the most prized of the snappers for home aquaria. Its bright red and white colors brighten up any aquarium. It grows slightly larger than the Red Snapper. The Red Emperor does best on a diet of live food (earthworms, brine shrimp, etc.).

SIZE: Attains a length of over three feet.

SCIENTIFIC NAME: *Lutjanus synagris* (Linnaeus).

POPULAR NAME: Lane Snapper.

Illustrated on page 317.

Cephalopholis argus has an attractive pattern of blue dots. Photo by Earl Kennedy.

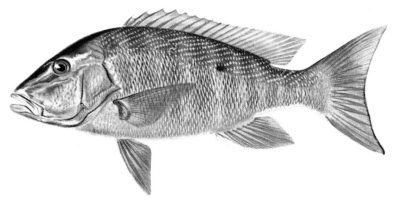

Lutjanus analis is known as the Mutton Snapper.

Ever see such bright blue stripes? This is *Cephalopholis boenacki*.
Photo by Dr. Herbert R. Axelrod.

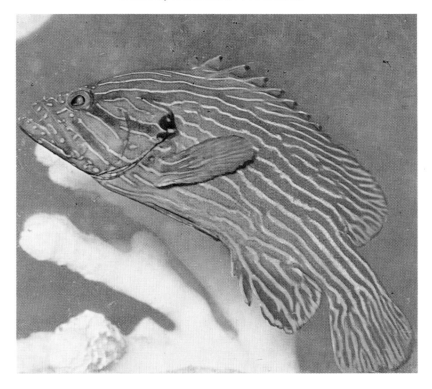

Epinephelus striatus, the Nassau Grouper.

Lutjanus jocu, the Dog Snapper.

Lutjanus apodus, the Schoolmaster.

Gaterin albovittatus, adult. Photo by Dr. Herbert R. Axelrod.

RANGE: Carolina and Bermuda south to Brazil.

REMARKS: The Lane Snapper is often found in schools of large numbers of fishes around reefs or in turbid waters over mud bottoms. It is found from shallow water down to 1,300 feet. The large black spot on the side aids in the identification.

SIZE: Attains a length of 14 inches.

THE GROUPERS AND SEA BASSES
Family Serranidae

Groupers and sea basses have among them the largest of fishes that might be considered for the home aquarium. Some species grow larger than a man and there are stories of such monsters eating divers or at least nibbling on them a little. Groupers are "friendly" fishes. Nearly every skin diver who has made a movie of underwater life on a reef has been able to bribe a grouper with bits of food to be the star of the show. The grouper may actually become a nuisance posing in front of the camera while waiting for more handouts. More than one diver had to "cage the beast" so he could continue his work unannoyed once he had befriended a grouper. These larger groupers often find themselves on the dinner table. The smaller ones, and juveniles of larger species, make very interesting pets in a large marine aquarium.

Gaterin albovittatus. Photo by Dr. Herbert R. Axelrod.

Gaterin albovittatus, young specimen. Photo by Dr. Herbert R. Axelrod.

Gaterin orientalis, young specimen. Photo by Dr. Herbert R. Axelrod.

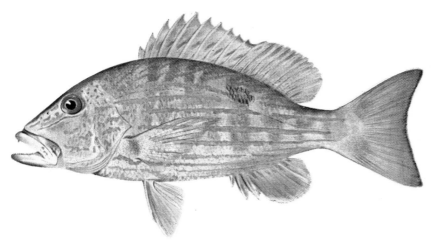

The Lane Snapper.

According to Dr. Leonard P. Schultz (Bull. 202, U.S. N.M.) " . . .
*the color pattern of groupers is of the utmost importance in distinguish-
ing the various species, but not too much value should be placed on the
presence or absence of the dark vertical bands; these appear to vary in
intensity with age, more or less disappearing in adults of certain species.
The dark blotches along the back, as well as the distribution of black
spots elsewhere on the head and body, are important characters.*" There
are probably a hundred or more species found in tropical waters all over
the world. The size of the family varies depending upon which groups
are included by a specific scientist and which groups are set aside in
their own families.

Groupers have large mouths (with appetites to match) and cardiform
(numerous, short, fine and pointed) teeth. A large piece of food, including a fish or two, will disappear in a flash down the throat of a grouper.
They seem to inhale it rather than break it down into smaller pieces.
There are one or two dorsal fins depending upon the species. Serranids
are protandric hermaphrodites, being males at first and later changing
into females.

SCIENTIFIC NAME: *Cephalopholis argus* Bloch & Schneider.
POPULAR NAME: Black Grouper.
   Illustrated on page 312.
RANGE: Throughout the central Indo-Pacific.

REMARKS: The background color of the Black Grouper in older specimens changes from a muddy, chocolate brown to a deep purplish-black. The eye has a brownish-red iris. What makes this species so attractive to marine aquarists are the bright blue spots covering the head and body. The Black Grouper is a voracious eater usually darting out from the protection of a rock to engulf its prey.

SIZE: Grows to over one foot in length.

SCIENTIFIC NAME: *Cephalopholis boenacki* (Bloch).

POPULAR NAME: Boenacki Grouper.

Illustrated on page 313.

RANGE: Western Pacific to East African coast.

REMARKS: The striped pattern makes this fish a favorite among marine aquarists. Like other groupers they like small fishes or shrimps. Members of this genus may start out life as females and wind up as males.

SIZE: Attains a length of about 1 foot.

SCIENTIFIC NAME: *Epinephelus adscensionis* (Osbeck).

POPULAR NAME: Rock Hind.

Illustrated on pages 310, 311.

RANGE: Tropical Atlantic.

REMARKS: This species can be distinguished by the spotted pattern and a large dark saddle on the upper edge of the caudal peduncle. Like many groupers it grows to a considerable size and soon outgrows the home aquarium.

SIZE: Reaches a length of about 2 feet.

SCIENTIFIC NAME: *Epinephelus flavocaeruleus* (Lacepede).

POPULAR NAME: Blue and Yellow Reef Cod.

Illustrated on page 347.

RANGE: Tropical Indo-Pacific.

REMARKS: This beautiful grouper unfortunately is not very common. It inhabits rocky areas and should be provided with some hiding places in the aquarium. The Blue and Yellow Reef Cod prefers live food but can be coaxed onto fish, shrimp, and some of the larger sized prepared foods.

SIZE: Attains a length of a foot and a half.

SCIENTIFIC NAME: *Epinephelus guttatus* (Linnaeus).

POPULAR NAME: Red Hind.

RANGE: Tropical Western Atlantic.

Grammistes sexlineatus. Photo by Gene Wolfsheimer.

REMARKS: The Red Hind is common, colorful, and very hardy. In addition it can be trained (like other fishes) to accept food from one's fingers. These attributes make it a welcome aquarium fish. As the species grows to a large size only the juveniles can be kept. The red spots covering this fish are diagnostic.

SIZE: Reaches about 2 feet in length.

SCIENTIFIC NAME: *Epinephelus morio* (Cuvier & Valenciennes).
POPULAR NAME: Red Grouper.
Illustrated on page 311.
RANGE: Brazil to Massachusetts.
REMARKS: In its mottled phase this species is often confused with the Nassau Grouper, *E. striatus*. However the Red Grouper has its membranes between the spines almost confluent with the tips of the spines, whereas the Nassau Grouper has deep notches.
SIZE: Reported in Dr. Randall's book (*Caribbean Reef Fishes*, T.F.H., 1968) to reach 50 pounds or more.

SCIENTIFIC NAME: *Epinephelus striatus* (Bloch).
POPULAR NAME: Nassau Grouper.
Illustrated on page 314.
RANGE: Tropical western Atlantic.
REMARKS: The Nassau Grouper is noted as a chameleon of the sea. Its most characteristic color pattern is vertically banded. A large black saddle on the caudal peduncle persists through the color changes and helps in identifying this species.
SIZE: Reaches a weight of over 50 pounds.

SCIENTIFIC NAME: *Grammistes sexlineatus* (Thunberg).
POPULAR NAME: Golden Striped Grouper.
Illustrated on page 319.
RANGE: Tropical Indo-Pacific.
REMARKS: The Golden Striped Grouper is one of the most popular groupers in the marine aquarium trade. It is hardy, colorful, and usually mild mannered. It accepts a variety of foods eagerly. The big problem with this species is that it will probably eat its way out of house and home.
SIZE: Reaches a length of about 10 inches.

SCIENTIFIC NAME: *Hypoplectrus unicolor* (Walbaum).
POPULAR NAME: Butter Hamlet.
RANGE: West Indies to Florida.

Not all of the cardinalfishes are red. Here is a black species, *Apogon brachygramma*, from the Philippines. Photo by Gene Wolfsheimer.

REMARKS: The Butter Hamlet is probably the most common hamlet in the West Indies, and is apt to be the species included in shipments from Florida. It has a large black spot at the base of the tail, otherwise it is yellowish gray with blue markings on its head.

SIZE: Reaches only 5 inches in length.

SCIENTIFIC NAME: *Serranus tigrinus* (Bloch).
POPULAR NAME: Harlequin Bass.
Illustrated on page 187.
RANGE: West Indies to Florida.
REMARKS: Members of the genus *Serranus* are small enough to be welcome in the marine aquarium. The Harlequin Bass is also colorful and hardy. When one of these fishes turn up in your aquarium shop, which is not very often, you can be sure it will cause a bit of excitement. The Harlequin Bass will eat small fishes and crustaceans.

SIZE: Reaches a length of 4 inches.

THE CARDINALFISHES
Family Apogonidae

Cardinalfishes are fishes of small size, small enough to reach maturity in a home aquarium. They are characterized by large eyes, a large mouth, and two separate dorsal fins, the second one equal in size and shape to the anal fin and opposite it in location. Most of the cardinal fishes are red as the common name indicates but some are black, yellow or other combinations of color. The black markings of these fishes are significant in the recognition of various species.

Apogonids, as they are sometimes called, are shy fishes, secretive during the day but active at night. They should not be kept with smaller fishes or the population of the tank will decrease rapidly each night. In nature some species make their homes in the hollows (pallial cavities) of large conchs. They are not parasitic but merely use these hollows as hiding places. The aquarium should be amply provided with areas for hiding. Once these fishes know that they can hide quickly if threatened, they will become less shy.

It is possible that cardinalfishes will spawn in home aquaria as they have done in public aquaria. Some species incubate their eggs in the mouth in a fashion typical of a mouth brooder whereas others build nests in abandoned mollusc shells. The eggs are deposited on the smooth surface of the inner part of the shell. In a single spawning there can be one hundred or more eggs.

Myripristis murdjan is simply called "Uu" by the Hawaiian natives. Photo by Dr. Herbert R. Axelrod.

This is the Deep Big-eye, *Pristigenys altus.* Photo by Robert P. L. Straughan.

SCIENTIFIC NAME: *Apogon brachygrammus* (Jenkins).

POPULAR NAME: Common Cardinalfish.

Illustrated on page 321.

RANGE: Tropical Pacific Islands to the Hawaiian Islands.

REMARKS: Although this is not a brightly colored species of cardinal-fish it is readily available from the Hawaiian Islands and handled by some dealers. Its pleasant disposition will make up for its lack of beauty. It can be recognized by the shortened lateral line, reaching only to the level of the soft dorsal fin. The Common Cardinal is found in shallow water, often in great numbers. It hides among the coral rubble.

SIZE: Reaches a length of about 3 inches.

SCIENTIFIC NAME: *Apogon erythrinus* (Snyder).

POPULAR NAME: Cardinalfish.

RANGE: Polynesian Islands including the Hawaiian Islands.

REMARKS: This is a typical red cardinalfish although it does fade to a pink sometimes in captivity. This species is reported to be a mouth brooder and may possibly be spawned and raised in captivity. It is another shallow-water species.

SIZE: Attains a length of 3 inches.

We kept these *Apogon orbicularis* for a long time in our office marine aquarium. Photo by Dr. Herbert R. Axelrod.

SCIENTIFIC NAME: *Apogon fraenatus* Valenciennes.

POPULAR NAME: Cardinalfish.

RANGE: Pacific Islands including Guam and the Hawaiian Islands through the East Indies.

REMARKS: This species is quite hardy and adapts well to captivity. It is nocturnal but can be seen hovering in open water in nature during the evening and early morning. The longitudinal black stripe and spot at the base of the caudal fin are shared by several other species of cardinalfishes. The width of the line and shape of the spot are usually helpful in identifying this species.

SIZE: Adults measure 4 inches in length.

SCIENTIFIC NAME: *Apogon maculatus* (Poey).

POPULAR NAME: Flamefish.

Illustrated on page 350.

RANGE: From Brazil to Florida, occasionally straggling northward.

REMARKS: Chances are that a cardinalfish coming from the Florida shippers will be this species. It is easily distinguished by the solid red color with a black spot at the base of the second dorsal fin in addition to other markings. The Flamefish is a mouth brooder, the male fish carrying the eggs.

SIZE: Up to 4 inches.

Myripristis murdjan. Photo by Dr. Herbert R. Axelrod.

Aren't they the strangest-looking things? These are Orange-Spotted Filefish, *Oxymonocanthus longirostris*, from the Philippines. Photo by Gene Wolfsheimer.

Part of the *Hemipteronotus taeniurus*, a juvenile in this photo, looks as if it has disappeared against the background. Photo by Earl Kennedy.

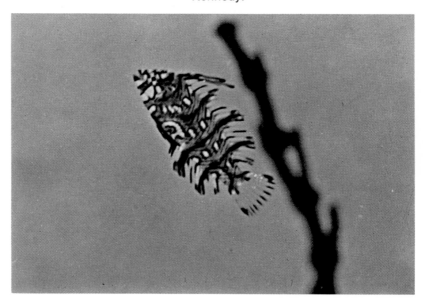

A young specimen of *Gaterin chaetodonoides*. Photo by Dr. Herbert R. Axelrod.

Moray eels are common in all tropical marine waters. This one is *Muraena helena.*

SCIENTIFIC NAME: *Apogon maculiferus* Garrett.

POPULAR NAME: Spotted Cardinalfish.

Illustrated on page 329.

RANGE: Hawaiian Islands.

REMARKS: The Spotted Cardinalfish is covered with dark spots arranged in rows. It is fairly common in Hawaii in shallow water hiding among coral rubble. They are hardy fishes as are most cardinalfishes but for some reason are not as popular as the red ones.

SIZE: Reaches a size of about 6 inches.

SCIENTIFIC NAME: *Apogon orbicularis* Cuvier & Valenciennes.

POPULAR NAME: Orbiculate Cardinalfish.

Illustrated on page 324.

RANGE: East Indies, Philippines, China and the Pacific Islands.

REMARKS: The Orbiculate Cardinalfish is the best known of the Pacific cardinalfishes. Its distinctive pattern and habit of hovering in the open spaces of the aquarium make this fish a very desirable addition. Like all cardinalfishes it easily disposes of small fishes.

SIZE: Reaches a length of 4-5 inches.

Apogon maculiferus has a spotted pattern rather than the bright red of many other cardinalfishes. Photo by Dr. Herbert R. Axelrod.

Looks more like a snake than an eel, doesn't it? This is *Myrichthys colubrinus*, from the Philippines. Photo by Gene Wolfsheimer.

SCIENTIFIC NAME: *Apogon waikiki* Jordan & Evermann.

POPULAR NAME: Waikiki Cardinalfish.

RANGE: Islands of the Pacific from Guam and the Marshall Islands to the Hawaiian Islands.

Not a very nice fish, but it has a nice pattern: *Echidna nebulosa.*

REMARKS: This little cardinalfish is common in the Hawaiian Islands. It is more rounded in outline than some other cardinalfishes and is brownish in color. Although the Waikiki Cardinalfish can be collected very easily the demand is very low and few individuals of this species are brought to the mainland from the Hawaiian Islands. The name Waikiki cardinalfish was given to this fish when it was first discovered in the Hawaiian Islands. Since it was later found in other areas the name is no longer very suitable.

SIZE: Maximum size of about 4 inches.

SCIENTIFIC NAME: *Apogonichthys stellatus* Cope.

POPULAR NAME: Conchfish.

RANGE: West Indies to the southern tip of Florida.

REMARKS: This little fish has the strange habit of concealing itself within the mantle cavity of the large Florida Queen Conch. When the conch is not available the cavities of sponges are acceptable. It feeds on small crustaceans such as shrimps.

SIZE: Only 2 inches at maturity.

330

Gymnothorax tesselata. You have to admit that the species is nicely colored. Photo courtesy of Alimenta-Brussels.

Gymnothorax eurostus, from Hawaii. Photo by Gene Wolfsheimer.

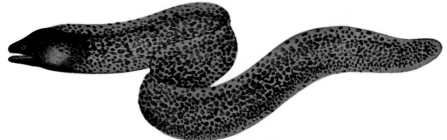

Gymnothorax thyrsoideus

MORAY EELS
Family Muraenidae

Moray eels seem to enjoy a high popularity with the marine aquarist. Perhaps this popularity is due not so much for the attractive color patterns but for the reputation of being such dangerous animals. Some are aggressive, almost savage, and have been known to attack without provocation. This is the exception and not the rule, however, morays generally being shy and retiring. They stay poised in their holes with only the head exposed waiting patiently for some food to pass by. At night one is more likely to encounter a moray out of its hole searching the reefs for its dinner of fish or crab. When working about warm water reefs it is not wise to poke a hand into blind crevices or holes. A moray eel, like many creatures, will defend its home and the intruding finger or hand is apt to be bitten.

An **odd** species from the Philippines. Photo by Gene Wolfsheimer.

Moray eels are often confused with other eels but can be distinguished by the following characters: anterior nostril with a tube and located near the end of the snout; posterior nostril located above the eye; mouth large, sometimes unable to close completely; teeth well developed, often fang-like; no pectoral fins; naked (scaleless).

Morays breath by leaving the mouth open almost continuously, the jaws opening and closing with the rhythm of the opercular pump, the device used to provide the flow of water past the gills. This motion, strictly for breathing purposes, has been falsely interpreted as a savage threat to anything or anyone who comes too close.

The moray's main diet consists of crustaceans (crabs, lobsters, shrimps, etc.), fish, squids, and octopuses. They rely largely on their senses of smell, taste, and touch to locate and catch their prey. Some morays actually leave the water to chase a crab, while others leap onto an exposed reef to capture their prey. As an adaptation to holding living prey the canines are hinged, able to fold backward under pressure of incoming food, but return and lock into the upright position when the movement is towards the mouth opening.

SCIENTIFIC NAME: *Echidna nebulosa* (Ahl).
POPULAR NAME: Snowflake Moray Eel.
    Illustrated on page 330.
RANGE: Throughout the coral reefs of the Indo-Pacific region.
REMARKS: There are many slightly different color variations of this fish certainly of interest to ichthyologists. It may be proven that each geographical race is a subspecies.

    Living animals have orange-tipped tails, orange eyes and anterior nasal tubes as well as centers of the black blotches sometimes orange. The Snowflake Moray has about 24 to 30 rows of "spots" in two rows.
SIZE: Less than two feet in length.

SCIENTIFIC NAME: *Gymnothorax eurostrus* Bleeker.
POPULAR NAME: Moray Eel.
    Illustrated on page 331.
RANGE: Indo-Pacific.
REMARKS: A long nasty moray that is even dangerous in the home aquarium. The author (HRA) received a shock one day when he arrived home to be greeted at the front door by a moray eel that had pushed off the cover glass and had sneaked his way to the front of the house some 50 feet from the aquarium.
SIZE: Maximum length of perhaps 2 feet.

SCIENTIFIC NAME: *Gymnothorax meleagris* (Shaw & Nodder).
POPULAR NAME: White Spotted Moray Eel.
  Illustrated on page 342.
RANGE: Tropical Indian and Pacific Oceans.
REMARKS: This species is probably one of the most wide ranging and
  common of the moray eels. It has white spots covering the head and
  body on a background of brownish or tan. In addition it has a
  blackish area marking the gill opening.
SIZE: Reaches a length of 3 feet or more.

SCIENTIFIC NAME: *Gymnothorax tesselata* Richardson.
POPULAR NAME: Leopard Moray.
  Illustrated on page 331.
RANGE: Tropical Indo-Pacific.
REMARKS: The Leopard Moray is one of the more attractive members
  of the moray eels. As with all morays it is quarrelsome and can give
  a person a nasty bite. Handle with care and keep your tank securely
  covered.
SIZE: Reaches a length of about 4 feet.

SCIENTIFIC NAME: *Gymnothorax thyrsoideus* (Richardson).
POPULAR NAME: Whitesnout Moray Eel.
  Illustrated on page 332.
RANGE: Tropical Indo-Pacific.
REMARKS: The snout and usually lower jaw are often white. The body
  is mottled with darker brown or paler spots, or plain colored.
SIZE: About 3 feet or more in length.

SCIENTIFIC NAME: *Muraena helena.*
POPULAR NAME: Painted Moray.
  Illustrated on page 328.
RANGE: Eastern Atlantic Ocean and Mediterranean Sea.
REMARKS: This moray is one of the cooler water species. The eggs
  of the painted moray have been collected in the Mediterranean Sea.
  They are large, 5mm in diameter, and usually hatch out in 10 days.
SIZE: Reaches a length of over 2 feet.

THE SWEETLIPS
Family Gaterinidae

Most sweetlips are shallow water species inhabiting the tropical Indo-
Pacific area. They are colorful and hardy, adapting well to captivity.

334

It is recommended that the tank be at least ten times as long as the fish.

There are great changes in the color pattern as the fishes grow from juvenile to adult. This of course led to the usual confusion in identification by early ichthyologists. Most of the outstanding problems of this sort have been solved at this time and the names should remain fairly constant.

Adult sweetlips are prized as food and the juveniles as aquarium fishes.

According to several observers in Ceylon, the juveniles of some species of the genus *Gaterin* have an extreme tolerance to fresh water and one of the authors (HRA) saw several specimens of *G. faetela* about three inches long (adults reach 20 inches in length) at the Lumbini Aquarium, Ceylon. They had been left out in an open aquarium which had been allowed to be diluted by the daily rains. According to Mr. Pererra, the aquarium owner, the fish were now in water which was fresh enough to support fresh-water aquarium plants.

SCIENTIFIC NAME: *Gaterin albovittatus* (Rüppell).
POPULAR NAME: Yellow-lined Sweetlips.
  Illustrated on pages 315, 316.
RANGE: Western Pacific Ocean to the Red Sea.
REMARKS: This fish changes from a longitudinally banded pattern to a spotted pattern with growth. The bands become more numerous and then break up into spots. The Yellow-lined Sweetlips will accept a wide variety of foods.
SIZE: Reaches a length of 8 inches.

SCIENTIFIC NAME: *Gaterin chaetodonoides* (Lacepede).
POPULAR NAME: Clown Sweetlips.
  Illustrated on page 327.
RANGE: Red Sea to the East Indies, Philippine Islands, and Caroline Islands.
REMARKS: The Clown Sweetlips is the most common species of this genus which has been imported as an aquarium fish. The characteristic large white spots or blotches are lost in the change to adult color pattern but by then the Clown Sweetlips has long outgrown the home aquarium.
SIZE: Grows to 3 feet in nature.

SCIENTIFIC NAME: *Gaterin orientalis* (Bloch).
POPULAR NAME: Oriental Sweetlips.
  Illustrated on page 316.

RANGE: East coast of Africa to the East Indies and Philippine Islands.

REMARKS: Feed this species of sweetlips an assortment of live and prepared foods including chopped fish, shrimps, earthworms, and *Tubifex*. They need lots of space and will do better if other members of their species were present.

SIZE: Attains a length of about 1 foot.

The Man-O'-War fish flirts with death underneath the stinging tentacles of the Portuguese Man-O'-War jellyfish. Photo by Dr. John E. Randall.

THE MAN-O'-WAR FISH
Family Nomeidae

The Man-O'-War Fish is a strange and beautiful fish that spends its entire life hiding among the deadly tentacles of the Portuguese Man-O'-War Jellyfish. It has almost perfect protection among the stinging tentacles that can kill a fish or painfully injure a human being. They are not at home in an aquarium, dashing back and forth, usually injuring themselves against the sides, and are among the more difficult fishes to keep. They adjust better if the jellyfish is with them but the latter does not adapt well to aquarium life and soon perishes. The Man-O'-War Fish eats small fishes and crustaceans.

SCIENTIFIC NAME: *Nomeus gronovii* Gmelin.

POPULAR NAME: Man-O'-War Fish; Rudderfish.

Illustrated on page 336.

RANGE: Warm seas of the world's oceans. In summer months they may be carried more northward.

REMARKS: The large, colorful pelvic fins are the outstanding physical characteristics of this fish.

SIZE: Does not exceed 8 inches in length.

THE SHRIMPFISHES
Family Centriscidae

The shrimpfishes are very strange fishes indeed! They constantly swim with their heads down. Their bodies have been highly modified through the process of evolution. The fins are up near the tail end, the ventral surface is compressed to a sharp knife-like edge, and their snouts are elongate. They generally swim in small schools. It has been theorized that they stay close to sea urchins and dash among the spines for protection. Recently much doubt has been cast on this theory.

Where the shrimpfishes fit into the general scheme of fishes is not known for certain. Perhaps it is near the pipefishes, perhaps not.

SCIENTIFIC NAME: *Aeoliscus strigatus* (Günther).
POPULAR NAME: Shrimpfish.
Illustrated on page 338.
RANGE: Red Sea to the Pacific Islands (not found in Hawaii since 1909).
REMARKS: The shrimpfishes do well in captivity. Several individuals should be purchased together so their schooling instinct will be satisfied. They are surprisingly fast in nature. One of the authors (WEB) has chased these fishes around coral rocks on the Great Barrier Reef. They were easily able to outdistance the swimmer, retaining their upright stance the entire time. Live or frozen brine shrimp and canned Norwegian brine shrimp are perfect foods for them.
SIZE: Reaches a length of about 4 inches.

THE JACKS AND POMPANOS
Family Carangidae

Although almost all of the species in this family are too large and therefore unsuitable for the home aquarium, some of the juveniles do very well. When several individuals of a species are kept together they usually form a school, constantly swimming back and forth across the aquarium reflecting the light rays off their sides as bright flashes of silver.

The carangids are usually silver or white and have scutes (modified scales) marking the curvature of the lateral line. Their caudal peduncle is very slender, but strong, and their caudal or tail fin is strongly forked, an adaptation for constant, rapid swimming in open water.

The jacks and pompanos, being food fishes for human consumption, are prime targets of some of the new aqua-culture programs. Two species of jacks were raised from eggs in Hawaii and some success was

The Shrimpfish, *Aeoliscus strigatus*, has a bizarre way of swimming. It is almost always seen in this position—with its head down!
Photo by Klaus Paysan.

Gnathanodon speciosus is one of the few carangids raised from the egg. Photo by Klaus Paysan.

Alectis crinitus. The Threadfin is well deserving of its name. Photo by Dr. Herbert R. Axelrod in Hawaii.

achieved with pompanos in Florida. Although these are large scientific programs the information obtained may eventually lead to success in the home aquarium.

SCIENTIFIC NAME: *Alectis crinitus* (Mitchill).

POPULAR NAME: Threadfin; Ulua Kihikihi; Kagami Ulua; Pennant Trevally.

Illustrated on page 339.

RANGE: Very widely distributed in warm waters of the Atlantic and Pacific Oceans.

REMARKS: The Threadfin is a very distinctive fish and is easily recognized by the long streamers on its dorsal and anal fins, an interesting oddity in the aquarium.

SIZE: Maximum length of about three feet.

SCIENTIFIC NAME: *Gnathanodon speciosus* (Forskål).

POPULAR NAME: Yellow Ulua (Hawaiian).

Illustrated on page 339.

RANGE: Tropical Pacific and Indian Oceans (including the Hawaiian Islands).

REMARKS: The Yellow Ulua, in contrast to other carangids which have a silvery color, is yellow with black bars crossing the body. Juveniles are lively, hardy, and colorful; excellent fish for the marine aquarium. This carangid is one of the species successfully raised from the egg in Hawaii.

SIZE: Attains a length of at least 3 feet.

SCIENTIFIC NAME: *Selene vomer* Linnaeus.

POPULAR NAME: Lookdown.

RANGE: Atlantic coast from Brazil to Cape Cod.

REMARKS: The aspect of this fish is similar to the preceding species but the head is deeper and almost vertical giving it a distorted appearance. The first rays of the dorsal and anal fins are also elongated.

SIZE: In nature it reaches a length of one foot.

SCIENTIFIC NAME: *Vomer setipinnis* Mitchell.

POPULAR NAME: Moonfish.

RANGE: Atlantic coast from Brazil to Cape Cod.

REMARKS: The head is very high and blunt, giving this fish a very sad and grouchy expression. The body is pancake flat and the fins are short. The Moonfish is a very odd but interesting fish.

SIZE: In the wild specimens attain a length of one foot.

THE BIG-EYES
Family Priacanthidae

The family Priacanthidae is a small family of deep water fishes. They are usually red and have, as the common name implies, very large eyes. These fishes are not too common and rarely become available to the marine fish fancier. Big-eyes are carnivores.

SCIENTIFIC NAME: *Priacanthus cruentatus* (Lacepede).

POPULAR NAME: Glasseye; Aweoweo (Hawaiian).

RANGE: Circumtropical.

REMARKS: The Glasseye, similar to the squirrelfishes, is red, large-eyed, and nocturnal. It can easily be caught during the day on shallow reefs in holes or caves where the light is at a low level. The bright red color can fade or change to a mottled pink and white. In Hawaii the Aweoweo is sought after as a food fish. The juveniles are not often available for the marine aquarist.

SIZE: Grows to about a foot in length.

SCIENTIFIC NAME: *Pristigenys altus* (Gill).

POPULAR NAME: Deep Big-eye.

Illustrated on page 323.

RANGE: Circumtropical.

REMARKS: This species is perhaps the most sought after aquarium fish among the big-eyes. It is short and deep, a pretty sight in an aquarium. It is nocturnal like the others but can be enticed out after food if the light level is low. They are generally found in deep water and only rarely find their way into an aquarium shop.

SIZE: About 8 inches.

THE SNAKE EELS
Family Ophichthyidae

Ophichthids or snake eels are easily distinguished from other eels. The dorsal and anal fins are not confluent around the tip of the tail, leaving a bare point. In addition the gill area appears swollen or pouch-like. The nostrils are in elongate tubes. These eels have the ability of

This Gold-spotted Snake Eel, *Myrichthys oculatus*, has taken a conch shell for its home. Photo by G. Marcuse.

Gymnothorax meleagris, the White-spotted Moray, in a typical moray eel pose. Photo by Rodney Jonklaas.

The Black Ribbon Eel, *Rhinomuraena quaesita*.
Photo by K. H. Choo.

The Blue Ribbon Eel, *Rhinomuraena amboinensis*, can turn very dark, almost black like the above species. Photo by K. H. Choo.

rapid burrowing or swimming through the sand *forward* or *backward*. Perhaps this is the reason for the blunt tail. They feed readily on various types of crustaceans (crabs, shrimps, etc.).

SCIENTIFIC NAME: *Myrichthys colubrinus* (Boddaert).
POPULAR NAME: Banded Snake Eel.
  Illustrated on page 329.
RANGE: East Indies, Philippines to the Pacific Islands (not including the Hawaiian Islands).
REMARKS: This strikingly patterned eel resembles the banded sea snakes and perhaps have been mistaken for the poisonous serpents. It is usually shy and will stay in its sand or gravel burrow with only its head sticking out.
SIZE: Attains a length of at least 2 feet.

SCIENTIFIC NAME: *Myrichthys oculatus* (Kaup).
POPULAR NAME: Gold Spotted Snake Eeel.
  Illustrated on page 342.
RANGE: Brazil to Florida and Bermuda.
REMARKS: The "gold" spots circled in black cover the head and body of this eel. It is also a good burrower and should be provided with a deep layer of sand or gravel. It feeds primarily on crabs.
SIZE: Reaches 3 feet in length.

THE RIBBON EELS
Family Rhinomuraenidae

The Ribbon eels are sometimes considered as part of the moray eel family. For convenience it shall be considered as a separate family here. The front end of these fishes is highly modified. The lower jaw has several fleshy extensions and the tip of the snout ends in a fleshy, pointed projection. But what really makes these eels stand out are the greatly developed fan-like extensions on the tubular anterior nostrils (from which the genus and family name is derived) and the long, compressed, ribbon-like bodies. Feeding habits are similar to that of moray eels. Crustaceans and fish provide the basic diet. Freeze-dried and frozen foods can help fill out the menu.

  Ribbon eels have been known to swim up the filter tubes and escape from their tank. If you don't want a dusty, dead eel make sure the filter tube and all small openings are covered or protected.

344

SCIENTIFIC NAME: *Rhinomuraena amboinensis* Barbour.

POPULAR NAME: Blue Ribbon Eel.

Illustrated on page 343.

RANGE: East Indies and Philippines.

REMARKS: The Blue Ribbon Eel is usually blue with yellow fins. It has reportedly darkened in a tank to a point where it greatly resembles the Black Ribbon Eel. The head however was said to remain blue. Other differences are in the robustness of the body and configuration of the greatly developed nasal tubes.

SIZE: Attains a length of over 3½ feet.

SCIENTIFIC NAME: *Rhinomuraena quaesita* Garman.

POPULAR NAME: Black Ribbon Eel.

Illustrated on page 343.

RANGE: East Indies, Philippines, Japan, and the Pacific Islands at least to the Marshall Islands.

REMARKS: The two species of ribbon eels most likely to turn up in the aquarium trade are easily separated on the basis of color. The Black Ribbon Eel is black with white fins, the Blue Ribbon Eel is blue with yellow fins. It has been reported that there is a single species which can change color while in the tank. If this were true there would be only one species of *Rhinomuraena* instead of two. Apparently this is not the case. Hiding places should be provided for the ribbon eels.

SIZE: Reaches a length of at least 3 feet.

THE GRUNTS
Family Pomadasyidae

It is rather difficult to precisely define the grunts without being highly technical. The grunts and snappers are closely related and resemble each other, at least superficially. One of the main differences is in the dentition. Conspicuously missing in the grunts are the enlarged, prominent canines of the snappers. Also lacking in grunts are what is referred to as vomerine teeth or teeth on a certain bone located in the roof of the mouth. They are present in snappers on the vomerine bone.

The grunts are able to produce audible sounds by grinding their pharyngeal (located at the throat) teeth together.

The adult Porkfish, *Anisotremus virginicus*, differs in color pattern from the juvenile. Photo by Dr. John E. Randall.

Three French Grunts, *Haemulon flavolineatum*, swimming about the reef. Photo by Walter A. Stark, II.

A large school of grunts, mostly *Haemulon sciurus*, the Bluestriped Grunt, milling about the reef. Photo by Walter A. Stark, II.

One of the more colorful groupers, *Epinephelus flavocaeruleus*. Photo by H. Hansen.

By day large schools of grunts may be seen near the reefs usually maintaining a position to the lee side. At night they scatter over the nearby sand or grass beds foraging for food. In general their diet consists of a wide variety of bottom invertebrates.

Juveniles are usually pale colored or white with horizontal stripes and perhaps a black spot at the base of the tail. They also feed on invertebrates but make greater use of the plantonic invertebrates than the benthic or bottom kind.

SCIENTIFIC NAME: *Haemulon flavolineatum* (Desmarest).
POPULAR NAME: French Grunt.
Illustrated on page 346.
RANGE: Tropical Western Atlantic.
REMARKS: A common species in the Caribbean area and Florida, the French Grunt is similar to the Bluestriped Grunt but does not have the horizontal blue and yellow stripes of that species. The stripes are more or less oblique below the lateral line though horizontal above it.
SIZE: Attains a length of about 1 foot.

SCIENTIFIC NAME: *Haemulon sciurus* (Shaw).
POPULAR NAME: Bluestriped Grunt.
Illustrated on page 347.
RANGE: Tropical Western Atlantic.
REMARKS: This species is very colorful once it gets its adult color pattern. It is yellow with blue stripes. The Bluestriped Grunt is very common in the Caribbean and will often be included in shipments of fishes from Florida. It is hardy, eats well, but may tend to be aggressive.
SIZE: Attains a length of somewhat less than a foot and a half.

SCIENTIFIC NAME: *Anisotremus virginicus* (Linnaeus).
POPULAR NAME: Porkfish.
Illustrated on page 346.
RANGE: Tropical Western Atlantic.
REMARKS: Young Porkfishes are very pleasingly colored with a bright yellow head and white body. They have a couple of horizontal black stripes and a black spot on the base of the tail. The adults have blue and yellow stripes on the body and two black vertical bands in the head region. Between these black bands is brilliant white. The young Porkfishes have been reported to be parasite pickers. The name

"Porkfish" seems to be referring to the taste of the flesh rather than the appearance of the fish.

SIZE: Up to 1 foot in length.

THE SPADEFISHES

Family Ephippidae

The spadefishes are closely related to the batfishes but differ from them in several respects. The most obvious differences are: (1) the dorsal fin of the spadefishes is notched, not elongate as in the batfishes; and (2) the juveniles are similar to the adults in spadefishes and do not undergo the metamorphosis of those of the batfishes.

Spadefishes do well in captivity, eating almost anything. Their diet should include some vegetable matter, such as lettuce, occasionally.

SCIENTIFIC NAME: *Chaetodipterus faber* (Broussonet).

POPULAR NAME: Spadefish.

RANGE: Brazil to Massachusetts.

REMARKS: Young spadefishes can turn almost solid black. A small school of them is a very pretty sight in an aquarium. They can be found in very shallow water over grass beds or sandy areas. When a seine is hauled over the grass several may turn up. Be sure to look closely as they bear a remarkable resemblance to small dead leaves or other debris.

SIZE: Reported to reach a length of about 3 feet although half that size is more likely.

SCIENTIFIC NAME: *Tripterodon orbis* Playfair.

POPULAR NAME: John Dory.

Illustrated on page 306.

RANGE: Indian Ocean along African coast.

REMARKS: This fish is closely related to the Atlantic spadefish and more remotely to the Batfishes of the genus *Platax*. The John Dory eats small invertebrates that it finds on rocks or around corals. It grows very large and is often sought after as a game or food fish.

SIZE: Reaches a length of about $2\frac{1}{2}$ feet.

Apogon maculatus is a common cardinalfish in the Florida area.
Photo by Wilhelm Hoppe.

The barbels of this goatfish, *Parupeneus pleurostigma,* are used fo
searching out food. Photo by Dr. Herbert R. Axelrod.

Acanthurus oli vaceous develops the orange band with age. Photo by Dr. Herbert R. Axelrod.

The young Bicolor Parrotfish, *Bolbometapon bicolor*, is unique in its color pattern among the parrotfishes.

DOTTYBACKS
Family Pseudochromidae

The dottybacks are grouper-like fishes in which the lateral line is in two parts, the second section extending along the middle of the caudal peduncle. Some ichthyologists still elect to keep them within the grouper family Serranidae.

Additional characters of these fishes are: body elongate, compressed; dorsal and anal fins each with only 2 to 3 spines; band of fine teeth in jaws, outer row enlarged.

The dottybacks are generally small fishes, some very brightly colored, which inhabit coastal waters around reefs, rocks, and weeds.

SCIENTIFIC NAME: *Labracinus cyclophthalmus* (Müller & Troschel).
POPULAR NAME: Philippine Mini-grouper.
  Illustrated on page 311.
RANGE: East Indies and Philippine Islands to southern Japan.
REMARKS: Sex distinction in this species may be possible by the color pattern of the dorsal fin. It has been reported that the males have a dark spot somewhere between the fifth and twelfth dorsal spines, whereas females have comma-shaped black spots at the base of the fin.
SIZE: Reaches a length of about 6 inches.

PORGIES
Family Sparidae

The porgies have many different names around the world, some of which are breams, stumpnoses, and hottentots. They are similar in appearance to the grunts and have about 10 to 13 dorsal spines, scaleless snout, and usually some molar teeth. Of particular importance is the fact that the maxillary slips under the suborbital for most of its length while the premaxillary has a groove in its posterior part into which a part of the maxillary fits.

Porgies are tropical and temperate fishes found in shore waters, including estuaries, mostly in shallow water but with a few species reaching considerable depths. They are sought after as food fishes, themselves feeding on invertebrates such as crabs, molluscs, and even sea urchins.

SCIENTIFIC NAME: *Argyrops spinifer* (Forskal).

POPULAR NAME: Roosterfish.

Illustrated on page 305.

RANGE: East Indies and vicinity to west African coast.

REMARKS: The common name roosterfish refers to the long anterior dorsal fin spines. Feed chopped shrimp, fish, clams, crabs, and some of the prepared foods.

SIZE: Reaches 2 feet in length.

THE HAWKFISHES
Family Cirrhitidae

The hawkfishes are related to the scorpionfishes but do not have their spinous nature. The lower rays of the pectoral fins are simple and thickened.

Hawkfishes are typically bottom type fishes often found sitting on top of coral heads. When approached they dart into the coral and remain between its branches, relatively safe from large predators. A collector can lift the piece of coral out of the water and shake it over a net. Within a few seconds the hawkfish will drop into the net.

The hawkfishes normally eat small invertebrates and fishes.

SCIENTIFIC NAME: *Cirrhitichthys aprinus* (Cuvier).

POPULAR NAME: Spotted Hawkfish.

Illustrated on page 354.

RANGE: Central tropical Indo-Pacific.

REMARKS: The Spotted Hawkfish is unusual in that it has small "tufts" at the top of each dorsal fin spine. That and its spotted or blotched pattern will make it easy to identify. Spotted Hawkfish are carnivorous and eat the usual fishfoods such as brine shrimp, Norwegian brine shrimp, freeze-dried *Tubifex* worms, and chopped shrimp.

SIZE: Attains a length of some $4\frac{1}{2}$ inches.

SCIENTIFIC NAME: *Oxycirrhites typus* Bleeker.

POPULAR NAME: Long-nose Hawkfish.

Illustrated on page 354.

RANGE: East Indies to Baja California, including the Hawaiian Islands.

REMARKS: Although the body shape is typically that of a hawkfish, the snout has become elongated like that of the Long-nose Butterflyfish, *Forcipiger*. It frequents the deeper parts of the reef at 100 feet or beyond. The Long-nose Hawkfish has been collected in Hawaii in

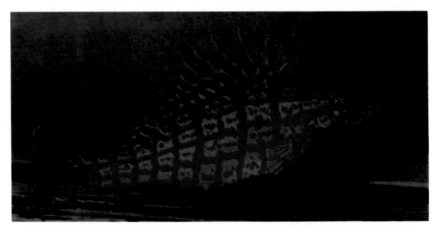

Oxycirrhites typus has an elongated snout in contrast to the other members of the hawkfish family. Photo by Morris.

Cirrhitichthys aprinus, the Spotted Hawkfish, remains near the bottom, which it probes with its sensitive fin rays. Photo by Klaus Paysan.

Synchiropus picturatus (Peters). Adult. Philippine Islands. Psychedelic fish. Photo by Dr. Herbert R. Axelrod.

deep water. It was perched among the branches of black coral. The elongate snout is used to pick small invertebrates out of the crevices or holes. Live brine shrimp is readily accepted.

SIZE: Does not reach over 5 inches in length.

THE DRAGONETS
Family Callionymidae

Dragonets are among the most spectacularly colored of fishes. Although they resemble blennies or gobies somewhat, they are quite different. The most distinctive characteristic is a strong preopercular process with a series of spines or hooks. It is used in conjunction with other features of the fish to separate the species.

In addition to the preopercular process dragonets have their gill openings restricted to small rounded holes located approximately above the process. There are two dorsal fins and the mouth is provided with small teeth. The ventral fins are placed well forward and are sometimes used by the fishes for "walking" along the bottom.

The sexes can easily be distinguished, the male fish having longer caudal and first dorsal fins. The color of the male is usually more brilliant. Spawning is unusual in these fishes in that although they are bottom dwellers the eggs are pelagic.

Dragonets inhabit coastal waters of tropical and temperate zones around the world. They are found in shallow waters as well as considerable depths. Since they also have a habit of partially burying themselves in the sand they can be collected by sieving or seining the sand at low tide.

SCIENTIFIC NAME: *Synchiropus picturatus* (Peters).
POPULAR NAME: Psychedelic Fish.
Illustrated on page 355.
RANGE: So far only known from the Philippines and New Guinea.
REMARKS: This species was unknown until recently when it appeared in numbers in the commercial market. It behaves much the same as its close relative *S. splendidus*. Only one fish per tank is recommended (even the Mandarin and Psychedelic fishes should not be mixed).
SIZE: Reaches a length of about 3 inches.

SCIENTIFIC NAME: *Synchiropus splendidus* (Herre).
POPULAR NAME: Mandarin Fish.

Illustrated on page 358.

RANGE: Indo-Australian Archipelago.

REMARKS: The Mandarin fish is rather peaceful except with members of its own kind. One per tank is suggested. It will eat a wide variety of food, picking it up off the bottom or even swimming up after it.

SIZE: Reaches 3 inches in length.

THE JAWFISHES
Family Opisthognathidae

Jawfishes have huge heads with large jaws. They live in burrows in the sand and rubble, lining the entrance with small pebbles or pieces of shell or coral. They can be seen hovering over these burrows into which they disappear tail first when they sense some apparent danger. The dorsal and anal fins are long and the eyes large. In some species the eyes are set at an angle so that they are more properly oriented when the fish is in its normal vertical position.

Jawfishes are highly territorial and even threaten members of their own species that approach too close. Behaviorists have experimented with the jawfishes by placing two of them in a tank separated by an opaque partition. When their burrows are completed the partition was removed. A rivalry was immediately set up with the line where the now absent partition was placed as the boundary line. No injury resulted but there was constant pilfering of rocks (deliberately in short supply) from each other. One jawfish usually became dominant over the other, keeping it in its burrow much of the time.

The large mouths are used not only for threat and burrow building but also for the incubation of eggs.

Their food generally consists of small animals which they select from the plankton as it is carried over their burrows.

SCIENTIFIC NAME: *Opisthognathus aurifrons* (Jordan & Thompson).

POPULAR NAME: Yellowhead Jawfish.

Illustrated on page 359.

RANGE: West Indies to the Florida Keys.

REMARKS: The Yellowhead Jawfish is a very popular aquarium fish and often is received in shipments from Florida. It is interesting to note the black markings on the chin like a painted on beard. For burrowing purposes about three inches of sand should be available to the jawfish in captivity. The Yellowhead Jawfish readily takes to live brine shrimp and can be coaxed onto many prepared foods.

SIZE: Reaches a length of about 4 inches.

Synchiropus picturatus, the Psychedelic Dragonet, was recently rediscovered in the Philippine Islands. Photo by Dr. Herbert R. Axelrod.

Synchiropus splendidus is very popular with aquarists. This Mandarin Fish is also a dragonet. Photo by Dr. Herbert R. Axelrod.

The Jawfish, *Opisthognathus aurifrons*, lives in burrows in the bottom sand or gravel. Photo by Craig Barker.

THE BLENNIES
Family Blenniidae

Blennies are small, interesting fishes well suited to the home aquarium. They have comical faces, as the accompanying photographs show, with fringes and cirri adorning their heads. They are often confused with the gobies but can easily be distinguished by their pelvic fins which have become reduced to a few rays. The pectoral fins have become enlarged and are used to aid in locomotion. Blennies will sit in the open with their tails curled towards their head. At the first sign of danger they straighten the tail giving them an initial fast start.

Blennies will feed on most small invertebrates. In the aquarium brine shrimp will be eaten along with most of the prepared foods.

SCIENTIFIC NAME: *Blennius nigriceps* Vinciguerra.
POPULAR NAME: Cardinal Blenny; Carmine Blenny.
Illustrated on page 362.
RANGE: Mediterranean Sea.
REMARKS: The Cardinal Blenny is very attractive. It is surprising that more of them have not been kept in home aquaria. They are bottom fishes and usually hide in and around rocks. Cardinal Blennies are not easy to collect. Food is no problem as they take very well to live brine shrimp and eventually to the prepared foods.
SIZE: Attains a length of about 1½ inches.

SCIENTIFIC NAME: *Ecsenius bicolor* (Day).
POPULAR NAME: Bicolor Blenny.
Illustrated on page 362.
RANGE: Tropical Indo-Pacific.
REMARKS: The purplish head and the orange posterior are quite distinctive. Bicolor Blennies are commonly found in rock crevices, the bright posterior in the hole hidden from view, in reef areas greater than 20 feet deep. Feeding should follow that prescribed for the other blennies.
SIZE: Grows to 4 inches.

SCIENTIFIC NAME: *Ophioblennius atlanticus* (Cuvier & Valenciennes).
POPULAR NAME: Atlantic Blenny; Redlip Blenny.
Illustrated on pages 300, 301.
RANGE: Tropical Western Atlantic (straggling northward to the Carolinas).

REMARKS: The Atlantic Blenny is common and appears often in shipments from Florida. It has the typical cirri of the blennies on the head and over the eyes. It feeds on filamentous algae so plant material is a must in its diet.

SIZE: Attains a length of 2-4 inches.

This blenny, *Blennius sphinx*, seems ready for a take-off with its "wings" spread and landing gear down. Photo by Hilmar Hansen.

The Cardinal Blenny, *Blennius nigriceps*, is very atractive. It is surprising that blennies are not more popular. Photo by G. Marcuse.

This blenny, *Ecsenius bicolor*, spends much of its time off the bottom compared to most other blennies. Photo by Dr. John E. Randall.

Most marine aquarists like to combine fishes and invertebrates in one aquarium. This combination of clownfish and sea anemone is the most popular means of doing this. Photo by Dr. Herbert R. Axelrod.

8

WHY NOT AN
INVERTEBRATE AQUARIUM?

Marine invertebrates are just as beautiful and just as interesting as the fishes, if not more so! Sea fans, corals, crabs, snails, sea anemones, and starfishes are only a few of the different kinds one is apt to keep in the home aquarium. Coral is one of the most popular decorations, however, it is always dead, bleached, and cured before being placed in the tank. How much more attractive it would be if it could be kept alive! Another popular invertebrate is the sea anemone, most often kept only as a refuge for the clownfish (*Amphiprion*) and not for their own aesthetic values.

Generally speaking invertebrates are animals without backbones or vertebrae. They constitute almost all of the animals in oceans except the fishes and marine mammals such as whales, porpoises, etc. They can be free-living and mobile as crabs, shrimps, and starfishes; or attached to the bottom or other substrate as sponges, sea fans, and barnacles. Unfortunately, some of their names are misleading, such as star*fish* and jelly*fish*, as these animals have nothing whatsoever to do with true fishes.

As there are dangerous fishes so are there dangerous and harmful invertebrates. There are those that sting (jellyfish, Portuguese Man-O'-War, cone shells, etc.), burn (fire corals, fire sponges, etc), puncture (sea urchins, etc), scrape or cut (corals, barnacles, etc.), and pinch or nip (crabs, shrimp, lobsters, octopuses, etc.) Most are not dangerous to the extent of actually killing a person. There has been some reported deaths from a poisonous octopus in Australia, a stinging jellyfish called the Sea Wasp, and various cone snails around the tropical reefs. So be sure to know something about the animals you keep and always handle them with care not only for the animals' sake but for your own as well.

Collecting marine invertebrates can be very easy. With the aid of a net, tennis shoes, and a little patience, a trip to a tide pool or shallow water can produce a wide variety of invertebrates that can be kept alive in a small marine aquarium. Seining is another popular method of collecting but it requires another person to pull the other side of the net. The more sophisticated collector will dive for his prizes using anything from net and gloves to full SCUBA regalia. In any collecting locale turning a rock over usually produces an abundance of different animals. It is strongly urged that all rocks be replaced in their original position to protect the animals that are left behind. If this is done, chances are a return visit next year will be just as rewarding rather than finding a desolate and ruined area.

Many invertebrates have found their way into the dealers tanks much to the delight of the hobbyist. As soon as shipping techniques are perfected many more will be available and marine aquaria will blossom with the new animals.

COELENTERATES (Sea Anemones, Corals, Jellyfish)

In tide pools which are famous for colorful occupants, none can challenge the gaudy beauty of the sea anemones. A sea anemone is a member of one of the major groups of the animal kingdom, the phylum *Coelenterata*. This phylum is broken down further into three classes, namely the *Scyphozoa* (the jellyfishes), the *Hydrozoa* (the hydroids) and the *Anthozoa* (the sea anemones).

Every coelenterate is outfitted with a characteristic set of stinging cells called, scientifically, nematocysts. These nematocysts are used for paralyzing food, as the coelenterates are very slow-moving creatures. The action of the nematocysts is much like a triggered spring mechanism, and any brushing movement will cause the threads to spring out and inject poison into the tissue to which contact has been made. In most cases the stinging cells are not sufficiently powerful to penetrate a human's skin, but there are painful exceptions to this rule. Many people are very familiar with the Portuguese Man-O'-War, *Physalia,* a hydrozoan (related to the fresh-water *Hydra* familiar to most aquarists), which has stinging cells powerful enough to put a man into the hospital.

Sea anemones, themselves, are equipped with nematocysts and our present knowledge is that none has sufficiently strong nematocysts to inflict any type of wound on a human being. They are usually found adhering to a rock or similar surface. For their attaching device to work, they must have a relatively flat and broad base upon which to anchor. Some species of sea anemones might be found in tide pools, clinging to pilings, seaweed, and eelgrass, while other species live in the mud.

Other animals are able to navigate through the stinging tentacles of sea anemones such as this porcelain crab, *Petrolisthes maculatus*, with the anemone *Stoichactis kenti*. Photo by U. Erich Friese.

The stalk of an anemone can be as brightly colored as the tentacles. This *Tealia coriacea* has an orange stalk. Photo by U. Erich Friese.

This delicate looking sea anemone is *Cerianthus membranaceus*. The tentacles are trailing to one side due to the water movements. Photo by U. Erich Friese.

Part of the Eniwetok, Marshall Islands coral atoll. The lagoon (center of the old volcanic cone) is to the left. Photo by Dr. Gerald R. Allen.

Locomotion among the sea anemones is limited to a slow creeping motion on a pedal disk. Constant observation over a period of 5 to 10 minutes might convince an observer that the anemone is a stationary flower that cannot move, but in reality this animal can really move great distances over periods of weeks or months. The fastest an anemone has ever been "clocked" is 4 inches in one hour. Several exceptional species move about by floating (the *Minyadidae*), while another moves by a flopping method.

The size of sea anemones varies from $\frac{1}{4}$ of an inch, to the 3-foot-wide giant *Stoichactis*, found on the Great Barrier Reef off Australia. Some anemones may live to 300 years old.

Corals are close relatives of the sea anemones, but secrete a calcium exoskeleton (shell) upon and in which the living parts of the animal are protected. These shells or skeletons give the animal its entire supporting structure and are the bleached part of the corals that are used as aquarium decoration.

The individual coral animals or polyps as they are called are like miniature sea anemones. They are the living parts of the coral which stretch their tentacles out into the water to catch the small animals of the plankton drifting past. They reproduce by dividing, thus enlarging the size of the colony, or by a larva called the planula, with which attached corals become distributed. Colonies of these tiny polyps have, over thousands of years, produced the massive coral reefs we know today.

Coral reefs are classified into three types of formation: barrier reefs, fringing reefs, and atolls. Barrier reefs are those that develop several miles from a land mass with a deep lagoon (usually suitable for large ships) between them. The Great Barrier Reef of Australia is the best known example of this type. Fringing reefs develop closer to land and are separated from this land by a shallow lagoon. The fringing reefs of Hawaii are well known. The third type of reefs are atolls which are oval or horseshoe-shaped and enclosing a lagoon shallower than the surrounding waters. Thousands of atolls dot the Pacific and Indian Oceans. The Darwinian Theory of atoll formation involves the other two types. It states that if a land mass is sinking and corals surround it a fringing reef develops (providing of course the sinking rate is slower than the coral growth). As the land continues to sink the reef gets more and more separated from it and the lagoon becomes wider and deeper. Finally the land mass sinks out of sight leaving only the surrounding reef or atoll remaining.

Reef type corals are found only where suitable conditions occur. These are high water temperature, strong light, and constant water motion. This limits them to the broad tropical zone surrounding the equator.

Cerianthus membranaceus looks like a tired feather duster.

This green anemone looks at if its tentacles were made of glass.
Photo by Dr. Herbert R. Axelrod.

Coral animals do not contribute all of the calcareous deposits that make up the reefs. As much as 50% is produced by calcareous plants (those capable of incorporating calcium in their tissues such as *Halimeda* and *Lithothamnion*).

Live corals for an aquarium need specialized care. Water temperature and light are easy enough to provide but feeding is more difficult. Without a current to bring food into reach of the polyps the aquarist must either supply the current or feed the coral animals individually. Brine shrimp in an eye dropper is the usually accepted method of feeding and can be varied using other types of food placed on the polyps themselves. Anchovy paste in tubes is a good food and easy to feed. When collecting live coral try to get a piece that is as free as possible from encrusting or boring animals. These can easily die and foul the tank in an amazingly short time.

When cured coral is desired there is a procedure to follow. Assume that you have collected your own piece of living coral. Under the coral, if it was a large, relatively flat piece (like brain coral), you might have

This Portuguese Man - of - War has caught a fish and is preparing to devour it. N.Y.Z.S. Photo.

Live corals and gorgonians decorate this marine aquarium. Sponges and other animals not suited to the inside of the aquarium can be seen in the shadow box in back. Photo by Robert P. L. Straughan.

noticed some small worms, or crabs. These must be removed. The best way to process the coral is to dry it thoroughly in the air and sun for a week or two at least. After all signs of life have disappeared and the coral is very hard and dry, it can be sterilized. It is best to boil the coral in a solution into which some chlorine bleach has been added. This bleach serves both as a disinfectant and as a bleaching agent. After the coral piece has been boiled for an hour or so it should be allowed to dry out again for a few days after you have washed it thoroughly in cool running water for a few hours. Once it has dried, bathe it again for a few hours in running water and then it is safe to put it into your marine aquarium.

If you want treated coral for decoration it is safest to purchase it from your pet shop. The treatment and preservation of coral pieces entail a lot of effort and time and they are much more costly when done on a piece by piece method than by volume, in huge pressure cookers.

You can see an *Amphiprion melanopus* among the tentacles
of this anemone.

Another of our nicely-colored anemones from Florida. Photo by
Robert P. L. Straughan.

These anemones come from the West Indies. Photo by Dr. Herbert
R. Axelrod.

Here is evidence of how deadly an anemone can be to its prey. The fish was caught and killed, and will be eaten. Photo RKO Radio Pictures, Inc.

MOLLUSCS (Chitons, Snails, Clams, Octopuses)

Chitons or Sea Cradles are sluggish, slow-moving creatures that crawl about on a large foot, much like a snail. Across its upper surface are eight calcareous plates, that articulate and overlap, forming a perfect protective shell if needed. The normal appearance of the chiton, uncurled, looks like the tail of a lobster, but when it curls up it has a completely different appearance, like a cradle, from which its nickname was derived.

Chitons have a rasping "tongue" which is used for scraping algae off rocks. The chiton will scrape an area clear and then move off to greener pastures. They browse at high tide and "hang on" when the tide drops, conserving water until it comes back.

One must strike fast when collecting these animals. If you don't get them on the first try they can clamp down on the rock very tightly. Once that happens they usually cannot be budged without damaging them.

Anyone who has walked along the beach has stopped to pick up and admire marine snails. Most were usually empty shells to be taken home and eventually discarded or put away in the back of some drawers. Other shells picked up and thought to be empty quickly walked away when placed back on the sand! These contained hermit crabs which, without a covering of their own, stick their soft and vulnerable abdomen into an abandoned shell and carry it with them as their home. A live snail can be recognized by the flat, tight-fitting "door" or operculum with which it blocks entry into the shell. This is its principal means of protection, not only from predators but from the danger of drying out (dessication). When tightly closed a small amount of water is kept inside to keep the gills moist in order to be able to get oxygen from the water.

Most snails feed with the aid of a rasping organ called the radula. It is used to scrape the fine algae off the surface of rocks. The "track" of a snail can easily be seen and its path for the past several hours indicated by the bare rock it has left behind. As the radula wears out new rasping teeth replace the worn ones.

Among the more prized snails are the cowries. These have smooth, colorful, oval shells which do not outwardly show the spiral structure common to all snails. A fleshy membrane, the mantle, covers the shell keeping it smooth and repairing any damage that occurs.

The hunters of the snail group are the cone shells. They hunt and capture other marine creatures including fish. Poison darts are jabbed into a victim by muscular action and the prey is engulfed by the muscular foot and feeding takes place at will. The poison from this snail can be dangerous to man — handle with care!

Reproduction in snails is well known. Some, like the top snail, release their eggs freely into the water. After a short pelagic life they metamorphose into recognizable snails, some drop to the bottom, and begin crawling. Most snails lay eggs enclosed in protective capsules or jelly-like masses. These are often found lying on the bottom around the reef or grass flats. If far enough along in development the miniature snails can easily be seen when the egg capsule is held up against the light.

The snails will probably make short work of the algae on the aquarium glass. They are, however, wanderers and if the tank is not covered they often disappear. It is also difficult to determine if they are dead and they can quickly pollute an aquarium.

In the Mollusca probably the most sought after animals are the nudibranchs, snails without shells and as the name implies with bare gills. They are sometimes called marine slugs and are often quite beautiful. The exposed gills add to their charm, being numerous and frilly giving the appearance of delicate feathers. Fortunately for them they have a

A beautiful coral piece.

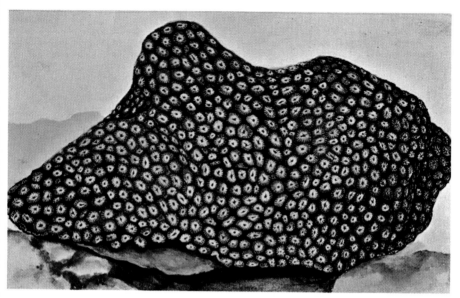

When dried and cured, this is known as "star coral."

Living coral looks a lot different from what we buy. Photo by Dr. Herbert R. Axelrod.

rather bad taste, an effective defense against a hungry fish. The nudibranchs are also provided with a radula and are therefore browsers.

Clams, oysters, mussels, etc., are related to snails but instead of having a single coiled shell, they have a pair of hinged shells. Their dreaded enemy, the starfish has been discussed above. These animals are usually not kept in the home aquarium because, as with snails, it is difficult to determine when they die and fouling of the tank can quickly occur. A closed clam shell gives no indication of whether it is alive or dead. However, there are attractive clams and some are well worth the risk. Foremost among these is the scallop. One species has a bright orange-red mantle with a long fringe and a double row of blue-green eyes at the edge. These animals are not attached and have the ability to "fly" through the water by clapping the shells together in combination with a sort of jet propulsion. A group of scallops quietly resting on the bottom of the tank will immediately "take off" the instant a starfish is placed near them.

Another favorite is the dwarf relative of the giant clam. Its fluted or scalloped shell is very attractive and the mantles come in a variety of colors.

Clams in general feed by pumping water into the shell, through a sieve-like structure, and out the other end. The edible particles caught in

A living filter, this young *Tridacna gigas* grows very large, weighing up to a ton or more. The mantle at the edge of the clam is brightly colored. Photo by G. Marcuse.

Squids are difficult to maintain in captivity. This *Sepia officionalis*, an inshore form, is one of the more hardy types. Photo by G. Marcuse.

the sieve are moved by cilia to the mouth and ingested while the inedible materials are moved also by cilia to the outside and discarded.

One character with a very bad reputation in fiction books is the octopus. It is a highly developed shell-less mollusc which has a mantle and a molluscan foot modified into eight arms with suckers. The octopus is a shy and retiring creature which normally lives in a hole. It sits at the doorway, strewn with all sorts of debris collected by the mobile arms, and will withdraw into the hole at one's approach. Their normal food are crustaceans, molluscs and sometimes fishes. They are intelligent animals that can be trained to do many tricks.

One can get a nasty bite from an octopus on account of the chitinous beaks very much like those of a parrot's. At least one species, the blue-ringed octopus of Australia, has a dangerously poisonous bite.

Their close relatives, the squids, are very difficult to keep in captivity. Both groups have the ability to squirt a dark substance (ink) into the water as a sort of "smoke screen" to confuse an enemy while they make their escape. In the confines of the tank the effects of the ink may be lethal not only to other animals in the tank but also to themselves.

One or two very small octopuses and squids from inshore waters can be fascinating animals to keep in your aquarium although they require high aeration, plenty of space and preferably live food.

1. Tide pool.

2. Blenny.

3. Peanut worms

4. Sea Bat starfish

5. Periwinkles

1. Coral polyp

2. Chiton

3. Shore crab

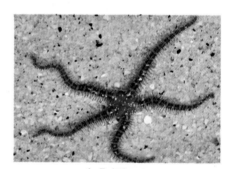

4. Brittle star

5. Chitons (curled for protection)

6. Chitons grazing.

This photo shows only one species of starfish, with from four to seven arms. N.Y.Z.S. Photo.

These are some of the things you might find on a beach. The upper two invertebrates are sea urchins (the one on the left is alive, but with most of its spines worn off; the one on the right is a "sand dollar", sand-smoothed remains of a sea urchin). The lower four figures are starfish. N.Y.Z.S. Photo.

1. Feather worm

2. Prying loose an abalone

3. Sea anemone

4. Sculpin

5. A tide pool teeming with life.

1. Limpet

2. Sea urchin

3. Whipping-top snails

4. Cancer crab

5. Six-armed starfish

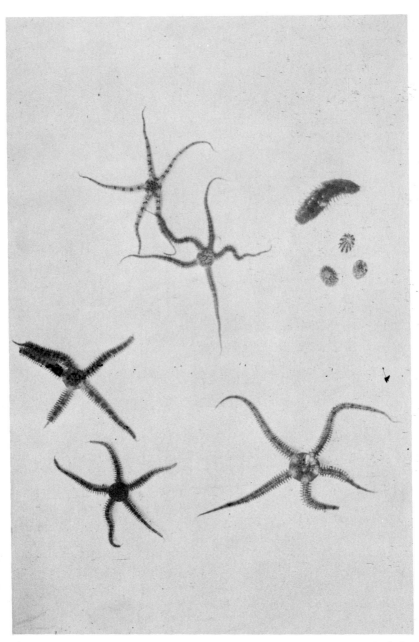

The broken-off arms of the brittle starfish are regenerated in remarkable fashion. It is interesting to observe the various ways in which the arms grow back. N.Y.Z.S. Photo.

Starfish feed mostly on clams and mussels, and are their worst enemy. Photo by Gunter Senfft.

CRUSTACEANS (Crabs, Shrimps, Lobsters)

There are many beautiful shrimps and crabs suitable for a home aquarium. They are generally hardy and eat almost anything. In nature they are scavengers and can provide this same service for the aquarist. When a fish dies, a crab will usually dispose of it before any fouling occurs. If there is not enough food available a crab might attack one of the other inhabitants of the tank.

Besides being scavengers, crabs can be entertaining creatures. Some species decorate their shells with bits of sponge and algae, often taking great pains to place the selected and trimmed item in exactly the right place. Other species have modified tips on their claws which enable them to pry attached sea anemones off the rocks. These sea anemones are held in the claws and used as weapons if danger threatens.

The small hermit crab, a highly specialized crab which lives in an empty snail shell, is immune to the poison of the sea anemone. It hunts out certain species of sea anemones and, once it has found one, gently

1. A crab smaller than a fingernail.

2. Porcelain crab.

3. Caprella shrimp.

4. Mussels and gooseneck barnacles.

5. A colony of sea urchins, not a pleasant place to step.

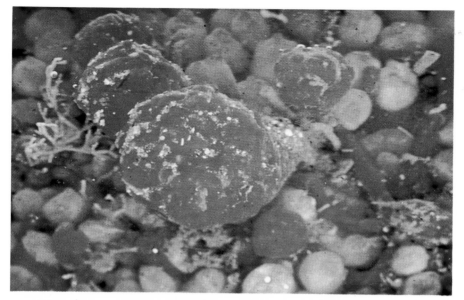

1. Sea squirt.

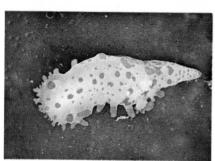
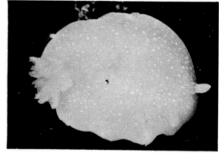

2 and 3. Sea slugs.

4. Starfish in motion.

5. Magnified section of a starfish's skin.

This tide pool is eight inches deep. It contains hundreds of tiny fishes, now hidden in coral crevices, plus some sea urchins.

tickles the anemone until it leaves the rock or piling to which it is attached. Then the crab maneuvers in such a way as to get the anemone to adhere to its own borrowed palace. With the anemone securely fastened to the snail's shell, the hermit crab goes off looking for food. Now, upon finding itself in the company of small fishes, the crab will provoke the fishes until they come in contact with the stinging cells of the sea anemones. Then both crab and anemone are able to feed.

The Candy Cane Shrimp (*Stenopus hispidus*) is a cleaning shrimp. It is allowed to crawl over a fishes' body searching for tiny parasites or anything else that it eats. Why a fish, which would make a quick meal of any other kind of shrimp, allows this particular one to take such liberties is still a mystery. There is some mutual agreement in which both partners gain something (the shrimp gets food, the fish gets rid of its parasites). It has been stated that the bright colors or the long white feelers of the shrimp is a "signal" to the fish that this little daredevil will be helpful and is not to be eaten.

BRYOZOANS or MOSS ANIMALS

The bryozoans (moss animals) as they are sometimes called belong to a very old group of invertebrates dating back to the Cambrian Age and some scientists claim they have lived in the same form for over 500,000,000 years.

Without a microscope it is difficult to appreciate the beauty of these animals. Each colony is composed of numerous small animals and each of them is surrounded by either a chitinous (horny) or limy (calcareous) shell. The colony grows by new members budding off and forming their own shells. When disturbed or stimulated the individual animals retreat into their shells, completely protected within by door-like structures. Bryozoans may be found attached on rocks, pilings, seaweeds, shells, other animals, driftwood, etc.

They are brightly colored animals and a small colony of moss animal could brighten up your tank. They are known to feed on plankton and detritus.

WORMS

Worms are probably the last thing you might want to keep in your marine aquarium, that is, until you've seen the magnificently beautiful Feather-Duster Worms. These Sabellids, as they are technically called, look like the old-fashioned feather duster, a bunch of feathers tied to a handle. Actually the Feather-Duster Worms live in limey tubes or holes bored in the reef. The feathery part is a set of gills which are ciliated and cause minute currents, sufficiently strong to swirl microscopic organisms against them trapping the small animals and bringing them into the mouth of the worm. The organisms are brought to the vicinity of the worm by water currents across the reef. Feather worms are very quick to react and disappear into their tube or hole at the slightest disturbance.

Peanut Worms are not true worms or segmented worms but a special group called sipuculids. They feed with the aid of ciliated tentacles, spending much of their time buried in the sand. They "eat" as much sand as they do other matter, passing it through the digestive system and it is eventually returned from where it came.

ECHINODERMS (Starfish, Sea Urchins, etc.)

The starfish is one of the best known invertebrates. It is not usually known, however, that starfishes can have more than five arms. Some species have many arms and at least one species is a perfect pentagon, without any at all. If an arm or two is lost the starfish has extraordinary powers of regeneration and will have its full complement in short order.

391

A sponge crab, with sponges attached. Photo by Robert P. L. Straughan.

Scallops, molluscs which can move rapidly through the water. Photo by Dr. Herbert R. Axelrod.

Alegonium palmatum, the sea hand or leather coral. Photo by Holzhammer.

The mat coral *Cladocera caespitosa.* Photo by Holzhammer.

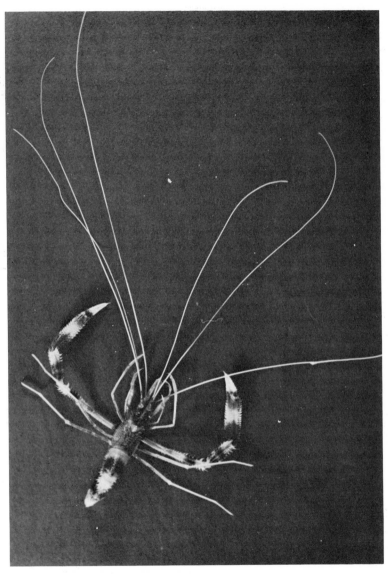

Stenopus hispidus, the banded coral shrimp.

Anyone collecting these animals is bound to come across some specimens with a short arm, the regenerative process in progress.

This peculiar animal is built with the destruction of shellfish in mind. Large numbers of mussels, clams, and oysters are destroyed by starfish each year and plans of eradication have been carried out in certain areas.

The starfish opens up the clam by clasping onto the shell with its tube feet (small suction cup structures on the ventral side of the arms) and applying pressure by pumping water out of the tube feet system. Since no muscles are used there is no fatigue for the starfish, only for the clam. Once the clam opens, the starfish everts its stomach and forces it inside secreting digestive juices, finishes its meal, recovers its stomach, and releases the clam shell, ready for another victim.

Brittle stars have a small central disk and five thin snake-like arms. Their name applies to the habit of these animals of discarding their arms when they are caught. There are some colorful brittle stars but they almost always hide from view so are not sought after for the aquarium.

Related to the starfish and having the same basic pentagonal symmetry are the sea urchins. This symmetry is usually hidden by the long sharp spines covering the calcareous shell or test. When touched the spines in the vicinity of the irritant all turn towards the direction of the expected assault. Between the spines sea urchins are provided with pedicillariae (beak-like jaws). These jaws, sometimes in three parts, are mainly used for crushing small animals that might try to attach themselves to the slow-moving sea urchins. They also have poison glands for stunning larger animals.

Sea urchins eggs are used in biology and embryology classes for studying embryonic development. The eggs and sperm are easily collected by placing sea urchins in a dish of sea water upside down. If they are ready to spawn the jostling of collecting will cause them to release the sexual products. They can be induced to spawn by several methods the most common being injection with a weak solution of potassium chloride (KCl). To distinguish the sex is simple; the males exude a white liquid, the female a cream or yellow colored liquid. A small amount of sperm solution can be used to fertilize a large number of eggs. Give them plenty of room and watch them grow.

INDEX

Page numbers marked with an asterisk denote illustrations.